India's Energy Security

India's Energy Security: Challenges and Concerns

By
Aleena Thomas
K. Jayaprasad

KALPAZ

First Published, 2020

Published by

Kalpaz Publications
C-30, Satyawati Nagar,
Delhi – 110052
Ph.: 011-47034999, 9811692060
www.kalpazpublications.com
E-mail: kalpaz@hotmail.com

Printed at: G. Print Process, Delhi

Cataloging in Publication Data—DK
Courtesy: D.K. Agencies (P) Ltd. <docinfo@dkagencies.com>

Dr. Aleena Thomas Jayaprasad, K. 1960- **author.**
India's energy security challenges and concerns / by Prof (Dr). K. Jayaprasad.
pages cm
ISBN 9789353242329

1. Energy security—India. 2. Energy industries—India. I. Title.
LCC HD9502.I42J39 2020 | DDC 333.7954 23

Contents

Abbreviations

$	-	United States Dollar
₹	-	Indian Rupee
°C	-	Degree Celsius
AC	-	Alternate Current
ACG	-	Azeri–Chirag–Gunashli
AERB	-	Atomic Energy Regulatory Board
AGE	-	Afghan Gas Enterprise
APL	-	Above Poverty Line
AREP	-	Accelerated Rural Electrification Programme
ASEAN	-	Association of Southeast Asian Nations
ASSOCHAM	-	Associated Chambers of Commerce and Industry of India
b/d-	-	Barrels per Day
BARC	-	Bhabha Atomic Research Centre
BBIN	-	Bangladesh, Bhutan, India and Nepal Initiative
BCCL	-	Bharat Coking Coal Limited
BCM	-	Billion Cubic Meters
BEE	-	Bureau of Energy Efficiency
BHEL	-	Bharat Heavy Electricals Limited
BIMSTEC	-	Bengal Initiative for Multi-Sectoral Technical and Economic Cooperation
BP	-	British Petroleum
BPCL	-	Bharat Petroleum Corporation Limited
BPD	-	Barrels per day
BPL	-	Below Poverty Line
BPRL	-	Bharat Petro-resources Limited
BT	-	Billion Tonnes
BTC	-	Baku-Tbilisi-Ceyhan Pipeline

Btu	-	British Thermal Unit
BU	-	Billion Units
BWR	-	Boiling Water Reactors
C	-	Symbol of Heat Capacity
CAGR	-	Compound Annual Growth Rate
Candu	-	Canada Deuterium Uranium
CASE	-	Commission for Additional Sources of Energy
CBM	-	Coal-bed Methane
CBRP	-	CO_2 Building Rehabilitation Programme
CCL	-	Central Coalfields Limited
CCO	-	Coal Controller's Organization
CEA	-	Central Electricity Authority of India
CEL	-	Central Electronics Limited
CESC	-	Calcutta Electric Supply Corporation Limited
CHP	-	Combined Heat and Power
CIAL	-	Coal India Africana Limitada
CIL	-	Coal India Limited
CIR	-	Canada- India Reactor
CIRUS	-	Canada India Reactor Utility Services
CMAL	-	Coal Mines Authority Limited
CMM	-	Coal-Mine Methane
CMPDIL	-	Central Mine Planning and Design Institute Limited
CO_2	-	Carbon dioxide
DAE	-	Department of Atomic Energy
DISCOM	-	Distribution Company (In India)
DNEP	-	Draft National Energy Policy
DNES	-	Department of Non-Conventional Energy Sources
DNI	-	Direct Normal Irradiance
ECBC	-	Energy Conservation Building Codes
ECL	-	Eastern Coalfields Limited
EIA	-	Energy Information Administration
EIA	-	Environmental Impact Assessment
ENVIS	-	Environmental Information System
EU	-	European Union
Euratom	-	European Atomic Energy Community

EV	-	Electric Vehicle
FAME	-	Faster Adoption and Manufacture of (Hybrid and) Electric Vehicles
FIT	-	Feed in Tariff
FOWFPI	-	First Offshore Wind Farm Project in India
FOWIND	-	Facilitating Offshore Wind in India
GAIL	-	Gail (India) Limited
GCC	-	Gulf Cooperation Council
GDP	-	Gross Domestic Product
GHG	-	Green House Gas
GOI	-	Government of India
GRIHA	-	Green Rating for Integrated Habitat Assessment
GSI	-	Geological Survey of India
GUTS	-	Green Urban Transport Scheme
GW	-	Giggawatt
GWh	-	Giggawatt hours
GWp	-	Global Warming Potential
HELP	-	Hydrocarbon Exploration and Licensing Policy
HEV	-	Hybrid Electric Vehicle
HPCL	-	Hindustan Petroleum Corporation Limited
HRIDAY	-	Heritage City Development and Augmentation
HV	-	Hybrid vehicles
HVO	-	Hydrotreated Vegetable Oil
IAEA	-	International Atomic Energy Agency
IBEF	-	India Brand Equity Foundation
ICVL	-	The International Coal Ventures Ltd
IEA	-	International Energy Agency
IEF	-	International Energy Forum
IESD	-	Indo European Union Sustainable Develop-ment
IGA	-	Inter-Governmental Agreement
IIT	-	Indian Institutes of Technology
INDC	-	Intended Nationally Determined Contributions
IOC	-	Indian Oil Corporation
IOCL	-	Indian Oil Corporation Limited
IPDS	-	Integrated Power Development Scheme

IPI	-	Iran-Pakistan-India Pipeline
IREDA	-	Indian Renewable Energy Development Agency Limited
IRENA	-	International Renewable Energy Agency
ISA	-	International Solar Alliance
ISGS	-	Inter State Gas Systems (Private) Limited
ISIS	-	Islamic State of Iraq and Syria
ISM	-	Indian School of Mines
ISTS	-	Interstate Transmission System
ITE	-	International Exhibitions and Conference Organizer in Russia
JCERDC	-	Joint Clean Energy Research and Development
JCPA	-	Joint Comprehensive Plan of Action
JNNSM	-	Jawaharlal Nehru National Solar Mission
JPOA	-	Joint Plan of Action
JV	-	Joint Ventures
KAPS	-	Kakrapar Atomic Power Station
KG Basin	-	Krishna Godavari Basin
KGS	-	Kaiga Generating Station
KM	-	Kilo Meter
KM^2	-	Square Kilometer
KUSUM	-	Kisan Urja Suraksha Evam Utthaan Mahaabhiyan
KV	-	Kilo Volts
KW	-	Kilowatt
KWh	-	Kilowatt hour
LED	-	Light-Emitting Diade
LNG	-	Liquefied Natural Gas
LPG	-	Liquefied Petroleum Gas
MAPP	-	Madras Atomic Power Plant
MAPS	-	Madras Atomic Power Station
Mb/d	-	Millions of Barrels per Day
MCL	-	Mahanadi Coalfields Limited
MECL	-	Mineral Exploration Corporation Limited
MMT	-	Million Metric Tonnes
MMtoe	-	Million tonnes of oil equivalent

MMTPA	-	Million Metric Tonne Per Annum
MNES	-	The Ministry of Non-Conventional Energy Sources
MNRE	-	Ministry of New and Renewable Energy
MS	-	Motor Spirit
MSW	-	Municipal Solid Waste
MT	-	Million Tonnes
MT	-	Metric Tons
MTOE	-	Million Tonnes of Oil Equivalent
MTPA	-	Million Tonnes Per Annum
MW	-	Megawatt
MWe	-	Megawatt electric
MWp	-	Mega Watt peak
NAPCC	-	National Action Plan on Climate Change
NAPS	-	Narora Atomic Power Station
NCDC	-	National Coal Development Corporation
NCEF	-	National Clean Energy Fund
NCL	-	Northern Coalfields Limited
ND TV	-	New Delhi Television Limited
NELP	-	New Exploration Licensing Policy
NEMMP	-	National Electric Mobility Mission Plan
NGO	-	Non-governmental organization
NIC	-	Nuclear Industrial Complex
NISE	-	National Institute of Solar Energy
NITI Aayog	-	National Institution for Transforming India
NIT	-	National Institutes of Technology
NIWE	-	National Institute of Wind Energy
NLCIL	-	Neyveli Lignite Corporation Limited
NMDC	-	National Minerals Development Corporation
NMEEE	-	The National Mission for Enhanced Energy Efficiency
NPT	-	Non-Proliferation Treaty (-Treaty on the Non-Proliferation of Nuclear Weapons)
NSG	-	Nuclear Suppliers Group
NTPC	-	National Thermal Power Corporation Limited
OECD	-	Organization for Economic Co-operation and Development

OIL	-	Oil India Limited
OLADE	-	Latin American Energy Organization
ONGC	-	Oil and Natural Gas Corporation
OPEC	-	The Organization of the Petroleum Exporting Countries
OPIC	-	Overseas Private Investment Corporation
ORKUSTOFNUN	-	National Energy Authority of Iceland
OVL	-	ONGC Videsh Limited
PACE	-	Partnership to Advance Clean Energy
PCRA	-	Petroleum Conservation Research Association
PDVSA	-	Petróleos de Venezuela
PGCB	-	Power Grid Company of Bangladesh Limited
PHEV	-	Plug in Hybrid Electric Vehicles
PHR	-	Pressurized Heavy Reactor
PHWR	-	Pressurized Heavy-Water Reactor
PM	-	Particulate Matter
POL	-	Petroleum, Oil, & Lubricants
POWERGRID	-	Power Grid Corporation Of India Limited
PPAC	-	Petroleum Planning and Analysis Cell
PSU	-	Public Sector Undertaking
PV	-	Photovoltaics
PWR	-	Pressurized water reactors
R&D	-	Research and Development
R&R	-	Resettlement and Rehabilitation
RAPP	-	Rajasthan Atomic Power Plant
RAPS	-	Rajasthan Atomic Power Station
REC	-	Rural Electrification Corporation Limited
REN 21	-	Renewable Energy Policy Network for the 21st Century
REST	-	Rural Electricity Supply Technology Mission
RGGVY	-	Rajiv Gandhi Grameen VidyutikaranYojana
RIL	-	Reliance Industries Limited
RINL	-	Rashtriya Ispat Nigam Limited
R-LNG	-	Re-gasified Liquefied Natural Gas
SAGE	-	South Asia Gas Enterprise Private Ltd

SAIL	-	Steel Authority of India Limited
SCCL	-	Singareni Collieries Company Limited
SCO	-	Shanghai Cooperation Organization
SEC	-	Solar Energy Centre
SECC	-	Socio-Economic and Caste Census
SECI	-	Solar Energy Corporation of India
SECL	-	South Eastern Coalfields Limited
SIMTARS	-	Safety in Mines Testing and Research Station
SO_2	-	Sulfur dioxide
SOCAR	-	State Oil Company of Azerbaijan Republic
SOS	-	Security of Supply
Soubhagya	-	Pradhan Mantri Sahaj Bijli Har Ghar Yojana
SPLA	-	Christian Sudanese People's Liberation Army
SPR	-	Strategic Petroleum Reserve
SRISTI	-	Sustainable Rooftop Implementation for Solar Transfiguration of India Scheme
STEC	-	Solar Thermal Energy Centre
TAP	-	Turkmenistan, Afghanistan and Pakistan pipeline
TAPI	-	Turkmenistan-Afghanistan-Pakistan-India pipeline
TAPS	-	Tarapur Atomic Power Station
Tcf-	-	Trillion cubic feet
TERI-	-	The Energy and Resources Institute
TW-	-	Terawatt
TWh	-	Terawatt Hours
UAE-	-	United Arab Emirates
UDAY-	-	Ujwal DISCOM Assurance Yojana
UJALA-	-	Unnat Jyoti by Affordable LEDs for All
UK-	-	United Kingdom
UN-	-	United Nations
UNCLOS	-	United Nations Convention on the Law of the Sea
UNCTAD	-	United Nations Conference on Trade and Development
UNDP	-	United Nations Development Programme
UNFCC	-	UN Framework Convention on Climate Change
UP	-	Uttar Pradesh

UPL	-	United Phosphors Limited
URJA	-	Urban Jyoti Abhiyaan
US	-	United States
USA	-	United States of America
USACEP	-	US-Asia-Pacific Comprehensive Energy Partnership
USGS	-	United States Geological Survey
USICEF	-	US-India Clean Energy Finance
UV	-	Utility Vehicle
VAT	-	Value-added tax
VVER	-	Vodo-Vodyanoi Energetichesky Reaktor
W	-	Watt
WBREDA	-	West Bengal Renewable Energy Development Agency
WCL	-	Western Coalfields Limited
WTO	-	World Trade Organization

List of Table

List of Figure

Preface

Energy security is an area of significant concern for India, especially for the last couple of decades. Energy demand and consumption have risen rapidly in the 21st century. It has a significant place in the development of human history. To a great extent, the social and economic growth of society depends on energy sources and the sustainability of this growth is determined by the way of energy usage as well as the type of energy resources.Energy security has been a significant practical concern for every human being, nations as well as world. The energy transition is not only the installation of renewable energy systems, but it consists of energy efficiency measures, sustainable urban planning, research and development on renewable energy sources and their business models, technological advancement in storage sector and integration of end use sectors for efficient usage of clean energy. The sustainable planning will help to improve the transport, agriculture, industrial and building sectors to implement the environmental friendly options.

The book focuses on some important concerns of Indian energy scenario. While taking into consideration the potentials and constraints of its energy profile, it deals with the challenges of India's energy security, the human environmental and societal security impacts of India's energy security goals and the policy options or remedies intended to tackle the present day energy insecurities.

The first chapter is introduction and the second chapter provides a detailed outlook on energy profile of India and explains history of India's energy searches, composition of energy mix, the institutional structure and the new initiatives on renewable energy. The same is justified with tables and figures. The third chapter deals with India's energy engagements with foreign nations and explore the opportunities of diversification of energy resources in international realm. It discusses the changing dynamics of India's energy engagements, focusing on main global energy institutions like OPEC, IEA, IAEA, ETC etc which shows the role played by them in shaping the prices of energy, particularly oil. This chapter focuses on the wide energy searches of India. It discusses human environmental and societal security questions in India's energy security framework. It delves into the challenges and constraints to India's energy sector like coal, oil, natural gas, solar, wind, and others. The fourth chapter catalogues some sustainable models and new initiatives in India's energy sector. And it analyses the prospects of green initiatives. The work put forward certain sustainable options in all end use sectors of energy. The final chapter brings together the observations and findings.

There is a visible growth in the field of renewable energy and sustainable development under Narendra Modi Government. He promises a 450 GW renewable target at UN Climate Action Summit in this year. Atal Mission for Rejuvenation and Urban Transformation, HRIDAY, Draft National Automotive Policy 2018, National Electric Mobility Mission Plan (NEMMP) 2020, GUTS 2017 (Green Urban Transport Scheme), UJALA Scheme, Energy Conservation Building Codes 2017, International Solar Alliance, low carbon pathways for industry initiative with Sweden and other countries etc. are some of the Green Initiatives during his tenure. The book underlines the need of energy transition as well as provides a comprehensive approach on all end use sectors of energy.

The book would not have been accomplished without the support and encouragement of so many people who came across this long effort. We would like to place on record our gratitude to Prof. (Dr). G. Gopakumar, Hon' ble Vice Chancellor, Central University of Kerala.Our sincere gratitude to the faculties and researchers of Department of International relations and Politics, Central University of Kerala, who provided the warm support and encouragement during the completion of this work. We would like to acknowledge Prof. (Dr). M. S John, Department of International Relations, Central University of Kerala, Kasaragod, for his untiring support and invaluable suggestions. Sincere thanks to Dr. Reinhart Philip, Assistant Professor, Central University of Kerala for his timely help and assistance in this endeavor.We express my sincere gratitude to Librarians of Central University of Kerala, Mahatma Gandhi University Kottayam, Kerala and Jawaharlal Nehru University, New Delhi for their courteous help to complete this book. Further we thank our families for their unwavering support.

We thank them all for their magnificent contribution.

Prof. (Dr.) K Jayaprasad

Dr. Aleena Thomas

Chapter - I

Introduction

Introduction

Energy has a significant place in the development of human history. To a great extent, the social and economic growth of society depends on energy sources and the sustainability of this growth is determined by the way of energy usage as well as the type of energy resources. Mankind made use of various types of energy resources in each stage of development. The primitive societies used energy from the sun without knowing its importance and they solely relied on their somatic energy[1] (Smil 2004, 549-50). The somatic energy is acquired by human beings through food such as plants, fruits, seeds and meat etc., and which is also derived from the sun. Likewise, almost all the energy resources are the reservoirs of energy from the sun through photosynthesis or some other ways. During hunting and gathering period, humans used the muscle force and some simple tools accelerated the reach of the muscles. Ultimately, the sun was the energy provider for them and they had been worshipping the sun for a long period of time. So, the earlier period's energy sources were the sun and various food items. And, the sun acts as the fundamental element in the food chain also. Even now, the commercial energy resources like fossil fuels are also the result of photosynthesis of plants. The wind, water and the rest of the resources are indirectly linked with the sun. Then fire was discovered and came to provide a wide variety of uses such as for heating, cooking and safety from predators. The burning of biomass and wood provided heat and light. It was one of the major developments in the human history. It was accessible to everyone, due to the abundant availability of biomass including dead wood and leaves from the forest. Further, the domestication of fire led to other developments such as invention of pottery, agricultural growth and secure human settlements (Bithas and Kalimeris 2015, 5-10).

Agricultural era contributed to the large production of food, permanent settlements, domestication of animals, expansion of energy sources and so forth. Hence the settlers had to depend on more new sources of energy for their advanced purposes. The power of muscles was very limited for their bulk farming, so that they used tamed animals, better tools and human labour for cultivation. Exploiting human labour force through slavery was one of the primary energy source for ancient Egypt as well as Greece. Human and animal powered tread wheels boosted the progress of mankind in the middle ages. According to Smil (2004, 549-53), a good horse was considered to be equivalent to 10 men, or at least 700 W. Later, water and wind mills were introduced as energy sources. Wind was behind the sailings, discoveries of new land and trade routes through seas. It marked a spot in the history and helped the European voyages and the following Western dominance over far away lands.

The steam engine and the Industrial Revolution transformed the organic economy to the fossil fuel economy. Organic nature of traditional society (Fouquet 2009, 1-19) changed due to population growth and the resulting need for more economic development (Krausmann et al. 2011, 877-892). Biomass driven energy delivery had been suffering from low efficiency. Since early 13th century, coal was recognized as a new energy source and began to be used as an alternative to wood. The coal deposits are formed by the geological transition of biomass for a long period of time. Shortage of wood and the need to preserve the forest were the reasons behind the transformation of wood to coal. The invention of steam engine which converts chemical energy to mechanical energy facilitated major advancements during the Industrial Revolution (Bithas and Kalimeris 2015, 5-10). The steam engine was helpful to drain the water from coal mines, and it reduced the effort and saved time. By 1900, the two thirds of power services were done by steam engines.

Oil discovery was another momentous and great milestone in the history of energy. In 1859, Edwin Drake drilled the first oil well in Pennsylvania and well along the first petroleum fuelled internal combustion engine was made in Japan in 1876. Initially, kerosene was distilled from oil for lighting purpose and petrol was considered as a waste and became popularized only during the commercialization of internal combustion engines. The invention of bulb was followed by alternate current (AC) for transmission, steam turbine, efficient transformer and electric motor. The development and spread of radios, televisions, cooking gadgets, air conditioners and computers were wholly relied on electricity. Massive coal plants, power plants and hydroelectric dams were built in the course of time. So, fossil fuels and electricity have driven the modern world in an advanced manner with lots of technologies and facilities. However, the strategic use of energy was getting significant only during the time of World Wars and it changed the course of history.

In the First World War, lesser amount of energy was used, compared with the Second World War. The importance of fossil fuel in the war was found and recognized the imperative of this strategic resource for everyone's benefit. Obviously, energy security was closely associated with military necessities during wars. For example, British Navy converted coal to petroleum for retaining the dominance. Germany and Japan had less petroleum resources during the Second World War and they designed their war strategies in order to get access to it. Earlier, Japan attacked Manchuria in 1931 for getting its coal reserves. In 1940, the US suspended its gasoline and aviation fuel export to Japan. Therefore, Japan invaded Indonesia for oil resources and then attacked Pearl Harbour. Similarly, Germany attacked the Soviet Union for oil, and in Romania, Hitler launched operation Blau to secure its oilfields. Finally, the first practical application of a new form of energy- nuclear energy- sealed the fate of the Second World War. Those two atomic bombs ever used were instrumental in creating the everlasting awareness among the whole humanity about the consequences of the destructive usage of energy sources.

The creation and usage of weapons are also related with energy as it uses energy during the time of production as well as after the usage of it (Sovacool 2011, 12-13). Also, wars can damage energy infrastructure causing the disruption of emergency services and other losses. Further, energy resources can also be conquered by insurgents and can be used as financial resources for their bargaining. Hence, energy is closely linked with or can be part and parcel of wars and violent conflicts.

After the Second World War, many countries looked upon nuclear energy for their survival. Electricity production and medicinal purposes increased the popularity of nuclear energy, but every nation has been trying to achieve it as a strategic source as well. The Three Mile Island nuclear accident reduced the interest on nuclear energy for a while, however the climate change concerns and defensive purposes facilitated the development of the nuclear sector. Transportation sector grew so rapidly and the usage of petroleum also increased correspondingly. During the 1970s, the concerns on climate change and environmental pollution contributed to the growth of the concept of clean energy.

The energy scenario drastically changed after the 1973 oil crisis. The Organization of Arab Petroleum Exporting Countries (OPEC) implemented a selective embargo on oil exports after the Arab–Israeli conflict and raised the price of oil. It stopped the oil exports to the United States and a few other western nations. It was against the support extended by the United States towards Israel in the Yom Kippur War. It quadrupled the oil price and so many gasoline stations became barren with many people waiting in the long queue for several hours. The 1979 Iranian Revolution too disrupted oil production and again an energy crisis occurred. The Iran-Iraq war also contributed to the energy price hike. These two crises questioned the reliability of supply and price mechanism. Thus, energy became an important aspect of national security for almost all nations. Consequently, every nation recognised and accepted the need for rethinking on energy policy. One way or the other, the crisis also affected even the daily lives of millions of people all over the world (Barton et al. 2005, 5-9).

After 1980s, because of the oil glut, oil price dropped drastically. However, the crisis generated serious concern about the need for energy diversification and nations were engaged with more research and development on finding out alternatives. The 9/11 terrorist attack and the resulting conflicts Afghanistan and Iraq put energy security in the top agenda. The abundant production of shale gas from the USA also affected the oil market. The world oil price was increased from $27.73 per barrel in 2003 to $35.00 per barrel in 2004 ($5.86 per million Btu), from $95 per barrel in 2007 to $135 a barrel in 2008 and then declined to $25.00 per barrel in 2010 ($4.18 per million Btu). Increasing demand from non OECD countries and unstable situations in countries like Iraq, Venezuela and Nigeria contributed to the price fluctuations. The Fukushima accident caused widespread concern and anguish over the use of nuclear energy. As a result, renewable energy is gaining greater attention and acceptance. Now the installed capacity and production of renewable energy increased considerably all over the world. Even though the dependence on fossil fuel is very high, the diversification of energy is a noticeable feature of the current energy scenario.

There is a vast literature dealing with energy and related issues. However, most of the works in this category are adopting a state centric perspective and the rest are mainly related with secure and reliable supply aspects. It can be observed that the mainstream literature does not fittingly address the environmental and human security issues of the energy searches and usages. Certain works bring up these aspects, such as environmental pollution as well as climate change. But, the current energy scenario needs a comprehensive approach on energy security, especially for the sustainable development of humanity.

Energy security scenario has mainly two dimensions, one is national security which is political or military and the other is economic. There are a lot of studies dealing with the issues of each energy source. In the case of coal, the environmental concerns and in the case of oil, supply disruptions and market failures are major issues. In the nuclear sector, the military dimensions and risk factors occupy the main focus. However, the new energy sources and the modern technologies adopted for the production, transmission and use of energy are instrumental in creating a changed energy scenario. More than any times, nations achieve and maintain power and influence on the basis of ownership and access to energy resources. In fact, today energy plays a critical role in the international realm as well as in the life of every individual. Hence, there are numerous works cantered around this field of study.

In *A Brief History of Energy Use,* Bithas and Kalimeris (2015) provides an overview about the development of human history and the role of energy in it. The energy use of traditional society was started from the sun which is the whole source of energy behind almost all forms of energy sources directly or indirectly. He stresses the significance of energy in the evolution of modern society and the depth of human dependence on energy. He also provides a clear picture on the evolution of energy usage. Fouquet (2009) argues that energy is the source for all human progress and survival. He examines the role of food as a major source of energy for human beings. According to him, sophisticated energy usage improves the quality of life and the source and forms of energy are different in different periods. By focusing on the similarities between societal metabolism and human metabolism, Krausmann (2011) argues that the environmental problems in societal metabolism, if unchecked, can destroy the entire living system in nearby future. During the time of evolution of society, the disposal of wastes, emissions and other pressures on environment are increasing. The study uses Material Flow Analysis from the history.

Smil (2004) in *World History and Energy*, sketches out a detailed history of energy. He deals with earlier, medieval and modern evolution of energy usage. In the earlier historical phase, the sun, fire, slaves, animals and biomass etc., were used while water and wind mills, tread wheels were in use at a later stage. Afterwards, the use of various sources like fossil fuels, coal, oil, nuclear energy and new technologies on renewable energy constitutes the history of energy.

As it is pointed out by Nakamura (2002), the control over these resources for the strategic achievement changed the energy dynamics in the 20th

century. After 1980s market became liberalized and industrial countries focused on supply and demand of energy. The removal of restrictions and allowing freedom in the energy trade happened during these days. The dynamics of the market approach, globalization and interdependence changed the oil industry. Besides, the threat of environmental hazards renewed the importance of renewable energy.

Yergin (1991) in the monumental work entitled *The Prize: The Epic Quest for Oil, Money, and Power* narrates the oil history from World Wars to 1990s and argues that the energy will be shaping our future international arena. The discovery of oil in Pennsylvania in 1859 created the history of modern day world. The Kerosene replaced whale oil as lighting fuel and since 1865, the gasoline changed the concept of energy resources. John D. Rockefeller monopolized the oil market in the early years. The book provides a broad history of energy and explains the dynamics of oil politics during the two World Wars. Less oil was used in the First World War, but the large usage of tanks and airplanes increased the dependency on oil in the Second World War. The book is more or less a history of the 20th century and recounts the incidents during the war period through the perspective of energy. Germany needed more oil reserves during the Second World War and they captured Maikop in 1942 but they had lost Rumanian oil fields due to the bombings from Russia. They failed in the attack on Baku and Grozny oil fields of Russia. The tensions in Crimea and Caucasus region in these times were due to the issues relating with access or control over the oil fields. In 1956, Nasser nationalized the Suez Canal, which was the main route of Arab Oil to the Europe and gave momentum to the other wars in this region. So, the twentieth century history could be explained through the lens of energy and it is more accurate than others.

While attempting to redefine energy security, Yergin (2006) argues for diversification of energy such as oil, natural gas, nuclear energy and renewable sources. The investments in new technologies help to increase the energy production as energy interdependence is an essential requirement for nations. So, the foreign policy strategies should be shaped by energy availability. It analysed the major disruption after 2000 on energy security. Yergin (2011) in yet another monumental work, *The Quest; Energy, Security, and the Remaking of the Modern World,* captures the energy scenario after the first Gulf War. By stating that energy is an element to shape the world, he deals with various issues like the reduction or scarcity of oil, the consumption growth of China and disruptions in the Middle East. The growth of the US and Europe after the Industrial Revolution and the impact of oil for the development of these economies are also discussed. The impact of energy on the environment is also dealt with. Since the First World War, energy is considered as a strategic component for attaining national power and energy is crucial in the war and conflicts. So, the powerful countries struggle to get access and control over these resources. Energy security is vital for the economic development. Energy and economic development together constitutes military strength.

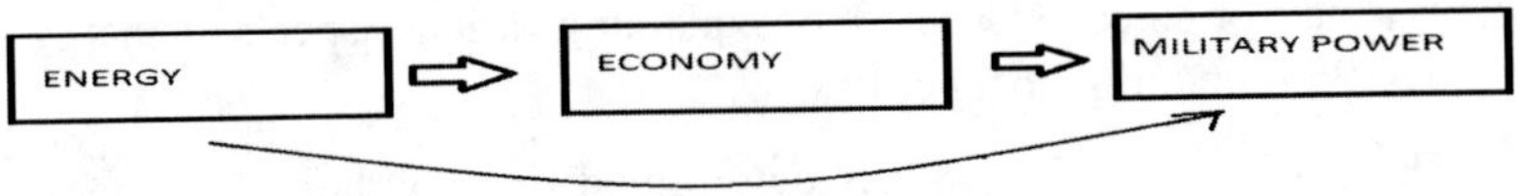

Figure 1.1

Energy independence and self-sufficiency are a matter of concern of national interest. Because of the scarcity of energy resources, states are competing to get access and control of energy sources. Michael T. Klare has done elaborate analysis of the energy interest behind foreign interventions and conflicts. In *Global Petro-Politics: The Foreign Policy Implications of the Bush Administration's Energy Plan,* Klare (2002) pointed out that the growing dependence of foreign oil creates more political and military interventions in resource rich areas. During the American intervention in Iraq, Klare (2003) criticised that the US intervened in the affairs of Iraq not becuase of the concern for democracy, but for the achievement of oil security. In another noted work titled as *Blood and Oil: The Dangers and Consequences of America's Growing Dependency on Imported Petroleum,* Klare (2004) bserves that the natural resources of a nation infuence the international realm. Oil resurce is the reason behind so many conflicts in the post cold war world. Alliances with certain Arab countries and conflict with some others explain the role of petroleum in the world politics. Klare (2008) in *Rising Powers, Shrinking Planet: The New Geopolitics of Energy,* argues that oil is a strategic componenet for all nations for their survival. He explains the new geopolicts after the cold war. Russia, emerging China and India plays a critical role in the energy scenario. In most of his articles he emphasised the importance of oil in the international politics. The issue of peak oil, increasing demand from non OECD nations and unstable oil regions lead to the disruptions in the supply side. Most of the oil rich nations are affected by inter-state conflicts, ethnic unrests and religious extremism or political turmoil etc. At the same time, they use their oil wealth as a powerful tool to achieve position and its power in the international realm. Energy has a vital role in the post 9/11 growth of radical Islam and the threat of international terrorism. He argues that the concept of energy security is evolved historically and geopolitically. The US traditionally considered energy as a security issue and maintains the availability without any disruption. So it intended to gain control over the Persian Gulf Region, announced the Carter Doctrine and engaged in fights with Russia, Iran and Iraq. Operation Desert Storm (1990-91) and the US invasion in Iraq (2003) reflected the energy thirst of the US. Central Asia, West Africa, Artic Region etc. are the new regions in the focus of energy searches and the US involves there also with military engagements. Klare adopts a state oriented perspective in explaining various aspects of energy in the background of global politics.

The geopolitics of energy is determined by geographical factors. Nakamura (2002) adopts a realist framework of energy security with geopolitical factors. Oil played a dominant role in the Second World War and the resource was concentrated in the Caribbean Sea. After 1950s, oil production has been shifted from Caribbean Sea to the Gulf of Mexico and then to the Persian Gulf region. The formation of OPEC and resulting politics revealed the significance of oil as a non- military weapon. The Soviet Union became the largest oil producer in 1980s and price fell down significantly after the oil glut. North Sea oil production also increased due to the energy crisis in 1980s. Further, Europe shifted its dependence from oil towards natural gas and other alternatives. According to Nakamura, when market oriented pricing system and the oil global market system were arranged by 1986, then the energy became a commodity from a strategic resource. The oil market gained dominance over the OPEC resources also at the end of the Gulf War. The energy policy of the US in 2001 was mainly concentrating on adequate supply of energy for its needs. Nakamura used the market analysis approach in analysing the geopolitics of energy. Similarly, Mamdouh (1988) also agrees that the geographical factors influence the new geopolitics where energy resources play a decisive role. Deudney (2000) projects security materialism as a new version of geopolitics of energy security. In his *Geopolitics as Theory: Historical Security Materialism,* explains the concepts of neoclassical geopolitics, historical security materialism, historical protection materialism, and structural-functional security materialism as well as attempt in presenting geopolitics as historical security materialism.

The sufficient and reliable supply of energy is the prior goal for every nation and it is the major requirement for maintaining the national interest. The earlier writers prefer state owned energy related activities and the object is always the state. They portray an anarchical world system with scarce resource. Therefore it is presumed that always there is a chance for states to engage in conflicts for energy resources and it always become a zero sum competition. The Report of an Independent Task Force, *National Security Consequences of U.S. Oil Dependency,* emphasises the role of state ensuring the regular supply with affordable price will be the duty of every state (Victor 2006). Energy security is a key to dominate the world with power, so that it is to be achieved by any means. There is a vast literature indicating the significance of the connection between energy resources and geopolitical issues. For instance, Jafar (2004) explains in *Kazakhstan: Oil, Politics and the New 'Great Game* about the oil politics in the Caspian sea region. Karasac (2002) in *Actors of the New Great Game* provides insights into the new geopolitics in the Caspian oil reserves. Blank (1995) in *Energy, Economics and Security in Central Asia: Russia and its Rival,* discusses about the role of energy sources in the geopolitics of central Asia and the role of Russia and the US in the region.

From the Neorealist perspective, energy security is a zero-sum game, in which each actor seeks gains and giving a relative advantage over the other. The security dilemma is playing a major role in the neorealism, so the military capacity of each actor is significant in the achievement of their interest. The destruction of pipelines by Russia in Russian-Georgian conflict in 2008 resembled the neorealist policy and also it used its Pipeline Diplomacy with European countries (Blinik 2008). Thus energy becomes a vital part of diplomacy as the demand of energy continues to increase.

Since 1980s, globalization and market approach have taken place in the energy field. The consumer countries are in vulnerable stage during this time. The market adjustment mechanisms changed the situation and realized the significance of cooperation between states in the reduction of supply disruptions. Now it is more or less a controlled system and can absorb shocks and balance supply and demand in a controlled manner. But it concentrates on reliable supply with reasonable price. Oil became a commodity and we can buy it at any time from the market. It influenced the diversification of energy and new technologies in this sector. Deregulation is a need for the stable supply of energy resources. According to market approach, militarization is not the solution for energy access. It is interdependence, integration and especially liberalization which will provide security of supply (SOS) with availability, accessibility, affordability and accessibility of energy sources (Kruyt et al. 2009). Free market with environment tax is also considered in this aspect and it is more open and cooperative rather than realist arrangements. International regulations, good governance and corporate social responsibility are helping hands to avoid the illicit practices of the market. International regimes and treaties such as IEA and Energy Charter Treaty regulate the market function.

Liberals consider oil as a commodity in the global market place. Verrastro and Ladislaw (2007) in *Providing Energy Security in an Interdependent World* attributed the complex interdependence and the international institutions are significant in energy security. The market approach of energy security emphasizes more on market as a suitable mechanism for the distribution of oil as for any other trade good. Oil is a unique natural resource and a trade good that can be the object of negotiation. Liberals point to the advantages of multilateral and institutionalized cooperation. This will make a trade web through which regimes and states will engage in cooperation and get benefitted from it. Cooperation is more significant than conflict for achieving energy security. Promotion of regional and international energy regimes such as IEA or the Energy Charter Treaty and institutions is the main characteristics of this approach. Srivastava and Misra (2007) advocate proposals for regional energy cooperative institutions, such as those proposed for South Asia or for North-East Asia to bring together Russia, China and Japan into a mutually beneficial rather than competitive energy relationship. The EU is an example for this and liberal and institutionalized energy policies enhanced the solutions to its energy security concerns.

Gault (2006) observes that the relationship in this is does not produce a zero sum outcome as "the improvement of one country's energy security need not be at the expense of other countries." Neoliberals argue for amity of democracies, Free trade for free countries, the importance of interdependence, international institutions and the value of community (Ikenberr 1999). The proper working of global energy market could resolve many energy security issues. In such a framework, the *laissez faire* principle is not an option to fight against market failures; instead governmental intervention is needed to solve them. The institutionalized framework and cooperation are the major factors in it. Goldthaugh and Witte (2009) are of the opinion that the economic liberalization of energy with principles of comparative advantage will ensure the efficient energy supply without any geopolitical compulsion. The object of this approach includes not only state but also global economy. Bielecki (2002) in the article *Energy security: Is the wolf at the door?*, concentrates on uninterrupted energy for global economy and the relevant market mechanism for the availability of the commodity. Pascual and Zambetakis (2009) in a report titled *The Geopolitics of Energy: From Security to Survival,* upholdsthe need of strategies for national, regional and international cooperation on energy. To them, economic growth and economic development are closely related with energy security in the liberalized world.

The phrase 'resource mercantilism' was first coined by Leverett (2007) in *The Geopolitics Oil and America's International Standing* for describing the use of economic and foreign policy instruments by national governments to help their state owned national energy companies to secure access to overseas hydrocarbon resources on more privileged bases than simply supply contracts. He stressed that the non OECD nations, such as China and India, are now energy hungry nations and argued that the Sino-Russian cooperation would be a threat to the US from the energy angle. China, Japan and India are more reliant on imports so that the import dependent nations try to own resources abroad. The diplomatic relations and financial aid help to invest abroad. Though the crude oil is a global commodity, the natural gas is delivered in regional markets. The new demand centres can change the price of oil and it was revealed during price rise in the 21st century. The states equity stakes in abroad played the crucial role in it. The resource mercantilism of these states support the state owned energy companies in foreign countries for exploration. Firstly, the states build a diplomatic rapport to key energy producing regions to pave the way for National Energy Companies to develop its access in these regions. Such an arrangement help the Chinese and Indian companies to secure equity stakes in oil and gas deals in the upstream and develop strategic assets in the downstream. Thus, they can achieve positions in the energy sector of those countries. The states provide financial and political aid to companies to explore in an effective manner and these neo mercantilists use market serving their state's interest. The disputes in the East China Sea between China and Japan were influenced by natural gas reserves. China is becoming a growing threat to the US for its energy searches. The shifting American policies towards Iran, Sudan and Syria are backed by its energy intentions in the changing world. In the same manner, India and China also compete to gain hold on energy fields in Africa and Central Asia. Ziegler and Menon (2014) in their paper *Neomercantilism and Great-Power Energy Competition in Central Asia and the Caspian* provide an account of the attempts by countries vying for control over alien energy resources from a neo-mercantilist perspective.

The producing nations use this tactic as a national government's ownership rights over oil and gas reserves within their territorial boundaries. It contradicts liberalization principles and international investments, and work against the interest of the international energy companies (Stevens 2008). The international oil companies had control over major oil producing nations or its assets in the 1970s and 1980s. After 1980s, the market took control and cooperation was visible in this field (Vivodo 2009). Deregulation and privatization took place in 1990s and the price fell down. However, the resource nationalism came back because of the 21st century price hike and increased taxes and royalties (Vivodo 2008). The Latin American states such as Bolivia, Venezuela and Ecuador paved the way for it. They increased their share in oil sector and Yemen stopped the operation of some International Oil Companies. In 2007, Zimbabwe used the nationalization technique to threaten foreign companies involved in uranium, coal and methane projects. After 2003, Russia renationalized their companies and increased their taxes. Nigeria, Angola, Chad and Sudan also demanded large share in oil sector. The supply states stressed the need to strategic influence over the production and marketing of the hydrocarbon reserves. The supply cut offs, from both Hugo Chavez of Venezuela and President Mehmoud Ahmadinejad had threatened the consumer nations. The oil producing countries and IOCs changing relations turned as an anti-western campaign and the Persian Gulf, North Africa and Latin American countries were part of it. Mamadouh (1988) in *Geopolitics in the Nineties: One Flag, Many Meanings* explains the '90s oil politics in the international landscape. Walde (2008) also focuses on the changes of the oil producing nations and analyses the present day challenges in the investment in energy sector.

In the global capital system, there is an unfair economic distribution resulting in the North-South divide and the critical theory is concerned largely about this. The energy rich nations export raw materials to core western world and are exploited by the latter. Some of the OPEC countries are benefited from the oil, hence they differ from the common pool of South or peripheral countries. Therefore, in the opinion of Sekhri (2009), there is a South -South divide as well as a result of the high oil revenue. However, even these resource rich countries are also depending on the North for their market, stability and other benefits. They are deprived of the core countries due to its lack of knowledge and technological advancement. In the case of oil and other energy resources, developing and underdeveloped nations are dependent on the North or the core countries. In every field of energy, the global West played a significant part and they take maximum resources and the rest gets only the left over. The big nuclear business nations sell their nuclear technologies to the underdeveloped nations. As far as the South is concerned, energy availability is confined mainly for the privileged strata. There are millions of people who have no access to electricity or clean fuel.

As mentioned earlier, the concept of energy security is part and parcel of national security. However, the energy searches of nations to achieve their national security lead to creation of new insecurities. The world is turning out to be insecure due to the unscientific usage of energy resources.

Therefore, the need of this security is also questioned in terms of, for whom or for what purpose. Dalby (1997) underlines the importance of a rethinking about the state centric security discources. In *Security and Environmental Change,* Dalby (2009) gives an account of the risks assosiated with the global economic development and the relationship between the climate change and human interventions on the ecosystem. He mentions the problems of environmental change and its impact on human security also. Dalby (2010) in *Critical Geopolitics and Security,* highlightes the weakness of traditional geoplitics and stresses the importance of environmental factors in the new geopolitics. Dalby's works elucidate environmental security aspect and it is very useful in the energy studies. His submits that the mainstream approaches neglected the individual and climate security. The policies of energy from the states are relied on the state security approach and neglected the marginalized sections.

Similarly, Trombetta (2008) argues that the environmental factors must be given a relevent concern in the new security discourses. In *Rethinking the Securitization of the Environment,* Trombetta (2010) examines the securitisation theory and the problems of the inclusion of environmrntal and other current security threats inthe theory. Vanderheiden (2011) in *The Politics of Energy: An Introduction,* points out the challenges of sustainable energy infrastructure. He warns that a cautious research is needed at the time of choosing alternate options, otherwise it will be catastrophic like Fukushima.

The concern over ecology and the human insecurity leads to the clean energy options. Simpson (2013) holds the view that the marginalized communities lack access to energy for their personal needs. Around 1.5 billion people in developing countries are suffering from lack of access to electricity and about 3 billion people rely on fuel wood and biomass for cooking. The energy rich nations in Africa grieve with poverty. Most of the local people staying nearby energy resource suffer from poverty and health impacts. The workers in energy industry are also deprived sections. In another article Simpson (2007) explains the love of dominant classes towards large scale projects. Mostly, the resulting issues affect the deprived sections. The state centric security discources are largely addressing the needs of elites. Dannreuther (2010) in *Energy Security* also holds the view that elites enjoy modern energy facilities and the neglected poor people have less access to these resources Mulligan (2010) in *Energy, Environment, and Security: Critical Links in a Post-Peak World* discusses the issues of peak oil, climate change and environmental considerations by the energy usage. Mulligan (2011) in another study points out that the finite nature of energy sources creates significant threats to human ecology. It necessiates the need of critcal security perspecctive rather than state centric discourse, in addressing such an issue. It is in this context, Barnet (2001) poses questions such as security from what and for whom?

India is the fourth leading consumer of oil and depends on import for its 80% of oil. Pant (2008) in the work titled *India: The Emerging Energy Player* portrays the energy landscape of India and its energy searches in domestic fields as well as abroad. In another work titled *India's Emerging Energy Relations*, Pant (2015) examines India's energy policy towards foreign countries. These books provide a vast picture about India's energy searches with different types of resources and policies with different nations.

Looking into the energy history of India, Ebinger (2012) states that energy acts as one of the prime concerns in India's foreign policy formulations and in the diplomatic relations. Noronha and Sudarshan (2009) in *India's Energy Security* analyses the economic growth of India and the corresponding life style changes. They argue that increasing usage of energy intensity products such as cars, air conditions, home appliances etc., by the middle class is a major compulsion behind India to be a major energy consumption country. The urbanization and the spread of globalization increased the energy consumption of India. The transport sector consumes one fourth of India's energy consumption. Addressing energy poverty as a significant issue in the case of India, Gupta (2009) in *Life Style and Energy Consumption* says that in rural areas, energy consumption is mainly occurs from direct usage. In urban areas, people consume energy directly and indirectly. Direct and indirect consumption of energy for the household activities are immensely high. The indirect usage consists of production of home appliances and it consumes more energy at the industrial level.

At present India is largely relying on coal and it has critical challenges on environmental pollution and affect the health of the people. Price fluctuations, global warming, fossil fuel burning, import dependence and instabilities of oil rich regions are challenges before India's energy searches. The diversification of energy resources turned India's attention towards natural gas and nuclear energy searches. Natural gas will contribute a major share in the future energy demands of India and at global level because of its abundance and less polluting characteristics. However, the security of energy transit route, extracting procedures and its geological impact are challenging factors. Since 2005, India again concentrated on nuclear energy without signing the NPT and the NSG waiver created a boom in this industry. But the liability issues and risk factors are the major concerns here. However, it contributes only 3% of its energy needs and it could not achieve the predicted targets in the stipulated period. Cherian (2017) in the article *From Non Alignment to Strategic Partnership,* explains India's new partnerships towards other states. Chari (2009) in *Indo-US Nuclear Deal: Seeking Synergy in Bilateralism,* analyses the developments of the Indo-US nuclear deal and Rajagopalan (2008) in a special report titled as *Indo-US Nuclear Deal Implications for India & the Global N-Regime,* emphasizes the benefits of the Indo-US nuclear deal. On the other hand, Seethi (2008) in *Perils of Nuclear Renaissance and the Indo US Civil Nuclear Deal,* points out the critical issues of the nuclear deal. Nuclear energy is not a viable option for human being as an energy source. Its eternality cost is much higher than other renewable sources. Global and national level renewable energy developments enhance the hope on clean future.

The literature on India's energy sector resembles mainly on basis of the economic growth and economic development. Reliable supply with affordable price is the main concern, so India's energy searches like oil and coal extraction are rarely addressing the future concern over environment and humanity. The energy exploration of Indian companies abroad, considers China as a critical competitor for India and the United States also poses challenges in India's energy aspirations. Majority of Indians have no access of sophisticated energy and they use fuel wood and biomass as cooking fuel. Per capita energy consumption is also very law. However, India's energy searches mostly satisfies the aspirations of state elites. The fossil fuels contribute to the major share of energy mix and the dependence on it is another challenging aspect of India's energy landscape. So the insecurities resulted from the quest for energy security are least addressed in India's energy security studies. Areas like the human security and environmental security in this sector are also largely neglected.

Energy security is an important consideration for India, especially for the last couple of decades. Energy demand and consumption have risen rapidly in the 21st century. Economic growth, growing transport sector, industrial growth, strong demand for infrastructure, housing, media, entertainment services and IT, economic reforms and etc., after the 1990s, the growing service sector and aspirations of more than one billion people together contribute the growing concern of energy in India.

Three-quarters of Indian energy demand is depended on fossil fuels and India was the world's third-largest importer of crude oil in 2014. It is estimated that oil demand may increases to 10 mb/d by 2040 and natural gas consumption may triple to 175 bcm. It is the third largest economy, but it can not provide access to electricity to 240 million people. Still the fuel wood and solid biomass are the major source of energy for rural areas in India which is the primary cooking fuel for around 840 million people and the usage of traditional cooking stove makes indoor pollution also. Even though the overall energy consumption is very high in India comparing to the other countries, the per capita energy usage is very low.

India lacks clean and sophisticated energy for majority of its population. Coal and oil are the major resources in India's energy mix and the environmental as well as health concerns of them cannot be avoided for the immediate short term goals. The impact on climate change, global warming and peak oil consideration compel to make a rethinking on oil, however it has a major share in India's energy mix. Energy infrastructure and its threats lead to human and social insecurity, so that energy security holds the meaning of energy insecurity also. It is more important for the rural people because they are very susceptible, marginalized and lack of access to most of the resources. A majority of rural the households depends on traditional fuels like fuel wood to meet most of their energy requirements, supplemented by small amounts of kerosene and electricity for lighting. Oil and other fossil fuel depletion, reliance on foreign source of energy, geopolitical reasons, and economic efficiency vs population growth, environmental issues like climate change are also certain challenges in this sector. Environmental and socio economic perspectives lagged in the India's energy scenario. One way or the other, the extraction, conversion, transformation or use of the energy cause challenges to environmental and societal security. These challenges started from the very beginning of human being, but in the initial stage the need was limited to sun as well as biological energy which is in the form of food, then it extended to wood when the use of fire was discovered, then to fossil fuels which made industrial revolution and urbanization. These together promoted transportation used by fossil fuels. Even so, the newer materialistic culture also promotes energy hungry approach and the pressure from this over usage made disastrous condition towards the environment and it is the high time for cleaner energy. Most importantly, the poor world still depends on poor resources so there is a need to intervene the energy usage pattern of them. Implementation of major energy projects causes besides the environmental problems displacement, livelihood, deforestation, health concerns etc. are some other issues for humanity. India faces challenges in meeting lifeline energy needs of all citizens to address social development, health and safety of the energy poor with a sustainable manner. In this backdrop the study analyses the challenges in the changing dimensions of India's energy security with a focus on the social and environmental factors.

Energy Security: The Concept

According to the International Energy Agency's (IEA) World Energy Outlook of 2012, the global energy demand is likely to grow by more than one-third over the period to 2035, with China, India and the Middle East accounting for 60% of the increase. The energy security, traditionally addresses the relative availability, affordability and safety of energy fuels and services. The World Bank expressed that energy security is based on the three pillars such as energy efficiency, diversification of supply and minimization of price volatility (World Bank 2005). Consumers view energy security as affordable price and without supply disruption. So they want to avoid the risks from the supply nations and they promote investments in different energy resources domestically as well as internationally. Producers focus on access to new reserves, reliable price and safety of energy infrastructure from terrorism and war (Stringer 2008, 121-142). Some energy abundant African countries considered energy as a burden for them. On the other hand, a country like the US is not only the consumer but also a significant producer of energy after the oil crisis. Similarly, Russia is largely an energy exporter and it need to maintain the market. It asserts state influence over strategic resources to gain primary control over the infrastructure. Restricting foreign investment in domestic oil and gas fields is an important element of this strategy (Brown & Sovacool 2011, 215-39).

Countries with limited energy resource like Japan adopted energy security strategies of diversification, trade, and investment, as well as selective engagement with neighbouring Asian countries to jointly develop energy. Earlier, they engaged in conflicts with other countries for accessing energy resources. Countries like China approach energy security towards energy scramble for resources and buying stakes in foreign oil fields, militarily protecting vulnerable shipping lanes and more on nuclear energy to meet their high demand. Even if various countries stress on different aspects of energy security, still energy is critical, directly or indirectly, in the entire process of evolution, growth and survival of all living beings and it plays a vital role in the socio-economic development and human welfare of a country. Energy security means having access to requisite volumes of energy at affordable prices (Ebinger 2012, 2-4). According to Hancher, energy security can be defined as "a condition in which a nation and all, or most, of its citizens and industries have access to adequate energy resources at reasonable prices for the foreseeable future, free from serious risks of major disruption of service" (Barton et al. 2004). Energy security is reliable supply at affordable prices from the side of the consuming nations and as reliable demand at sustainable prices in the case of producing nations.

Problems of energy security interact with social, cultural, political, economic and military aspects of national security concerns (Dees 1979). Security of physical supply, affordability and sustainability create energy security and it is linked with energy, economic growth and political power (Stringer, 2008, 122).

It is observed that energy security as the ability of an economy to guarantee the availability of energy resource supply in a sustainable and timely manner with the energy price being at a level that will not adversely affect the economic performance of the economy. Thus, there are several factors that can influence the 'security' of energy supply, such as: (1) the availability of fuel reserves, both domestically and by external suppliers; (2) the ability of an economy to acquire supply to meet projected energy demand; (3) the level of an economy's energy resource diversification and energy supplier diversification; (4) accessibility to fuel resources, in terms of the availability of related energy infrastructure and energy transportation infrastructure; and (5) geopolitical concerns surrounding resource acquisition (APERC 2007, 6).

Thus energy security spreads across the four 'A's of *availability, accessibility, acceptability* and *affordability*. Energy security has been a significant practical concern for every human being, nations as well as world. Energy engages almost every aspect of human endeavour in modern times. It has also emerged as a distinct area of scholarly studies in the last several decades. Energy is the prime determinant aspect behind economic and social development. Accessibility and adequate supply of energy is the key to sustainable development. It has direct impact on the quality of service in the fields of education, health and, even food security. Almost all mainstream studies focused on the energy security from the state perspective. Since 1970s oil crisis, the studies are relating with the supply disruption and security concern.

According to Leal-Arcas & Filis (2013, 5) "energy security is a condition in which a nation and all, or most, of its citizens and businesses have access to sufficient energy resources at reasonable prices for the foreseeable future free from serious risk of major disruption of service." It needs to address three challenges. The first involves limiting the vulnerability to disruption given rising dependence on imported oil from an unstable Middle East. The second, is to ensure the adequate supply for rising demand at reasonable prices. The third face of energy security is the energy related environmental challenge.

As a country with a population of 1.3 billion, energy security is a critical part of India. However, even today its 70% of energy mix is depend upon fossil fuel resources. The resulting environmental hazards and human security are countless. In the global level, India is third in the case of carbon emission and primary energy consumption, even though several people still have no access to electricity and most of the rural people are using traditional biomass for cooking. Affordability is a main factor for access of energy for common people. And the per capita energy consumption is very low compared to other countries. However, access of energy without any supply disruption is considered as an integral factor of national security and every nation tried to maintain its energy security. But during this journey to fulfil the target, there are several issues that could be neglected or marginalized. Environmental concerns are one among this; especially climate change, pollution of all kind, risks to the biodiversity etc. Health concerns of human being and livelihood and displacement issues of certain societies are also emerged out from the search of energy security.

Energy security in the Indian context or the context of the developing world at large is a complex issue that goes well beyond the typical understanding of what it is. It dwells upon assuring "sufficient" supply at "reasonable" prices. Such a traditional understanding of energy security was relevant only when the currently developed world enjoyed unconstrained growth by depleting the world's resource endowments and destroying our global commons. Today 'reasonable' prices and the definition 'sufficient' varies with the level of economic development and resulting patterns of production, consumption and lifestyles. The increased use of commercial energy by those who still use more than a 'sufficient' requirement simply because they can afford to do so, threatens the very existence of those who never used it in the first place, or used it in insufficient quantities and at reasonable prices. Thus, in the current context, energy security has strong overtones of equity and implies a moral responsibility towards reversing the historic impact on our global commons (Sethi 2009, 20-21).

So, the concept of energy security itself is a constructed one and it addresses only the present day needs. It rarely concerns the human and environmental aspect. So, we need to understand the effects of present day energy consumption pattern and change this towards a green and clean energy future. Nationalized as well as decentralized minor renewable energy programs will help to accomplish our domestic energy needs. The solar and wind energy promoting policies of the government is a significant achievement in this scenario. Green energy can provide a brighter future with clean environment for the next generations. Access to clean and modern energy will improve the education, health and overall development of individual and the society.

This study is organized into six chapters. The first chapter provides an introductory overview of the study. It introduces the concept of energy security and provides the conceptual framework of the study. The chapter also includes a review of literature and theoretical discourses, research questions, research objectives and methodology. The second chapter categorizes the energy profile of India. The chapter examines history of India's energy searches, composition of energy mix, the institutional structure and the new initiatives on renewable energy. The third chapter deals with India's energy engagements with foreign nations and explore the opportunities of diversification of energy resources in international realm. The fourth chapter focused on the challenges from energy searches of India. It discusses human environmental and societal security questions in India's energy security framework. The fifth chapter catalogues some sustainable models and new initiatives in India's energy sector. And it analyses the prospects of green initiatives. The final chapter brings together the observations, findings and recommendations.

In this study, an analytical, historical and descriptive methodology has been adopted. The data for the study has been collected from primary and secondary sources. Personal interviews were conducted with selected persons working in this field. These were unstructured interviews with open ended questions. Data from various libraries and other knowledge repositories has been comprehensively surveyed for this work. Different documents including statistical as well as other reports, official statements, interviews, agreements, working papers and studies published by government and non-governmental agencies, and international institutions have also been referred. Data has also been collected from the Ministry of Petroleum and Natural Gas, Ministry of Coal, Ministry of New and Renewable Energy, Ministry of Power, External Affairs Ministry, NITI Aayog, International Energy Agency and International Renewable Energy Agency etc.

Reference

APERC (Asia Pacific Energy Research Centre). 2007. *A Quest for Energy Security in the 21st Century: Resources and Constraints*. Japan: APERC. https:// aperc.ieej.or.jp/file/ 2010/9/26/APERC 2007 A Quest for Energy Security.pdf.

Barnett, Jon. 200. *The Meaning of Environmental Security: Ecological Politics and Policy in the New Security Era.* London: Zed Books.

Barton, Barry, Catherine Redgwell, Anita Ronne, and Donald N Zillman. 2004. *Energy Security: Managing Risk in a Dynamic Legal and Regulatory Environment.* New York: Oxford University Press.

Bielecki, J. 2002. "Energy Security: Is the Wolf at the Door?." *The Quarterly Review of Economics and Finance* 42(2): 235-50.

Bithas, Kostas, and Panos Kalimeris.2015. "A Brief History of Energy Use." In *Revisiting the Energy-Development Link: Evidence from the 20th Century for Knowledge-based and Developing Economies,* edited by Kostas Bithas and Panos Kalimeris. 5-10. London: Springer.

Blank, Stephen. 1995. "Energy, Economics and Security in Central Asia: Russia and its Rival." *Central Asian Survey* 14(3): 373-406.

Blinik, Adam. 2008. "Pipeline Diplomacy." *The New Atlantis 21(Summer): 122-27.*

Brown, Marilyn A., and Benjamin K. Sovacool. 2011. *Climate Change and Global Energy Security: Technology and Policy Options.* Massachusetts: Cambridge.

Chari, P.R. 2009. *Indo-US Nuclear Deal: Seeking Synergy in Bilateralism.* New Delhi: Routledge.

Cherian, John. 2017. "From Non-alignment to Strategic Partnership". *Foreign Policy,* September 1, 2017.

Dalby, Simon. 1997. "Contesting an Essential Concept: Reading the Dilemmas in Contemporary Security Discourse." In *Critical Security Studies: Concepts and Cases,* edited by Keith Krause, & Michael C. Williams. Minneapolis: University of Minnesota Press.

Dalby, Simon. 2009. *Security and Environmental Change.* Cambridge: Polity Press.

Dalby, Simon. 2010. "Critical Geopolitics and Security." In *Handbook of New Security Studies*, edited by J. Peter Burgess, London: Routledge.

Dannreuther, R. 2017. *Energy Security*. Cambridge: Polity Press.

Deudney, Daniel. 2000. "Geopolitics as Theory: Historical Security Materialism." *European Journal of International Relations* 6 (1):77-107.

Doyle, Michael W., and G.John Ikenberry, ed. 1997. *New Thinking in International Relations Theory,* Colorado: Westview Press.

Ebinger, Charles. K. 2012. *Energy and Security in South Asia: Cooperation or Conflict.* Washington DC: The Brookings Institution.

Fouquet, Roger. 2009. "A Brief History of Energy." In *International Handbook on the Economics of Energy,* edited by Joanne Evans, and Lester C. Hunt. 1-19. Cheltenham, UK: Edward Elgar Publishing.

Gault, John C. 2006. "*Energy Security, Globalization and Global Security.*"In the Program on the Geopolitical Implications of Globalization and Transnational Security GCSP Policy Brief Series.no.8. September 28. Geneva: Geneva Centre for Security Policy.

Goldthau Andreas, and Jan Martin Witte. 2009. "Back to the Future or Forward to the Past? Strengthening Markets and Rules for Effective Global Energy Governance."*International Affairs* 85(2) March: 373-90.

Gupta, Mitali Das. 2009. "Life Styles and Energy Consumption." In *India's Energy Security,* edited by Ligia Noronha and Anant Sudarshan. Abingdon, Oxon: Routledge.

Ikenberry, G John. 1999. "Why Export Democracy? The 'Hidden Grand Strategy' of American Foreign Policy." *The Wilson Quarterly* 23(2): 56-65.

Jafar, Majid. 2004. "Kazakhstan: Oil, Politics and the New 'Great Game." In *The Caspian: Politics, Energy and Security*, edited by Shirin Akiner. London: Routledge.

Karasac, Hasene. 2002. "Actors of the New 'Great Game' Caspian Oil Politics." *Journal of Southern Europe and the Balkans* 4(1): 15-27.

Klare, Michael. T. 2002. "Global Petro-Politics: The Foreign Policy Implications of the Bush Administration's Energy Plan." *Current History* 101(653) March: 99-104.

Klare, Michael. T. 2003. "For Oil and Empire?Rethinking War with Iraq."*Current History* 102(662) March: 129-35.

Klare, Michael. T. 2004. *Blood and Oil: The Dangers and Consequences of America's Growing Dependency on Imported Petroleum.* New York: Metropolitan Books.

Klare, Michael. T. 2008. *Rising Powers, Shrinking Planet: The New Geopolitics of Energy.* New York: Henry Holt and Company.

Krausmann, Fridolin, Simone Gingrich, and Reza NourbakhchSabet. 2011. "The Metabolic Transition in Japan: A Material Flow Account for the Period From 1878 to 2005."*Journal of Industrial Ecology* 15(6): 877-92. Yale University.

Krausmann, Fridolin. 2011. *The Socio-Metabolic Transition. Long Term Historical Trends and Patterns in Global Material and Energy Use.Institute of Social Ecology.* Vienna: Institute of Social Ecology.

Kruyt, Bert. *D.P. van Vuuren, H.J.M. de Vries*, and *H. Groenenberg.*2009. "Indicators for Energy Security." *Energy Policy, Elsevier* 37(6) June: 2166 -2181.

Leal-Arcas, Rafael, and Andrew Filis. 2013. "The Fragmented Governance of the Global Energy Economy: A Legal-Institutional Analysis." *Journal of World Energy Law & Business* 167/2014: 1-59.Queen Mary School of Law Legal Studies.

Leverett, Flynt. 2007. *The Geopolitics of Oil and America's International Standing.* United States: Committee on Energy and Natural Resources, US Senate. January 10.

Mamadouh, V. D. 1988. "Geopolitics in the Nineties: One Flag, Many Meanings." *Geo Journal.* 46(March): 237-253.

Mauawad, Jad. 2006. "Western Firms Feel a Pinch from Oil Nationalism." *The New York Times.*May 7.

Mulligan, Shane. 2010. "Energy, Environment, and Security: Critical Links in a Post-Peak World." *Global Environmental Politics.* 10(4), November: 79-100.

Mulligan, Shane. 2011. "Energy and Human Ecology: A Critical Security Approach." *Journal of Environmental Politics* 20(5) September: 633-649.

Nakamura, Yuji. 2002. *The Historical Flow of Black Gold: Two Approaches to Energy Security.* Institute for International Policy Studies Policy Paper. 282 E(January). Tokyo: IIPS.

Noronha, Ligia and Anant Sudarshan. 2009. *India's Energy Security*. Abington, Oxon: Routledge.

Pant, Girijesh. 2008. *India: The Emerging Energy Player.*Delhi: Dorling Kindersley.

Pant, Girijesh. 2015. *India's Emerging Energy Relation: Issues and Challenges.*New Delhi: Springer.

Pascual, Carlos and Elkind, Jonathan. 2010. *Energy Security: Economics, Politics, Strategies and Implications*. Washington DC: Brookings.

Pascual, Carlos, and Zambetakis E. 2009.*The Geopolitics of Energy: From Security to Survival.* Washington DC: Brookings.

Rajagopalan, Rajeswari Pillai. 2008. *Indo-US Nuclear Deal: Implications for India and the Global N-Regime.* New Delhi: Institute of Peace and Conflict Studies.

Rasizade, Alec. 2002. "The Specter of a New 'Great Game' in Central Asia." *Foreign Service Journal* 79(11) November: 48-52.

Seethi, K.M. 2008."Perils of Nuclear Renaissance and the Indo US Civil Nuclear Deal."*Indian Journal of Politics and International Relations.* 1(1):129-40.

Sekhri, Sofiane. 2009. "Dependency approach: Chances of survival in the 21st century." *African Journal of Political Science and International Relations.* 3(5): 242-52.

Sethi, Surya. 2009. "India's Energy Challenges and Choices" In *India's Energy Security*, edited by Ligia Noronha and Anant Sudarshan. 19-28. Abington, Oxon: Routledge.

Simpson, A. 2007. "The Environment: Energy Security Nexus: Critical Analysis of an Energy 'Love Triangle' in Southeast Asia." *Third World Quarterly.* 28(3) April: 539 – 54.

Simpson, A. 2013. "Challenging Inequality and Injustice: A Critical Approach to Energy Security." In *Environmental security: Aapproaches and Issues,* edited by Rita Floyd, and Richard Mathew, London: Routledge.

Smil, Vaclav. 2004. "War and Energy." *Encyclopedia of Energy* 6: 549-61. Elsevier.

Sovacool, Bennjamin. K. 2011. "Introduction: Defining, Measuring, and Exploring Energy Security." In *The Routledge Handbook of Energy Security*, edited by Benjamin. K. Sovacool, 1-42. London: Routledge.

Srivastava, Leena. and Neha Misra. 2007. "Promoting Regional Energy Co-operation in South Asia." *Energy Policy* 35(6) February: 360-368.

Stevens, Paul. 2008. "National Oil Companies and International Oil Companies in the Middle East: Under the Shadow of Government and the Resource Nationalism Cycle." *Journal of World Energy Law & Business* 1(1) May: 5-30.

Stringer, Kevin. D. 2008. "Energy Security: Applying a Portfolio Approach." *Baltic Security & Defence Review.* 10: 121-142.

Trombetta, Maria Julia. 2008. "Environmental Security and Climate Change: Analyzing the Discourse." *Cambridge Review of International Affairs* 21(4):585-602.

Trombetta, Maria Julia. 2010. "Rethinking the Securitization of Environment: Old Beliefs, New Insights." In *Securitization Theory: How Security Problems Emerge and Dissolve,* edited by Thierry Balzacq. New York: Routledge.

Vanderheiden, Steve. 2011. "The Politics of Energy: An Introduction." *Environmental Politics* 20(5): 607–16. Routledge.

Vanderheiden, Steve. 2014. *The Politics of Energy: Challenges for a Sustainable Future*. New York: Routledge.

Verrastro, Frank, and Sarah Ladislaw. 2007. "Providing Energy Security in an Interdependent World." *The Washington Quarterly* 30(4) November: 95-104.

Victor, David. G. 2006. *National Security Consequences of U.S. Oil Dependency.* New York: Council on Foreign Relations.

Vivoda, Vlado. 2008. *The Return of the Obsolescing Bargain and the Decline of Big Oil: A Study of Bargaining in the Contemporary Oil Industry.* Saarbrucken: VDM Verlag.

Vivoda, Vlado. 2009. "Resource Nationalism, Bargaining and International Oil Companies: Challenges and Change in the New Millennium." *New Political Economy* 14(4) December: 517–34.

Walde, T. 2008. "Renegotiating Acquired Rights in the Oil and Gas Industries: Industry and Political Cycles Meet the Rule of Law." *Journal of World Energy Law & Business* 1(1) May: 55-97.

World Bank. 2005. "Energy Security Issues." Accessed April 23, 2018. http://documents.worldbank.org/curated/en/464811468175435408/Energy-security-issues.

Yergin, Daniel. 1991. *The Prize: The Epic Quest for Oil, Money, and Power.* New York: Free Press.

Yergin, Daniel. 2006. "Ensuring Energy Security." *Foreign Affairs* 85(2) March/April: 69-82.

Yergin, Daniel. 2011. *The Quest; Energy, Security, and the Remaking of the Modern World.* New York: Penguin Books.

Ziegler, Charles. E, and Rajan Menon. 2014. "Neomercantilism and Great- Power Energy Competition in Central Asia and the Caspian." *Strategic Studies Quarterly* 8 (2): 17-41.

Chapter - II

India's Energy Profile

Introduction

The continuous availability of energy in different forms in sufficient quantities with reasonable price is one of the primary interests of every nation. So India, which is the third among the primary energy consumer countries, has adopted an energy policy with the key objectives such as access at affordable prices, improved security and independence, greater sustainability and economic growth. The changing dynamics of India's economy and growing aspiration of 1.32 billion people have made the energy aspect a complex one. As energy consumption is in a rapidly growing stage in India, it must be managed efficiently and responsibly to ensure the overall quality of life, including the protection of the natural environment.

Energy production, transportation and use have significant impact upon the environment, so assurance of clean energy is an integral element of sustainable development. Energy is a prime factor behind sustainable development as well as improved standard of living, especially for development in health, food security and etc. However, India is heavily dependent on fossil fuel resources, especially coal and oil. The huge dependence on import for these resources is also a major hurdle to the clean energy future. Even after the Pradhan Mantri Sahaj Bijli Har Ghar Yojana, several households are unelectrified and the electrified rural poor enjoys only the accessibility. The costly electricity and related equipment are still far away for them. And unhealthy cooking practices are existing in rural and urban areas. The biomass such as firewood and dried cow dung as well as fossil fuels like coal and kerosene are the major source in almost all the rural area. The improvement of energy efficiency on supply and demand side is also a significant factor in the path of achievement of India's energy security goals (NITI Aayog 2017, 4-7).

India's Energy History

The current energy landscape is the outcome of the events and policy decisions of India's energy history. The uneven and limited supply of energy was the major characteristic of the pre independence period of the country. More than 80% of people were residing in the rural areas and they were using non-commercial energy for their daily activities. The six major cities consumed around 70% of commercial energy such as coal, oil and hydroelectricity. Most of the energy productions were carried out in the private sector. British owned electricity was used in the industries. The British started the coal mining in 1774 in the Raniganj Coal field of the Damodar River Valley (Ministry of Coal 2018, 17-23). However, the low quality, weak extraction methods and poor rail facilities had been causing a slow growth in this sector. In fact, oil production was relatively very low. Digboi field in Assam as well as Attock in North-Western part of undivided India were the only major oil fields in the colonial period.

Hydel project started in 1896 with the establishment of Sidrabong power station in the Darjeeling hill area of West Bengal (Kesharwani 2006, 44-57). The availability, low cost and huge demand from industrial sector forced them to choose coal powered thermal power plants. In 1899, the Calcutta Electric Supply Corporation Limited (CESC) Ltd, a private company established the first thermal power station in Kolkata. Under the British India the power supply was limited to cities and industrial areas, especially Bombay, Calcutta, Ahmadabad and Kanpur. The demand from industries increased the thermal power stations and large scale coal mining. The electricity generation and distribution were done by private players before independence (Saini 2018, 275-78) Lignite and diesel also contributed a share to the thermal power plants. The production of energy was very low in the earlier period even after independence as the technologies and geographical data were neither updated nor revised after the colonial rule. Electricity generation and energy searches were poorly funded and manned. At the time of independence, the power generation mix constituted coal and small hydro in the ratio of 50:50 (Sudarshan & Noronha 2009, 3-19). For a country like India, coal mining was comparatively easier than exploration of other sources of energy. The coal industry became nationalized in 1970s. The coking coal industry was nationalized in 1972 and non cooking coal in 1973. However, in 2018 it was privatized for better efficiency, technology and investments for the sector (*The Hindu* 2018).

The oil exploration from Assam, Bombay High Field and West Bengal Basin continued after the independence. Canada and the Soviet Union were assisting these projects. Privately owned groups made more production than the public sector. The necessity of industrial and economic development together with defence purpose influenced the establishment of the Oil and Natural Gas Commission (ONGC) and then oil and gas development became under the public sector (Chauhan 2006, 5-6) Electricity sector became under public control by the Indian Electricity Act 1948. Electricity is in the concurrent list according to the constitution. The Central Electricity Authority of India (CEA) advices and implements the electricity policies and various State Electricity Boards maintain the electricity sector of concerned states.

Jawaharlal Nehru and Homi J. Bhabha were behind the India's nuclear programme and they perceived that was required for the industrial and agricultural development of the country. Thorium deposits in India enhanced the nuclear research. To attain long term energy independence the three stage nuclear power programme was formulated. In 1974, India held its first nuclear exploration and described it as the "peaceful nuclear explosion." The Atomic Energy Act was passed in 1946 and the Atomic Energy Commission was established in 1948. The Apsara Research Reactor started in 1956 which is the first reactor in India (BARC 2006).The first nuclear explosion proved that India could develop nuclear weapons with the technology transferred for peaceful purposes. As a result, the United States isolated India for twenty five years, refusing nuclear cooperation and trying to convince other countries to do the same (Gopalakrishnan 2002, 369-95). The Indo-US nuclear deal, 2008 and the NSG waiver removed all the interruptions in the field of nuclear industry. Now India can access the technology and nuclear materials from nuclear supplier countries.

The renewable energy is growing at the rate of 20%, from 14,400 MW to 50,068 MW in the period of 2009 to 2016 (MNRE 2017, 2-6). The Electricity Act, 2003 decentralized the rural electrification process. It enables the Panchayats, NGOs and other private players to contribute to this sector. The higher subsidies in solar and wind technologies also enhance the renewable sector (Bhushan 2015). Department of Non-Conventional Energy Sources (DNES) was started its functioning to give funds for R&D in renewable energy. Indian Renewable Energy Development Agency Limited (IREDA) maintains the commercialization of these energy sources. Now as a separate ministry, the Ministry of New and Renewable Energy (MNRE) handles the renewable energy sector by facilitating research, manufacture and development.

India adopted the Integrated Energy Policy in 2006 by promoting energy with the least cost in a technically efficient, economically viable and environmentally sustainable manner. The policy consists of certain recommendations which help to reduce greenhouse gas (GHG) emissions and addressing the growing energy demand of India. It proposed market driven energy prices and reduction of subsidies with identification of targeted population. It recommended a competitive atmosphere for energy resource access. It aims at maximum exploitation of domestic energy and enhancement of the foreign exploration. The policy emphasises the importance of energy transfer and its cost. The Manmohan Singh government commissioned an expert committee to prepare a comprehensive energy plan and launched the policy known as Integrated Energy Policy 2006. It aimed at promotion of energy diversification and efficiency, reduction of energy intensity and secure supply of renewable energy. The policy proposed some liberalization measures, including in the coal sector. It also looked at climate change implications. The National Clean Energy Fund (NCEF) was created in 2010-11 period as an Inter-Ministerial Group, chaired by the Finance Secretary in the Ministry of Finance. The fund consists of the carbon tax which is a clean energy cess and meant for funding research and innovative projects in clean energy technologies of public sector and private sector entities, up to the extent of 40% of the total project cost (Planning Commission 2006, 57-147).

Niti Aayog Draft was another milestone in the energy scenario announced for energy security of the nation. It pointed out concern over the heavy reliance on oil import and expressed the need to reduce it. The draft also advocated the necessity for increasing the domestic production as well as renewable energy. It also stressed the need for diversification of the sources of energy supply. The policy also suggested to connect the renewable power with the public electricity grid. It also proclaimed the aim to electrify all houses by 2022 and to increase the renewable power production to 175 GW by 2022 (NITI Aayog 2017).

Institutional Mechanism of Energy in India

The management of energy in India is performed mainly by five ministries such as the Ministry of Power, the Ministry of Coal, the Ministry of New and Renewable Energy, the Ministry of Petroleum and Natural Gas and Department of Atomic Energy. Besides, certain advisory agencies, regulatory bodies, public sector undertakings, research institutions, the Ministry of External Affairs, and the Ministry of Environment, Forest and Climate Change are also having a significant say in the matters connected with energy sector. The Ministry of Coal is responsible for exploration and development of coal and lignite reserves. Coal India Limited and Neyveli Lignite Corporation undertake the exploration of coal and lignite. The

Ministry of Petroleum and Natural Gas holds the responsibility for the exploration, production, refining, distribution, marketing, import, export and conservation of petroleum, natural gas, petroleum products and liquefied natural gas. It also monitor and regulate the oil and gas price mechanism. The Oil and Natural Gas Corporation (ONGC) is India's largest state owned oil company and Indian Oil Corporation (IOC)is also a significant player in the Indian oil industry. They have achieved Maharatna status. ONGC Videsh Limited and ONGC Mittal Energy Limited explore overseas resources. The Gas Authority of India Limited is transporting and distributing the natural gas produced by ONGC. Bharat Petroleum Corporation Limited, Hindustan Petroleum Corporation Limited and Oil India Limited are the other state owned oil companies. Ministry of New and Renewable Energy deals with the policies relating with the renewable energy resources. The Commission for Additional Sources of Energy (CASE) was established in 1981, acknowledging the significance of renewable energy. It became as Department of Non-Conventional Energy Sources (DNES) in 1982. The Ministry of Non-Conventional Energy Sources (MNES) was formed in 1992. It was renamed as the name Ministry of New and Renewable Energy (MNRE) in 2006. The ministry promotes research and development, international cooperation and coordination in renewable energy sources (Ebinger 2013, 28-33).

The Department of Atomic Energy was established in 1954 under the direct control of the Prime Minister. It undertakes the development of nuclear power technology and its application in the fields of agriculture, medicine and industry (Singh 2010, 81-85). The Ministry of Power was established in 1992. It maintains the development of electricity sector of India and deals with production, generation, transmission, delivery and infrastructure development. The Ministry administers the Energy Conservation Act 2001 and the Electricity Act 2003. Also, it handles hydroelectric power and rural electrification. The Rural Electrification Corporation is the nodal agency of this ministry. The Electricity Act in 1910 was the basis for the generation and supply of electricity in pre-independence India. There was no consideration of conservation, environmental security, planning and etc., during that period.

The same was the case with the initial stages of post-independence era. The supply of electricity, coal and oil were included in the policies and programmes without adequate conservation strategies till the 1970s. The Working Group on Energy Policy was constituted in 1977 during the Fifth Five Year Plan which undertook the analysis of the present and future energy scenarios of India. In 1981, the Inter-Ministerial Working Group on Energy

Conservation (IMWG) was established and formulated energy saving targets and policies.

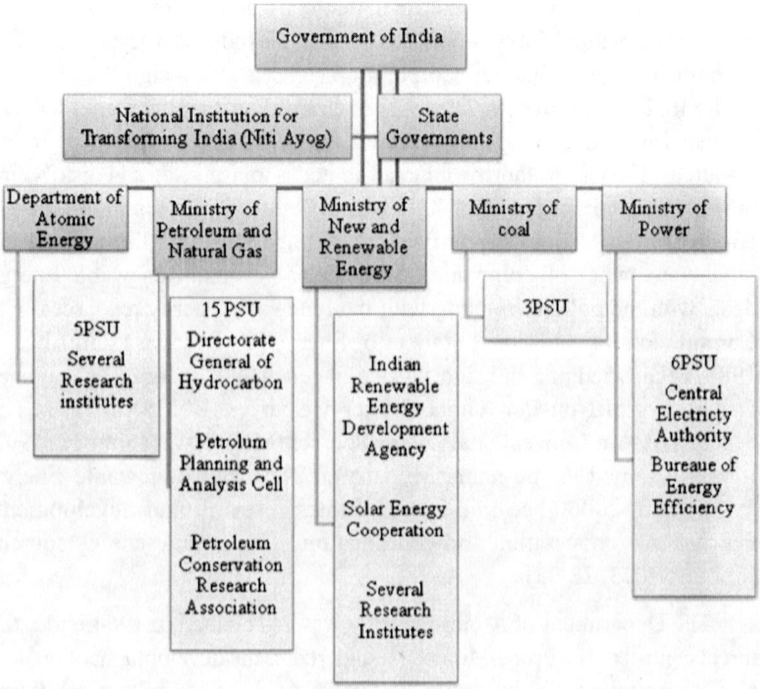

(IEA 2015)

Figure 2.1 Institutional Mechanism of India's Energy Sector

The Saubhagya Scheme or Pradhan Mantri Sahaj Bijli Har Ghar Yojana launched by the Union Ministry of Power launched in Manipur with the aim of providing electricity to all households. It is based on Socio-Economic and Caste Census (SECC) data 2011 and Rural Electrification Corporation Limited (REC) is maintaining the scheme. Through this BPL card holders can get free electricity and APL families can access it with Rs.500/- with 10 instalments. The FAME India scheme (Faster Adoption and Manufacturing of (Hybrid &) Electric Vehicles) supports electric vehicles or eco-friendly vehicles. Technology development, demand creation, pilot projects and charging infrastructure for building awareness and increasing utilisation of eco-friendly vehicles are the initiatives of this project. Now India pushes for methanol as the alternative source for transportation sector. It can be used in railways, marine sector, power generation, cooking fuel, hybrid and electric mobility (Ministry of Road

Transport & Highways 2017). It is cost effective than electricity vehicles. It is sustainable and obtained from natural resources (Sharma 2018).

The Ministry of New and Renewable Energy (MNRE) is the apex body and each state has department for carrying out the programmes and policies of renewable energy. National Institute of Solar Energy, earlier known as Solar Energy Centre, is an autonomous institution which helps to implement National Solar Mission and to coordinate research, technology and other related works. It has the full facility to test every thermal system and assess the solar potential of the country. National Institute of Wind Energy, National Institute of Bio-Energy, Solar Energy Corporation of India and Renewable Energy Development Agency have been established to provide technical support to the renewable energy sector in the country. The reputed technical institutions i.e., IITs, NITs and Universities provide support for research and development work, capacity building of stakeholders, potential assessments, monitoring and evaluation etc. Renewable energy database is updated regularly in the country. The National Institute of Wind Energy (NIWE), formerly known as Centre for Wind Energy Technology, has developed the Wind Atlas of India. NIWE also collects data from Solar Radiation Resource Assessment stations to assess and quantify solar radiation availability and develop Solar Atlas of the country (Awasthi 2018, 207-10). The Indian Institute of Science, Bengaluru has developed Biomass Atlas of India, and the Alternate Hydro Energy Centre, Indian Institute of Technology, Roorkee has assessed small hydro potential in the country.

New Initiatives in Indian Energy Scenario

India's energy scenario accounts new initiatives in the last few years due to the influence of global and local changes. Energy became a significant agenda in domestic as well as foreign policy of India. India announced its Draft National Energy Policy (DNEP) in 2017 and it proposes increased domestic production, diversification of the energy sources and the development of clean energy. India's energy mix is in a transitional phase. The dependence on coal for power and industrial purpose, biomass for cooking and oil for transport lead to high carbon emission. So, India is in a process to reduce the emission by improving the energy efficiency and renewable energy sector. 'Coal Vision 2030' gives an assessment of the future demand scenario for the coal sector in India up to 2030 (CIL 2018). About 500,000 people are directly employed in coal mining and coal thermal power generation and these sectors contribute approximately 10% to India's Index of Industrial Production (Coal India Limited 2018). Government opened the mining of coal for private players for better result. Land acquisition, environmental regulations, increasing cost of production, significant growth in renewable energy etc., are being the challenges to this sector. The government announced a new coal linkage policy named SHAKTI (Scheme for Harnessing and Allocating Koyala (Coal) Transparently in India) in 2017, which guarantees sufficient supply of fuel to power plants and ensure the coal transparency.

The Petroleum and Natural Gas Ministry initiated the *#GiveItUp* campaign in 2015 which was aimed at motivating users who can afford to pay the market price for LPG to voluntarily surrender their LPG subsidy. As a result of the campaign, it is reported that more than a million users had given up their LPG subsidy. PaHaL or Pratyaksha Hastaantarit Laabh, is a Direct Benefit Transfer Scheme introduced for the subsidy in LPG in India. Under this scheme, users get their subsidy amount to their bank account. The diesel price regulation linked the price of diesel to the global market without any government intervention. Pradhan Mantri Ujjwala Yojana, launched in 2016, targets to give five crore LPG connections to beneficiary women in Below Poverty Line (BPL) households (Ministry of Petroleum and Natural Gas n.d).

Renewable energy expansion programme undertaken by the Ministry of Renewable Energy aims to achieve 175 GW by 2022. Solar Park, Solar Roof Top Scheme, Solar Defence Scheme, Solar Scheme for CPUs, Solar PV Power Plants on canal banks and canal tops, solar pumps etc. are some of the major initiatives under the solar energy promotion scheme. Ujwal DISCOM Assurance Yojana is the revival package for state electricity distribution companies (DISCOMs) at the financial and operational levels. The Ministry of Power implements the Energy Conservation Act which reduces the energy intensity of Indian economy. Bureau of Energy Efficiency (BEE) is responsible for energy efficiency in the economy through various regulatory and promotional instruments. Deendayal Upadhyaya Gram Jyoti Yojana aims to provide continuous power supply to each rural households. Pradhan Mantri Sahaj Bijli Har Ghar Yojana (Saubhagya) is also designed with the objective to deliver electricity connections to all the remaining un-electrified households in rural as well as urban areas. 'Power for all' is also an initiative of the government for 24x7 accesses of electricity to all. Integrated Power Development Scheme (IPDS) is for urban power distribution sector. Urban Jyoti Abhiyaan (URJA) Mobile application enhances consumer connect with the Urban Power Distribution sector by providing information of IT enabled towns. Under the Unnat Jyoti by Affordable Lighting for All (UJALA) Scheme, 20 W LED tube lights and BEE 5-star rated energy efficient fans are distributed to the consumers for energy efficiency and preservation of environment. The Ministry of Petroleum is targeting reduction of oil imports by 10% from 2014-15 level by 2022. India submitted its nationally determined contributions (INDCs) with the target of 20-25% intensity reduction by 2020, at the UN Framework Convention on Climate Change (UNFCCC) in 2015 (MOEF 2015). It promised to reduce the emissions intensity of its GDP by 33-35% from 2005 levels by 2030 and to increase the share of non-fossil fuel based capacity in the electricity mix above 40% by 2030 The policy guarantees that electricity reaches every household by 2022 and clean cooking fuel to all.

India's Energy Landscape

India's energy mix is largely relied on hydrocarbons. Though coal and oil are the major sources, natural gas, which is cleaner energy than other hydrocarbons, contributes higher share in the recent energy landscape of India. The renewable energy sector is also growing rapidly. The nuclear energy is very low in the energy mix, but the coal based power generation is critical to the energy scenario of India. Nearly 175 GW, over half of the country's total installed electricity capacity of 288 GW, is produced from coal. India has about 5.7 billion barrels of proven crude oil reserves and 40% of crude oil production is from Mumbai High Basin (Ebinger 2016, 12-13). It is estimated that the share of coal in India's energy mix will be 42%-50%. Availability and lower price are the main reasons for relying on this energy source (Thambi et al. 2018). Now, 75% of our power generation and 58% energy dependence are related to coal. The following chart depicting India's energy mix shows that coal constitutes the largest share and oil is at just below.

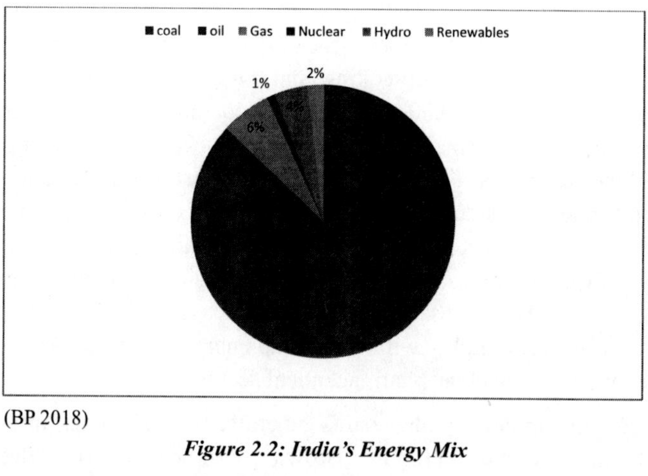

(BP 2018)

Figure 2.2: India's Energy Mix

Coal

Coal is the primary energy source since the industrial age. It is the cheapest and the most important sources of energy. As far as India is concerned, it is the primary source for the power generation. Ninety per cent of the domestic production comes from public sector and 10% from private sector. In power generation today, the share of coal in total capacity is about 62%, but the share in generation is about 80%. Coal deposits are concentrated on the eastern and south central parts of India, such as in the states of Jharkhand, Odisha, Chhattisgarh, West Bengal, Madhya Pradesh, Telangana and Maharashtra. They have the capacity of 98.58 % of the total coal reserves. Jharkhand and Odisha have 26.29% and 24.58% respectively. The country has around 315.14 billion tonnes coal reserves and 44.70 billion tonnes Lignite reserves (Central Statistics Office 2018, 1). India has 7% of world coal reserves and it has the fifth position in this regard. The estimated consumption of raw coal is 832.46 MT in 2016. India is the second largest consumer behind China and the third largest coal producing country in the world after China and the US, however it depends on around 25% of its demand on imports.

Around 90% of India's production is non-coking coal. The coal industry aspires to meet 1.5 billion tonne target by 2020. It expects 1BT by CIL and the remaining 500 MT by Singareni Collieries Company Limited (SCCL) and other public and private sector producers(ICC 2016). Coal production was 639.23 MT in 2016. The rest of coal demand of the country is addressed by the import from Indonesia (55%), Australia (23%), South Africa (14%), Mozambique, Colombia, the USA and Canada. Coal can be freely imported by the consumers for their needs. Coking coal is being imported mainly by Steel Authority of India Limited (SAIL) and coal based power plants, cement plants, captive power plants, sponge iron plants, industrial consumers, while coal traders are importing non-coking coal (GOI, Ministry of Coal 2018). India imported around 199.88 million MT of coal in 2016. Most of India's thermal coal imports depend on Indonesia and several Indian companies own Indonesian mines. Electricity generation mostly depends upon coal availability and it is a significant raw material for steel and cement industry. Coking coal is used in steel production and thermal coal is used in power generation. Cement industry also mostly depends on coal and the by by-products of burned coal is used in concrete production. Paper and aluminium industries also relate highly with this cheap energy resource. Coal is also used in chemical as well as pharmaceutical sectors.

Depending upon its grade, coal is generally categorized as Anthracite Coal, Bituminous Coal and Lignite (Brown Coal). The Indian coal deposits are mainly found in the Gondwana sediments in the Eastern and Central parts of Peninsular India and the varieties are bituminous and sub-bituminous that rank below anthracite coal found in Damodar valley, the Godavari, the Mahanadi, the Son and the Wardha valley (Sarolkar 2007, 70-72). Further, the Tertiary Coal of Meghalaya, Assam, Arunachal Pradesh and Nagaland in the North-Eastern India is low quality coal with 30-50 % carbon content. India produces coking coal and non-coking coal. the former is used in steel making and metallurgical industries and the latter is used for fertilizer, glass, ceramic, cement, paper, chemical and brick manufacturing, and for other heating purposes.

Table 2.1: Sector wise consumption of Coal

Sector	*Coal use in Million Tonnes*
Electricity	527.26
Steel and Washery	54.15
Cement	6.43
Sponge Iron industries	5.68
Paper	1.18
Textile	0.24
Fertilizers & Chemicals	3.33
Brick	0.10
Others	246.83
Total	845.39

(Central Statistics Office 2018)

Raniganj fields of West Bengal, near the Damodar River, is the birth place of coal mining in India. The systematic geological surveys of 1845-46 and 1860 by the English East Company exposed the fifty collieries in the area producing 28,200 tonnes of coal. At the beginning of 20th century, many coal fields of Bengal and Bihar were found out and 'Jharia' field especially for cocking coal was one among them. Establishment of railway lines increased the output. The emergence of World War increased the demand of coal and the production rose to 21 million tonnes (Prasad 1986,113). Aden, Ceylon and Straits Settlements were the major coal markets for India. The period 1928-29 witnessed a boost of Indian coal industry. The number of coal mines was increased to 547 and production rose above 23 million tonnes. Later, low price affected the industry and production fell down to 21 million tonnes during 1931. Consequently, Government of India had set up a committee to report all the problems affecting the industry, including the safety of employees. During 1937-42, the production again increased and the Singareni Collieries Company Limited (SCCL) was formed as the first government owned coal company in 1945. Government of Nizam of Hyderabad bought all the shares of the company and brought the company under India Trust Fund of the Nizam Government (Vasudevachary 1994, 31). Five year plans in post-independence era paid attention on coal mining and took necessary actions to improve the efficiency. National Coal Development Corporation (NCDC) was set up in 1956 and several mines transferred from Indian Railway to this corporation. At the end of oil crisis, coal industry acquired great demand and attention.

Nationalization of coal mines took place in two phases. The Coking Coal Mines (Emergency Provisions) Act, 1971 and Coking Coal Mines (Nationalization) Act, 1972 nationalized coking coal mines and the Coal Mines (Taking over of Management) Act, 1973 and Coal Mines (Nationalization) Act, 1973 nationalized all the coal mines of India. Department of Coal, Ministry of Energy and Government of India incorporated the Coal India Limited (CIL) as a holding company in 1975. Bharat Coking Coal Limited (BCCL) and Coal Mines Authority Limited (CMAL) for non-coking mines were incorporated as subsidiaries of CIL. Eastern Coalfields Limited (ECL), Western Coalfields Limited (WCL), Central Coalfields Limited (CCL) and Central Mine Planning and Design Institute Limited (CMPDIL) along with planning, design and engineering consultancy services of the coalmines were also incorporated to CIL. In 1986, South Eastern Coalfields Limited (SECL) and Northern Coalfields Limited (NCL) and in 1992, Mahanadi Coalfields Limited (MCL) were also added to CIL and now it consists of 8 subsidiaries (CIL 2017). Now, the Ministry of Coal maintains the policies and programmes relating with the exploration and development of coal and lignite resources. It is operating through public sector undertakings such as Coal India Limited (CIL), Neyveli Lignite Corporation Limited (NLCIL)and Singareni Colleries Company Limited (SCCL). The Geological Survey of India (GSI), the Mineral Exploration Corporation (MEC), SCCL, and CMPDIL conduct surveys and identify coal resources. The Coal Controller's Organization (CCO) gives permission for opening new mines, collects and publishes data on the coal sector, collects excise duties and monitors progress in captive mining. The Coal Ministry is held responsible for all the administrative control (Ministry of Coal 2017).

The International Coal Ventures Ltd (ICVL) is a joint venture of five companies owned by the Indian government comprising Steel Authority of India (SAIL), Coal India (CIL), Rashtriya Ispat Nigam Limited (RINL), National Minerals Development Corporation (NMDC) and National Thermal Power Corporation(NTPC) (ICVL n.d). Working together to ensure the exploration of coal from abroad, these companies jointly or single-handedly operate in countries like Mozambique, Australia, Canada, the USA etc. Coal India Africana Limitada (CIAL), a subsidiary of of CIL began its operation in Mozambique from 2009. Essar Energy, Tata Steel and Jindal Steel & Power have their share in Mozambique. Adani group owned one of the largest coal mine and railway project in Galilee Basin in Queensland region of Australia and Bunyu coal mine in Indonesia. Lanco Infratech has also investments in Australia. GVK Group also started its investments in Australia since 2011.

Institutional delay, problems of land approvals, poor transportation system and low productivity with weak production technologies affect the growth rate of coal production. Environmental concerns are high in this resource usage. The removal and processing of coal at the mining site and its transportation to a power station disturb the environment. Methane, nitrogen oxides and sulphur dioxide which are produced during the mining of coal pollute the surrounding air and contribute to greenhouse gas emission and global warming. Combustion also emits Carbon dioxide to the atmosphere. Dust particles and gaseous pollutants create complications to mining workers and other living things in the nearby area. Changing land use pattern causing the land cover variations is a major environmental concern as it leads to environmental problems like water pollution and decreased soil quality etc. Calamities like mine wall failures and vehicle collisions, suffocation, gas poisoning, roof collapse and gas explosions are common in this sector.

Petroleum

Crude oil is oil in its crude or unrefined state and it is separated into constituents such as gasoline, aviation fuel, fuel oil, etc., in a refinery. Petrol is used in transportation requirements. Diesel fuel is used in the diesel engines of heavy construction equipment, trucks, buses, tractors, boats, trains, some automobiles and electricity generators. Fuel oil is used in boilers and furnaces for industrial heating, and for producing electricity in power plants. Lubricating oil is used in the smooth functioning of machines and tar is used in the construction of roads. Paraffin and Petroleum jelly are used in the manufacturing of candles and pharmaceuticals and naphtha is used to make synthetic rubber, plastics, paints, fertilizers, detergents, cosmetics, nylon, insecticides, food supplements etc.

In India, the oil production started in 1889 at Digboi in Assam. Assam Railways & Trading Company Limited changed to Assam Oil Company and built a refinery in Digboi in 1901 (Madhrey 2014, 1-20). The company was taken over in 1917 by Burmah Oil Company. Then it became Burmah Shell and transferred as Shell. In 1961, Oil India Limited (OIL) was built as a joint venture with Burma Oil Company. It became a government owned company in 1981. In West Bengal, another company known as the Indo-Stanvac Petroleum Project, a joint venture between Government of India and Standard Vacuum Oil Company of USA, was engaged in exploration work.

After independence, India was very much in need of oil and gas for the industrial development of the country. The Oil and Natural Gas Directorate was set up in 1955, as a subordinate office under the then Ministry of Natural Resources and Scientific Research. In 1956, the Directorate was raised to the status of a commission with enhanced powers. Finally, the Oil and Natural Gas Commission (ONGC) was established with statutory authority in 1959. Discovery of oil in Bombay high was a significant achievement of ONGC.

Table 2.2: Production and consumption of petroleum products, 2016-17 (MMT)

Petroleum products	*Production*	*Consumption*
High speed Diesel	102.1	76.0
Petrol/MS	36.6	23.8
Naphtha	19.7	13.2
Petroleum Coke	12.9	24.0
Fuel Oil	12.0	7.20
LPG	11.3	21.6
Bitumen	5.2	5.9
Lubricants	1.0	3.5
Light Diesel Oil	0.6	0.4
Kerosene	6.0	5.4
Aviation Turbine	13.8	7.0
Others	22.3	6.6
Total	243.5	194.6
Growth	5.0%	5.4%

(Central Statistics Office 2017)

Gail (India) Limited (GAIL), formerly known as Gas Authority of India Limited, was formed in 1984 to maintain the transportation, processing and marketing of natural gas. While ONGC and Oil India Limited have Maharathna status, GAIL has Navarathna status. ONGC is India's largest state owned oil company. Bharat Petroleum Corporation Limited and Hindustan Petroleum Corporation Limited are the state owned downstream petroleum companies. Now the Ministry of Petroleum and Natural Gas deals with the exploration and production of Oil and Natural Gas, refining, distribution and marketing, import and export and conservation of petroleum products. Hydrocarbon Exploration and Licensing Policy (HELP) is the new policy initiative which allows uniform licensing system and provides single licensing to cover all hydrocarbons such as oil, gas, coalbed methane etc. Earlier, the New Exploration Licensing Policy (NELP) existed and had separate policies and licenses for different hydrocarbons. The Petroleum Planning and Analysis Cell (PPAC) is responsible for revising natural gas prices and Petroleum Conservation Research Association (PCRA) promotes policies which helps to reduce India's dependence on oil.

Table 2.3: Domestic Crude oil production by companies

Companies	*2015-16*	*2016-17*
ONGC	21.1	20.9
OIL	3.2	3.3
Private/Joint Ventures (JV)	11.2	10.4
Total	35.5	34.5

(PPAC 2018)

ONGC Videsh Limited (OVL), Oil India Limited (OIL), IOCL, BPCL, Reliance Industries Limited (RIL), HPCL, GAIL and Cairn Oil & Gas vertical of Vedanta Limited have been actively involving in exploration of energy abroad. OVL has stake in 38 oil and gas projects in 17 Countries - Vietnam, Russia, Sudan, South Sudan, Iran, Iraq, Libya, Myanmar, Syria, Brazil, Colombia, Venezuela, Kazakhstan, Azerbaijan, Mozambique, Bangladesh and New Zealand (OVL, 2017). ONGC Mittal Energy Limited with ONGC operates in Nigeria and Syria.

Table 2.4: Production of Oil and Gas

	oil	*gas*
Total domestic production Oil and Gas in MMTOE	69.2	67.9
Overseas production	10.1	16.2
Overseas %	14.6	23.9

(Central Statistics Office 2018)

The maximum reserves of crude oil in India are in the Western Offshore (39.79%) followed by Assam (25.89%) and the estimated total reserves is 621.10 million tonnes (MT). During 2015-16, there was a decrease of 2.28% in the estimated reserve of crude oil and Arunachal Pradesh, Rajasthan and Assam witnessed a decrease by 44.75%, 17.04% and 2.11% respectively.

However, Tamil Nadu, Andhra Pradesh, Gujarat, Western Offshore and Eastern Offshore observed an increase by 18.42%, 15.30%, 2.58%, 1.88% and 0.59% respectively(GOI, Ministry of Statitistics and Programme Implementation, 2018). The country's crude oil production is less than 0.3% of global reserves. The crude oil production in 2015-16 is at 36.950 MMT with a decrease of 1.36% comparing to 2014-15. The consumption of crude oil is 183.5MMT due to increased land and air traffic, and irrigation usage. So, import dependence on oil rose to 81% in 2015-16 from 78.5% in the previous year. India imported 202 MMT oil in 2015-16. Oil and gas accounted for around 35 percent share in India's energy consumption. India became the third largest oil consumer in the world after the US and China and surpassing Japan in 2015. India aims to reduce import dependence from 77 % to 67% by the year 2022.

Table 2.5: Petroleum and Crude oil of India in MMT

	2015-16	*2016-17*
Crude oil production	36.9	36.0
Consumption of petroleum products	184.7	194.6
Production of petroleum products	231.9	243.5
Crude oil import	202.9	213.9
Petroleum products imports	29.5	36.3
Gross petroleum products& Crude oil	232.3	250.2
POL exports	60.5	65.5
LNG Imports	27.1	29.0
Import dependency of crude oil on consumption basis	80.6%	81.7%

(PPAC 2013)

The Natural Gas industry began in the country since 1960s. It started with the discovery of gas fields in Assam and Gujarat. It is the cleanest fuel with less carbon dioxide. Earlier, exploration activities were carried out by the National Oil Companies (ONGC & OIL) and now it is accessible for private companies as well. New Exploration Licensing Policy (NELP) allows 100% foreign participation(Ministry of Petroleum and Natural Gas 2017). Natural Gas reserves in India is 1227.23 Billion Cubic Meters (BCM) in 2016 and the production is at 32.249 Billion Cubic Meters (BCM) which is 4.18 % lower than 2015. Natural gas reserves were found in Gujarat, KG Basin, Cauvery Basin, Tripura and Assam. In 2004, liquefied Natural Gas was imported from Qatar and LNG terminal was set up at Dahej of 5 MMTPA capacity. Supply and distribution of domestic Natural Gas has to follow the policy guidelines of the Government and imported Regasified Liquefied Natural Gas (RLNG) follows Open General License Item and the marketers are free to import LNG and sell the RLNG to customers. It is used in various sectors like fertilizers, power, city gas supply, sponge iron etc. India has 16470 Km long Natural Gas pipeline network in operation (PPAC 2018) and Natural Gas accounts for 7% of India's energy consumption.

India's domestic production of Natural Gas rose in 2010 and has declined annually ever since. The consumption has also declined since 2010. It is the availability of cheap LNG from abroad which reduced the production and consumption rate of natural gas. In 2010-11, the gross domestic production of natural gas was 52.22 BCM and it became 32.25 BCM in 2015-16. The imported natural gas in 2015-16 was 16.58 BCM and the availability was 48.83 BCM. As far as its use is concerned, fertilizer industry has used 33.72%, around 22.76% has been used for power generation and 11.42% for domestic fuel. It means that natural gas is used for energy and non-energy purposes.

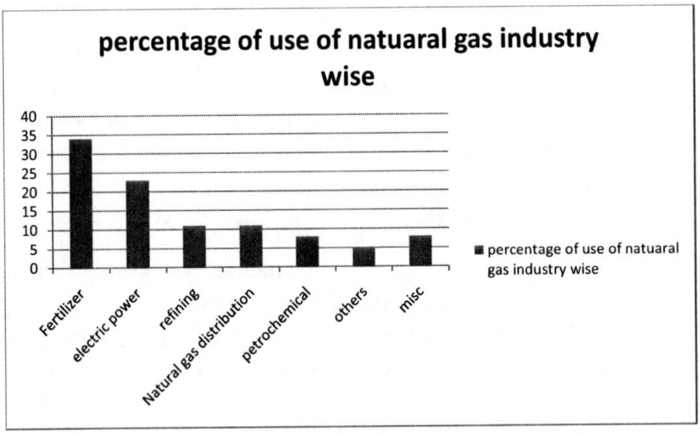

(Ministry of Petroleum and Natural Gas 2017)

Figure 2.3: Use of natural Gas Industry wise

CBM, Shale Gas and Coal Sand

Coal-bed Methane (CBM) is found in coal layers, generated during the process of the coalification. It is almost like natural gas and consists of methane, nitrogen, carbon dioxide and ethane. CBM exploration is reducing the greenhouse effect, and extraction of the CBM through degassing of the coal seams before the mining of coal enables in maintaining safe methane level in working mines. Countries with the largest proven coal reserves are the USA (28.6%), followed by Russia (18.5%), China (13.5%), Australia

(9.0%) and India (6.7%). India has the fifth largest proven coal reserves in the world. Andhra Pradesh, Assam, Chhattisgarh, Gujarat, Jharkhand, Madhya Pradesh, Maharashtra, Odisha, Rajasthan, Tamil Nadu and West Bengal are the states which have CBM reserves. The estimated CBM resources are 2,600 billion cubic metres (BCM) and 112.6 BCM of CBM is established as recoverable reserves. India has emerged as the fourth country in the world capable of producing CBM on commercial scale. The Gondwana sediments produce the largest share of CBM producing blocks in India.

Shale gas is methane rich natural gas found in shale rock. It was first found from the US in 1821. Now along with the US, China and Canada are also producing shale gas commercially. Shale gas exists in the form of micro-bubbles situated in rock with clay. Water is injected to the rock at very high pressure for releasing the bubble. This hydraulic fracturing is controversial due to the over usage of water, environmental concerns and seismic probabilities. The US is the major player in this field and the US State Department signed a Memorandum of Undertaking with India's Ministry of Petroleum and Natural Gas in 2010 for resource assessment, technical studies, regulatory framework consultations, training, and investment promotion etc., for India. It is discovered that there are shale gas reserves in Cambay, Krishna Godavari and Cauvery Basins. Carbonaceous shale occurs inter bedded with the coal and Assam Arkan and Damodar Basins have large shale deposits (Indian Bureau of Mines 2015).

Oil sands are geologic formations that include a mixture of thick and heavy oil, water and sand. The heavy oil is called bitumen. Surface mining and *in-situ* (producing in place) mining are used to produce oil from these sands. The oil sand is found in Canada, Russia, Venezuela and Congo. Though it is costlier, it can fulfil the energy needs for years. India is trying to get access to this source due to the low cost comparing to others. Since 1967, the Athabasca oil sands in Alberta, Canada is producing oil sands. Around 2.2 million barrels per day was produced from this region in 2014(Natural Resource Canada 2014). IOCL, RICL and Essar Oil are buying this with a subsidized rate. China and Japan are the major competitors to India in the trade in this field. Adani and Welspun have investments in Louisiana and Texas shale fields in the US and Alberta oil sands projects in Canada. India's ONGC has also investment in Canadian oil sands. Oil sands production also creates greenhouse gases and it uses more water and land. We need 13 to 14 barrels to get 1 barrel bitumen crude. The process of extraction and upgrading causes largescale air pollution and the mining leads to the damage of forest and wetland.

Renewable Sources

The Ministry of New and Renewable Energy (MNRE) is the concerned ministry for maintaining the renewable energy sector. India is a significant player in the Paris Climate Accord with the commitment to generate 40% of country's electricity from non-fossil sources by 2030. According to World Bank, India's current 102 GW installed renewable power generation will grow up to 347 GW by 2027. The estimated potential of renewable energy in the country is 10,01,132MW. It includes solar power potential of 649342 MW wind power 3,02,251 MW at 100 m height, small-hydro power 21,134 MW, Biomass 18,601 MW, 7,260 MW from bagasse based cogeneration in sugar mills, 2554 MW from waste to energy (Central Statistics Office 2018).

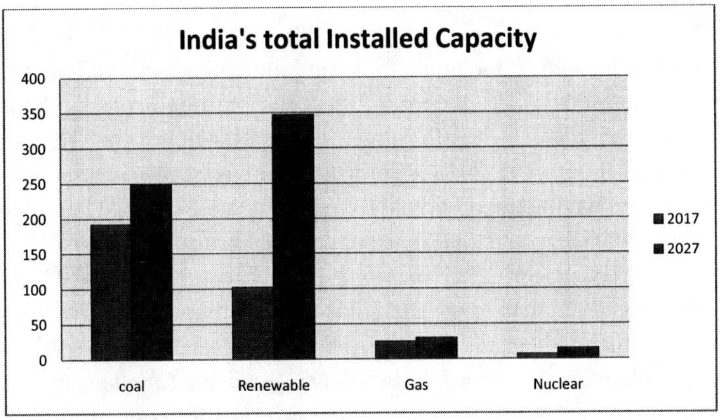

(World Bank 2017)

Figure 2.4: India's Total Installed Capacity

Renewable energy is being used in power generation, heating and cooling, transport and rural off grid energy services. Subsidy, fiscal incentives, preferential tariffs, affirmative action etc., are implemented for promoting a renewable energy future. Of India's current 50 GW installed renewable energy capacity, 57% of it is accountable to wind energy. India has the fourth position in wind installation with a capacity addition of 3,300MW in 2016. Around 1.2 million households are using solar energy to meet their lighting energy needs and cooking energy needs from biogas plants. There is an increase of 157% of solar power capacity addition in 2016. On 31st December 2017, the total solar power capacity installed is 17052.37 MW. Based upon availability of land and solar radiation, the potential of solar power in the country has been assessed to be around 750 GWp (MNRE 2018). India is targeting the installation of 175GW of renewable energy capacity by 2022, which will be 100GW from solar, 60 GW from wind, 10 GW from bio power and 5 GW from Hydro.

Table 2.6: India's Renewable targeted capacity for 2022

Resource	*Targeted capacity by 2022*	*Installed capacity in 2016*
Solar	100GW	6762.87MW
Wind	60GW	26866.66MW
Bio Power	10GW	483.33MW
Hydro	5GW	4273.48MW
Waste to Energy		115.08MW
Renewable	175GW	42849MW

(NITI Aayog 2017)

Solar

India is located in the equatorial sun belt of the earth and gets more than 300 sunny days. Production of electricity through solar is the most sustainable way and it has the greater potential than other renewable resources (Kapoor et al. 2014, 476-86). India has huge potential in solar energy as it is having good Direct Normal Irradiance (DNI).Though India possesses 750 GWp potential, it has now the capacity of 14 GW only. The government is planning to increase it up to 100GW by 2022. The technologies of solar thermal and solar photovoltaic are used to explore solar radiation into heat and electricity. Solar thermal is used in solar water heater, cookers, air heating and buildings. Solar photovoltaic is used in lighting, pumping and telecommunications. The Commission for Additional Sources of Energy (CASE) initiated the first program on solar energy which provided 10,000 solar cookers with subsidy. For research and development and promotional activities, one institution was established known as Solar Thermal Energy Centre (STEC). Solar water heater systems are used in industries like textile, dairy, bakery, brewery etc. Solar thermal pump was made by Bharat Heavy Electricals Limited (BHEL). Central Electronics Limited (CEL) is also engaged in manufacturing solar PVs and associated with Indian Antarctica Expedition and ONGC for their offshore activities. National Action Plan on Climate Change (NAPCC) established Jawaharlal Nehru National Solar Mission (JNNSM). It plans to install 22,000 MW through grid connected and off grid power plants. It is one of the eight missions under National Action Plan on Climate Change 2008. National Solar mission was launched in 2010 with the objective of grid parity and to achieve grid connected 20000MW power by 2022. In 2009, a state specific policy was started in Gujarat. Kurnool Solar Park in Andhra Pradesh with 1000 MW capacity has emerged as the world's largest Solar Park. National

Solar Mission fixed the target 20 GW by 2022 and Prime Minister Narendra Modi revised this target to 100 GW of solar power by 2022. It included 40 GW for rooftop solar electricity generation and 60 GW for large and medium scale grid-connected projects. India already achieved 20 GW by 2017. The price of solar photovoltaic (PV) has dropped by 60% between 2010 and 2014. So, it is expected that grid parity can be achieved in the near future. But, solar power plants need more land for installation. However, a solar power plant requires less land than that of a hydro plant needed but of a similar level as a coal or nuclear plant (Mitavachan and Srinivasan 2012).

Solar Energy Centre (SEC) which was converted into National Institute of Solar Energy (NISE), is an autonomous institution of the Ministry of New and Renewable (MNRE), and engages in doing major research and developmental activities in solar energy. Solar Energy Corporation of India (SECI) is engaged in the process of developing solar technologies and facilitates national solar mission targets. The National Action Plan on Climate Change (NAPCC) in June 2008 identified the development of solar energy technologies in the country to be pursued as a national mission. In November 2009, the Government of India approved the Jawaharlal Nehru National Solar Mission (JNNSM). The Mission aims at development and deployment of solar energy technologies in the country to achieve parity with grid power tariff by 2022. Earlier, Manmohan Singh government put a target of achieving 20000MW by 2022 and now Narendra Modi government raised the target to 1,00,000 MW. It consists of 40 GW rooftop and 60 GW through large and medium scale grid connected solar power projects (SECI 2017). The International Solar Alliance became a treaty-based international intergovernmental organization between solar rich countries and it aims to decrease the cost of solar technology and build up more solar energy before 2030. India has about 20GW installed solar generation capacity in 2017- 18 fiscal year and by 2022, India has to achieve 100 GW (*The Economic Times* 2018). Government decided to auction 30 GW in each fiscal year up to 2022. India has attained a record low tariff of Rs 2.44/unit for solar auction in Rajasthan. The cost of electricity from solar photovoltaic (PV) is currently descending and it is expected to be reduced 66% by 2040 (World Bank 2017).

Bio Energy

Biomass plays a vital role in India's rural area for cooking and heating. It is one of the oldest energy sources. Firewood and cow dung are the primary energy sources for many rural areas. Around 70% of Indian population depends upon biomass as their primary energy. Heat and electricity can also be made from biomass. It can be used in CHP plants. The combination of biomass and fossil fuels improve the efficiency. It can replace petroleum for transportation. It will provide self sufficiency and help to reduce waste materials. India produces about 450-500 million tonnes of biomass per year (EAI 2017). Around 32% of India's primary energy consumption constitutes biomass energy (MNRE 2017). It is estimated that 500 million metric tonnes biomass is available in India per year and an additional 100 million metric tonnes agricultural residue is also available. It has 18000 MW potential and bagasse based cogeneration in windmills can produce 5000MW each year. In biomass combustion, biomass is being burnt in high pressure boiler to generate steam. And this steam operates the turbine. Bagasse is the by-product of sugar production. Burning of bagasse produces steam and the mills through this process produce electricity for their own usage and rest for the sale to the grid. The state of Maharashtra has the highest installed biomass power capacity. Grid interactive power capacity of bio power includes biomass and gasification and bagasse cogeneration. It together produces 8181.70 MWp. It provides more than 14% of world energy usage.

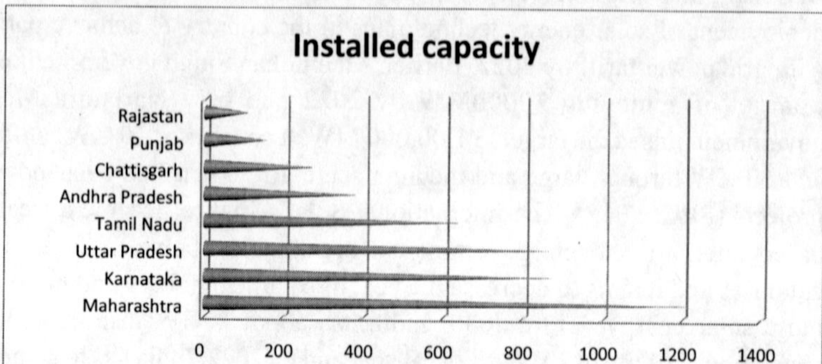

	Maharashtra	Karnataka	Uttar Pradesh	Tamil Nadu	Andhra Pradesh	Chattisgarh	Punjab	Rajastan
■ installed capacity	1220	872.18	870	641.9	380.75	279.9	155.5	108.3

(ENVIS 2016)

Figure 2.5: State wise installed capacity of Biomass Power

Hydro Power

Hydro electric power plant uses water with its high position as energy resource and it is converted to electricity. It produces less greenhouse emissions. In 1858, the first hydro electric power plant was installed. India has 47.1 GW installed hydropower electricity. It produces 11.1 Mtoe power production per year. India commissioned 1,909 MW of new hydropower projects in 2015. Small hydropower is in three categories, i.e., micro (less than 100 kW), mini (100 kW-1MW) and small (1MW-10 MW). Micro-hydro systems provide cheap power to the remote rural area. Hydropower is a sustainable energy source. It will not contribute to global warming. It can improve irrigation facility. India has abundant hydropower potential. However, the share of hydropower decreases gradually due to the rehabilitation and resettlement issues, environmental concerns and water sharing disputes. Huge hydro electric projects need river integration or consent of more than one state which is very difficult in the given situation. There is also mass protests against the implementation of projects as it causes ecological distractions and livelihood issues. The following figure indicates the declining share of hydropower share in India.

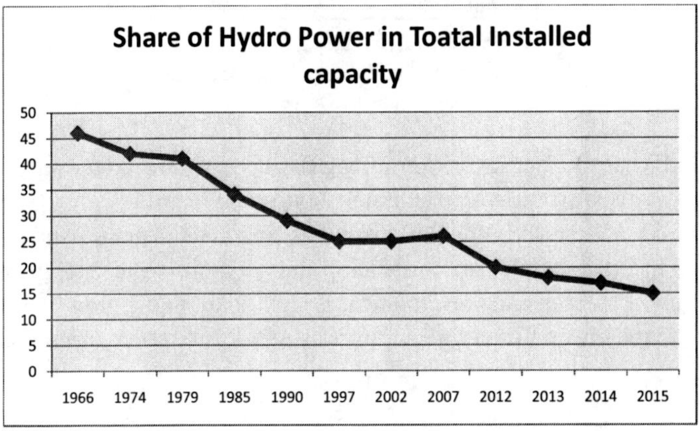

Source: (ASSOCHAM 2016)

Figure: 2.6: Share of Hydro Power in Total Installed Capacity

The Sutlej-Beas dispute between Punjab and Haryana and the Mullaperiyar Dam conflict between Kerala and Tamil Nadu occurred due to benefit sharing. Resettlement and rehabilitation(R&R) issue is very difficult in these types of projects. Hirakud Dam, Tehri Dam and some other dams are still facing the R&R issues, and safety and vulnerability concerns. Damage of flora and fauna of the region are also major concern in the big hydro projects. Geological weakness and seismic possibility also discourage the development of hydro project. India is in the seventh in ranking of hydro power projects in the world.

Wind Energy

The estimated potential of wind energy in India is around 1,02,788MW. There is an installed capacity of 32,380.18 MW wind energy in India. The sector is largely owned by private firms. Tamil Nadu is credited with the status of a world leader in terms of production of wind power renewable energy as its wind turbines have a combined installed capacity of 7.9GW, surpassing Sweden and Denmark (World Economic Forum 2018).India installed 5502.39 MW in the year 2016-17 itself (MNRE 2017).

Table 2.7: Estimated Capacity of Wind Power in India

Gujarat	84.40 GW
Karnataka	55.85GW
Maharashtra	45.39 GW
AP	44.22 GW
Tamil Nadu	33.79 GW
Rajasthan	18.77 GW
Madhya Pradesh	10.48 GW

(Central Statistics Office 2017)

India has the fourth position among countries with wind turbine power plants. The wind power producing states are Tamil Nadu, Gujarat, Karnataka, Maharashtra and Rajasthan. The National Offshore Wind Energy Policy in 2015 is released to develop the offshore wind energy in the coastline. Research and Development is significant in the growth of wind energy and more financial support is vital for more sophisticated

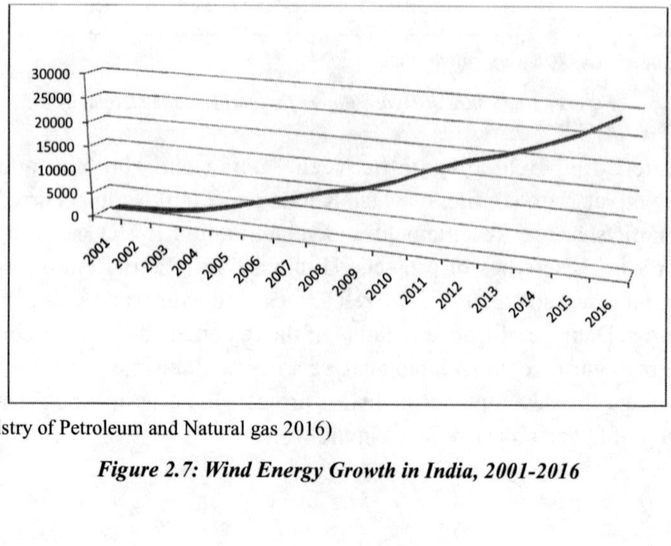

(Ministry of Petroleum and Natural gas 2016)

Figure 2.7: Wind Energy Growth in India, 2001-2016

technologies. Government intervention in R&D programmes, financial support and promotional activities will enhance the industry. India's estimated potential of wind energy is shown in the table 2.7.

Nuclear Energy

Nuclear energy brought a new hope in the energy sector during 1970s. The uranium fuel cycle for electricity generation is used in the production of nuclear weapons. So the developments in the nuclear technology became a necessity for developed and developing countries. Civilian Nuclear power was an "add on" or "spin-off" from, military weapons programmes (Willrich 1975).

The Tata Institute of Fundamental Research and Homi J. Bhabha initiated the nuclear power development in India. Atomic Energy Act and Atomic Energy Commission (1948) paved the way for the future growth of the resource. In 1954, Department of Atomic Energy was established. Bhabha Atomic Research Centre (BARC) carries out nuclear energy initiatives in different areas, such as health, medicine, industry, agriculture as well as in electricity sector. Recognizing the feasibility of nuclear power for electricity generation, nuclear power plants are installed in various locations in the country.

The three-stage nuclear power programme formulated by Bhabha was officially adopted in 1958. The programme has been based on the aim of exploration of India's thorium reserves instead of uranium for its energy requirements. A pressurized heavy reactor (PHWR) with uranium fuel was used in the first phase. Plutonium 239, which is the by-product from PHWR, uranium and thorium were used in the second phase in fast breeder reactors. Thorium 232 and uranium 233 are the fuels in the third stage nuclear programme. It is expected to be completed and planned to be self sufficient by 2050. The spent fuel of one stage is reprocessed to produce fuel for the next stage, so as to reduce the amount of waste. APSARA (1956), CIRUS (1960) and DHRUVA (1985) are the three reactors commissioned by BARC. CIRUS was built in association with the United States and Canada. Tarapur Atomic Power Station with small boiling water reactors became operational in 1969. Rajasthan Atomic Power Station (RAPS) was constituted in 1970s. Madras Atomic Power Station (MAPS) was completed in 1986 by the Power Projects Engineering Division of India. Narona and Karakpur atomic power stations were completed in 1992 and 2000 respectively.

India's civil nuclear programme had no assistance since 1974 due to its nuclear explosion. Non-signatory status of India on NPT has also been a hindrance to access nuclear raw materials. Russia assisted India during the isolation period. Unavailability of uranium and isolation from NSG weakened the level of growth of nuclear industry in India. Now there are 22 operating reactors from seven nuclear power plants such as Tarapur, Kalpakkam, Narora, Narona, Kakraparr, Kakrapar, Kaiga, Rawatbhata and Kudankulam with a total capacity of 6219 MWe. There are 6 reactors under construction in Kalpakkom, Kakrapar, Kakraapur, Rawatbhata, and Kudankulam with expected 4350 MWe production capacity.

Table 2.8: Nuclear Reactors in India

Reactor	*State*	*Type*	*MWe Net(each)*	*Commercial operation*
Tarapur 1&2	Maharashtra	GEBWR	150	1969
Kaiga 1&2	Karnataka	PHWR	202	1999,2000
Kaiga 3&4 (KGS)	Karnataka	PHWR	202	2007,2012
Kakrapar 1&2 (KAPS)	Gujarat	PHWR	202	1993,1995
Madras 1&2 (MAPS) Kalpakkam	Tamil Nadu	PHWR	202	1984,1986
Narora 1&2 (NAPS)	Uttar Pradesh	PHWR	202	1991, 1992
Rajasthan 1&2	Rajasthan	Candu PHWR	90 & 189	1973,1981
Rajasthan 3&4	Rajasthan	PHWR	202	1999,2000
Rajasthan5&6 (RAPS)	Rajasthan	PHWR	202	2010
Tarapur 3&4	Maharashtra	PHWR	490	2006,2005
Kudankulam	Tamil Nadu	PWR,VVER	917	2014,2017
Total			6219 MWe	

(NPCIL 2017)

The NSG agreement ended the 34 years isolation and opened up new opportunities. Now, India has signed deals with Canada, the United States, Russia, Namibia, the United Kingdom, France, Kazakhstan, Argentina, South Korea, Australia, Czech Republic, Magnolia, Vietnam, Japan and Uzbekistan. The government is planning to produce above 150 GW by 2050, 15 GW by 2020 and 27.5 GW by 2032. India is planning to build fifteen units of power reactors: three in Koodankulam (Tamil Nadu); four in Gorakhpur (Haryana); two in Chutka (Madhya Pradesh); four in Mahi Banswara and two in Kaiga and proposed power plants in two Kalpakkam (Tamil Nadu) four in Koodankulam four in Bhimapur (Madhya Pradesh) two in Chutka and two in Bihar, six in Jitapur (Maharashtra) four in Kovvada in Andhra Pradesh and one in Guntur (Andhra Pradesh), Orissa and Gujarat. India has not much uranium reserves and imports it from Russia, Kazakhstan and other countries. Uranium mines are operating in Jharkhand, Andhra Pradesh, Telangana, Karnataka and Meghalaya, Himachal Pradesh, Maharashtra and Rajasthan. It is estimated that India has 1,71,672 tonnes of uranium reserves.

The Indo-US Civil Nuclear Deal and NSG waiver helped India to cooperate with many countries and get access of sophisticated nuclear technology and uranium (Singh 2010, 83-85) . However, the current liability law provides insecurities to the foreign supplies with financial penalty in case of the occurrence of a nuclear accident. The current nuclear power generation capacity of all 22 nuclear power reactors are 6780 MW. Disasters like the Three Mile Island, Chernobyl and Fukushima warn about the dangers of nuclear option. It is not environmentally sustainable, as in every stage of nuclear fuel cycle, radioactive waste is produced. It affects human health, livelihood and nearby eco system. The cost of production, maintenance, transportation and waste management are higher than other energy sources. The close link with nuclear weapon production is another major threat emanating from the nuclear option for power generation.

Electricity Sector

At the time of independence, there were only 1500 villages had been electrified. Electricity Supply Act in 1948 promoted rural and semi urban electrical grid connectivity. Most of the electrification focussed on on irrigation projects. During 1960s, the rural electrification extended towards commercial activities. Agricultural productivity solely depended on irrigation and for this purpose, rural electrification has been enhanced. Government also provided subsidised electricity for farming. Earlier, household electricity was relatively secondary in priority. The Rural Electrification Corporation (1969) promoted investments in rural electrification. Household access to electricity became a priority in government policies only since 1980s. Integrated rural energy programmes and Kutir JyothyYojana are intended to provide improved energy provision in rural areas. Pradhan Mantri Gramodaya Yojana (2001) also helped the growth of rural electrification. Rural Electricity Supply Technology Mission (REST) and Accelerated Rural Electrification Programme (AREP) promoted the production of energy through renewable energy sources. Subsequently, electrification programmes extended to public places, Dalit hamlets and remote villages in this period. Rajiv Gandhi Grameen Vidyutikaran Yojana (RGGVY) planned for complete rural electrification within a span of five years. Electricity Act, 2003 and National Electricity Policy, 2004 improved the universal electricity access. As of now, 1370 more villages remain to be electrified (Ministry of Power 2017).

The Electricity Act, 2003 promotes the renewable sector and the National Electricity Policy, 2005 and the Tariff Policy, 2006 enhanced the renewable energy investment and made prices compatible with traditional energy. In electricity sector, India has installed a capacity of 3,44,002 MW. Now the installed capacity under the centre sector accounts 103,975 MW (30.2%), 84,571 MW by state sector and 155,510 MW (45.2%) by private sector. The power network of India constitutes five regions, namely Northern, North Eastern, Eastern, Western and Southern. As per the constitutional provisions, electricity is in the concurrent list.

Table 2.9: India: Power Sector

Total Thermal	*2,22,907*	*64.8%*
Coal	1,97,172	57%
Gas	24,897	7.2%
Oil	838	0.2%
Hydro	45,293	13.2%
Nuclear	6,780	2.0%
RES	69,022	20.1%
Total	3,44,002	

(GOI, Ministry of Power, 2017).

Table 2.10: Installed capacity in India: A Comparison between 1950 & 2016

	1950	*2016*
Installed Capacity of Power Plants	1713MW	302088MW
Electricity Generation	5.1BU	1107BU
Per Capita consumption of Electricity	15kWh	1010kWh

(CEA 2016)

The reform in 1998 opened up for private sector on transmission sector. World Bank assisted the Orissa Hydro Power Project and the state became the first state to enact its own reforms act. Several other states followed this path. The Electricity Act repealed the Indian Electricity Act, 1990 and the Electricity Supply Act, 1948. The act promoted the competition in the supply side. The reason is to ensure quality of supply and price. The Electricity Act, 2003 made significant changes in the electricity sector. India plans to achieve "24×7 Power for All" by 2022 and targets a 40% share of renewable based capacity by 2030.

Table 2.11: All India Installed Capacity MW (2016)

Source	*Percentage*	*Installed capacity in MW*
Coal	61%	185172.88
Hydro	14%	42783.42
Renewable	14%	42849.40
Gas	8%	24508.63
Nuclear	2%	5780.00
Diesel	1%	993.53

(CEA 2016)

Energy Efficiency

Energy efficiency is the usage of less energy for getting the same result. It reduces the global warming and greenhouse gas emissions. Energy efficiency is achieved through efficient technologies. Bureau of Energy Efficiency (BEE) was set up under the Ministry of Power in 2002 under the Energy Conservation Act, 2001 (Ministry of Power 2016). The Act intends to reduce energy intensity of India and instructs certain standards for all equipment, implementation of building codes and norms for industries. The Draft National Energy Policy suggested de-carbonization with the help of energy efficiency and renewable energy. Unnat Jyoti by Affordable Lighting for All (UJALA) provides LED lights at Rs. 38/- for all consumers. India wants to change all incandescent lamps by 2019. Distribution of LED bulbs, tube lights and energy efficient fans are encouraged, which may reduce 25 million tonnes of Carbon Dioxide per year. The National Mission for Enhanced Energy Efficiency (NMEEE) is one of the mission under the National Action Plan on Climate Change (NAPCC) (Bureau of Energy Efficiency 2017). Integrated Energy Policy predicts that India's energy demand will reach at 1500 million toe in 2030. Definitely, our energy consumption will increase in future. However, we can use energy efficient mechanism to reduce our carbon footprint. A close collaboration with energy supply and consuming sectors is needed for the achievement of energy efficiency.

The unexplored renewable energy is very high in India. The wind, solar, biomass and hydro resources can contribute more to the energy mix. India has a solar power potential of 748990 MW (62.48%),wind power potential of 102788 MW (8.57%) at 80 m hub height, 302235 MW (25.21%) at 100 m hub height, small-hydro power potential of 19749 MW (1.65%), biomass power of 17,538 MW (1.46%), 5000 MW (0.42%) from bagasse based cogeneration in sugar mills, 2556 MW (0.21%) from waste to energy (Central Statistics Office 2017). Being so, the sustainable energy sources with energy efficient technologies are the need of the time for a country like India.

Reference

ASSOCHAM (Associated Chambers of Commerce and Industry of India). 2016. *Hydropower @ Crossroads*. https://www.pwc.in/assets/pdfs/publications/ 2016/ hydropower-at-crossroads-pwc-assocham-report.pdf.

Awasthi, Shambhu Ratan. 2018. *Wind Power: Practical Aspects*. New Delhi: The Energy Resources Institute.

BARC (Bhabha Atomic Research Centre). 2006. *50 Years of Apsara Reactor*. http:// www.barc.gov.in/ publications/tb/apsara.pdf.

Bhushan, Chandra. 2015. "Growth of Renewable Energy in India." *Down to Earth.* https://www.downtoearth.org.in/news/growth-of-renewable-energy-in-india-43605.

BP (British Petroleum). 2018. *B P Energy Outlook.* B.P Energy Economics. https://www.bp.com/ content/dam/bp/business-sites/en/global/corporate/pdfs/energy-economics/energy-outlook/bp-energy-outlook-2018.pdf.

BP (British Petroleum). 2018. B P *Statistical Review of World Energy 2018.*https://www.bp.com/ en/global/corporate/energy-economics/statistical-review-of-world-energy.html.

CEA (Central ElectricityAuthority). 2016. *Draft National Electricity Plan.* Ministry of Power.http://www.cea.nic.in/reports/committee/nep/nep_dec.pdf.

Central Statistics Office. 2017. *Energy Statistics.* New Delhi: Ministry of Statistics and Programme Implementation, Government of India. http://www.mospi.nic.in/sites/ default/files/publication_reports/Energy_Statistics_2017r.pdf.pdf.

Central Statistics Office. 2018. *Energy Statistics.* New Delhi: Ministry of Statistics and Programme Implementation, Government of India. http://mospi.nic.in/ sites/default/files/ publication_reports/Energy_Statistics_2018.pdf.

Chauhan, D.S. 2006. *Non-Conventional Energy Resources.*Ernakulam: New Age International.

CIL (Coal India Limited). 2018. *Coal Vision 2030.* https://www.coalindia.in/ Desktop Modules/ DocumentList/documents/Coal Vision 2030 document for Coal Sector Stakeholders Consultation 27012018.pdf.

EAI (Energy Alternatives India). 2017. *India Biomass Energy.* Chennai: Energy Alternatives India.

Ebinger, Charles. 2016. *India's Energy and Climate Policy: Can India Meet the Challenge of Industrialization and climate change?* Brookings. https://www.brookings.edu/ research/ indias-energy-and-climate-policy-can-india-meet-the-challenge-of-industrialization-and-climate-change.

ENVIS (Environmental Information System Network).2016. *Statewise Installed capacity of Biomass Power in India 2012-2016 (Grid Connected).* Centre on Renewable Energy and Environment. Ministry of Environment, Forest and Climate Change (MoEFCC), Government of India, http://terienvis.nic.in/index3.aspx?sslid=3252 &subsublinkid=850 &langid=1&mid=1.

Gopalakrishnan, A. (2002). "Evolution of Indian Nuclear Power Programme." *Annual Review of Energy and the Environment* 27 (November): 369-395.

ICC (Indian Chamber of Commerce). 2016. *Bridging the Gap Increasing Coal Production and Sector Augmentation.* https://www.pwc.in/assets/pdfs/publications/2016/icc-pwc-coal-report-june.pdf.

ICVL (International Coal Ventures (P) Ltd). n.d. "*Company Background*" https://icvl.in/ aboutus.php?tag=company-background

IEA (International Energy Agency). 2015. *India Energy Outlook.*World Energy Outlook Special Report. https://www.iea.org/publications/freepublications/publication/ IndiaEnergy Outlook WEO2015.pdf

Indian Bureau of Mines. (2015). *Indian Minerals Yearbook 2015.* Indian Bureau of Mines, Government of India, https://ibm.gov.in/index. php?c = pages & m= index&id=852.

Kapoor, Karan, Pandey K. Krishan, A.K Jain, and Ashish Nandan, 2014. "Evolution of Solar Energy in India: A Review." *Renewable and Sustainable Energy Reviews* 40.475–87.

Kesharwani, Manoj Kumar. 2006. "Overview of Small Hydro Power Development in Himalayan Region." In International Himalayan Small Hydro power Summit. October 12-13: 44-57.

Malik, Priyanjali. 2016. *India's Nuclear Debate: Exceptionalism and the Bomb.* New Delhi: Routledge.

Ministry of Coal. (2018). "Production and Supplies." Accessed October 20 2018. https://coal.nic.in/content/production-and-supplies.

Ministry of Coal. 2017. *Coal Directory of India 2016-17.* Government of India. http://www.coalcontroller.gov.in/pages/display/16-coal-directory.

Ministry of Coal. 2019. *Annual Report 2017-18.* https://coal.nic.in/content/annual-reports.

Ministry of Petroleum and Natural Gas. n.d. **"**Pradhan Mantri Ujjwala Yojana.**"** National Portal, Government of India. https://www.india.gov.in/spotlight/pradhan-mantri-ujjwala-yojana#tab=tab-1.

Ministry of Power. 2017. "Power Sector at a Glance: All India*."* Governmant of India, https://powermin.nic.in/en/content/power-sector-glance-all-india.

Ministry of Road Transport & Highways. 2017. "Methanol Economy for India: Energy Security, Make in India and Zero Carbon Foot Print." 28-December, Government of India: Press Information Bureau. http://pib.nic.in/newsite/ Print Release.aspx?relid=174919.

Mitavachan, H, and J. Srinivasan. 2012. "Is Land Really a Constraint for the Utilization of Solar Energy in India." *Current Science*103(2), 163-68.

MNRE (Ministry of New and Renewable Energy). 2017. *Annual Report 2016-17.* Government of India. https://mnre.gov.in/annual-report.

MOEF (Ministry of Environment, Forest and Climate Change). 2015. "India First Biennial Update Report to the United Nations Framework Convention on Climate Change." http://www.moef.gov.in/sites/default/files/indbur10.pdf.

Natural Resource Canada. (2014). *What are the Oil Sands?* Government of Canada. https://www.nrcan.gc.ca/energy/oil-sands/18089.

NITI Aayog. 2017. *Draft National Energy Policy.* Government of India. June 27. https://niti.gov.in/writereaddata/files/new_initiatives/NEP-ID_27.06.2017.pdf.

NPCIL (Nuclear Power Corporation of India Limited). 2017. *Plants under Operation.* http://www.npcil.nic.in/content/302 1 AllPlants.aspx.

Planning Commission. 2006. *Integrated Energy Policy.* Report of the Expert Committee, New Delhi: Government of India.

PPAC (Petroleum Planning & Analysis Cell). 2018. *Ready Reckoner Snapshot of India's Oil & Gas Data.*Ministry of Petroleum & Natural Gas. https://www.ppac.gov.in/ WriteReadData/Reports/20190 12205 543813 40355 Snaps hot of India % E2 %80%99s Oil & Gasdata, December 2018.pdf.

PPAC (Petroleum Planning and Analysis Cell). 2013. "All India Study on Sectoral Demand of Petrol & Diesel." Nielsen, PPAC. Government of India. http://

ppac.org.in/ Write Read Data/Reports/20141 11103 294500 69740 All India Study on Sectoral Demand of Diesel. pdf.

PPAC (Petroleum Planning and Analysis Cell). 2018. *Monthly Report on Indigenous Crude Oil Production, Import and Processing & Production, Import and Export of Petroleum Products.* Ministry of Petroleum and Natural Gas, Government of India. https://www.ppac.gov.in/ Write Read Data/Reports/201902280 601098 725033 WebVersion Monthly Report Jan 2019.pdf.

Prasad, Anubhuti Ranjan. 1986. *Coal Industry of India.* New Delhi: Ashish Publishing House.

Rahman, Salma and Zaki Hussain. 2017. *Renewable Energy Governance in India: Challenges and Prospects for Achieving the 2022 Energy Goals.* Munich, Germany: Munich Personal RePEc Archive.

Saini, Sunita. 2018. "Evolution of Indian Power Sector at a Glance." *National Journal of Multidisciplinary Research and Development* 3(1): 275-278.

Sarolkar, P.B and K. Shivkumar. 2007. *Energy Scenario in 2020.* Nagpur: Gondwana Geological Society.

Sharma, Yogima. 2018. "Niti Aayog's new methanol push could be bad news for Modi's electric vehicles mission." *The Economic Times,* January 1, 2018. https://economictimes.indiatimes.com/ niti-aayogs-new-methanol-push-could-be-bad-news-for-modis-electric-vehicles-mission/articleshow/62323639.cms.

Singh, Bhupendra Kumar. 2010. "Energy Security Options." In *India's Energy Security: The Changing Dynamics,* edited by Bhupendra Kumar. 52-100. New Delhi: Pentagon Energy Press.

Sudarshan, Anand, and Ligia Noronha. 2009. "Contextualizing India's Energy Security." In *India's Energy Security,* edited by Ligia Noronha and Anand Sudarshan, 3-19, Abington, Oxon: Routledge.

Thambi, Simi, Anindya Bhatacharya, and Oliver Fricko. 2018. *India's Energy and Emissions Outlook: Results from India Energy Mode, Energy, Climate Change and Overseas Engagement Division.* NITI Aayog, Government of India. http://www.niti.gov.in/ writereaddata/files/document_publication/India%E2%80% 99s-Energy-and-Emissions-Outlook.pdf.

The Economic Times. 2018. "India set to achieve 20GW solar energy capacities this fiscal itself." March 8, 2018. https://economictimes.indiatimes.com/industry/energy/ power/india-set-to-achieve-20gw-solar-energy-capacities-this-fiscal-itself/articleshow/63218130.cms.

The Hindu. 2018. "Why has coal mining been opened up." February 25, 2018.

Vasudevachary, A. K.1996. *Problems and Prospects of Coal Industry in India: A Case Study.* New Delhi: Mittal Publications.

Willrich, Mason. 1975. *Energy and World Politics,* New York: Free Press.

World Bank. 2017. "Solar Powers India's Clean Energy Revolution "https://www.world bank.org/ en/news/immersive-story/2017/06/29/ solar-powers-india-s-clean-energy-revolution.

Chapter - III

Changing Dynamics of India's Energy Engagements: an Overview

Introduction

For developing as well as developed nations, energy is a significant factor to achieve its overall growth and welfare of the people. As time passes, energy sector undergoes unprecedented changes and the recent decades witnessed drastic transformations due to the invention of new fuel alternatives. The usage of coal, instead of wood was a more cost effective for the huge population of the earlier days. The steam engine increased the efficiency of coal powered industries and the discovery of oil boosted the transportation sector. The impact of climate change and other polluting factors contributed the growth of renewable energy.

There are transformations in the characteristics of nations in the energy scenario with changing times. The Europeans were the major consumers of energy during the period of industrial revolution and are now becoming the leaders in renewable energy and energy efficient technologies these days. China once was a sufficient producer of energy and now they are one of the largest importers among the world energy industry. On the other side, the United States as an energy starving country depended more on imports in the past and today they are self sufficient with their resources and are exporting a large share of energy to the rest of the world. The 1973 oil crisis has made lasting impact on the perspectives of every nation with regard to the energy policies and approaches. The availability and the price of the oil became the prime concern. As a result, nations included energy concern as a priority agenda in their foreign policy strategies to avoid supply disruptions. At suitable occasions, oil producing states and organisations used it as a tool for pursuing and protecting their vested interests as in the case of OPEC, the US, Russia, Venezuela, etc.

Global Energy Scenario

Global energy consumption shows an increasing pattern by 30% from 2015 to 2040 (IEA2017). However, the two third of energy consumption comes from the non OECD Asian countries such as India and China. Asia is the biggest consumer of oil, renewable power as well as hydro electricity and it consumes 3/4th of the global coal production (BP 2017). Even now coal, oil and gas remain the primary source of energy for the majority of nations. Its availability and low price help the natural gas industry to grow rapidly, however, the renewable energy industry also shows a considerable growth in this scenario. The renewable sector accounts 40% of the increasing primary energy (BP 2018). In the sector wise analysis, industrial sector consumes around 50% of the total energy consumption. The usages of energy by commercial and residential building are also contributing a considerable share. The advanced technologies and alternative fuels adopted in motor vehicles like bio-fuel, electricity and other options changed the transport sector and reduces the oil consumption in many nations. The rising GDP growth, population, industrial demand, and growth of transportation sector in emerging economies increases the energy demand of non OECD member countries.

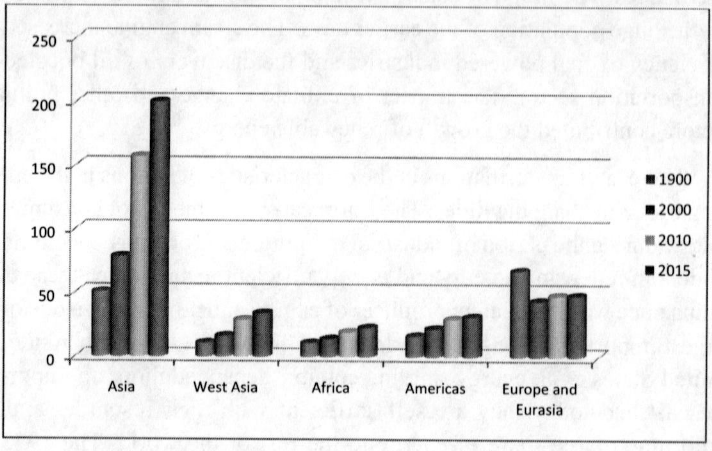

(EIA 2017)

Figure 3.1: Energy use in Non OECD nations by region

Figure 3.1 provides the clear picture about the energy consumption of non OECD nations by region. After 2000, Asia accounts for the largest share in the global energy consumption. China, India and other Asian economies consume major share of energy in the current energy scenario.

The other non OECD nations in various regions and the developed economies have a stable consumption pattern.

Energy Poverty and Access Challenge

There are 1.1 billion people still living without using electricity and 3 billion people using traditional fuel such as biomass and wood for cooking which affect the health and quality of life (World Bank 2018). Energy access and affordability are still problems for a large group of people. Even in energy rich nations, the people suffer from energy poverty and the health risks. Transportation, electricity, industry and heating or cooling are the major sectors which consume energy largely. Fossil fuels are the major provider of energy to these sectors.

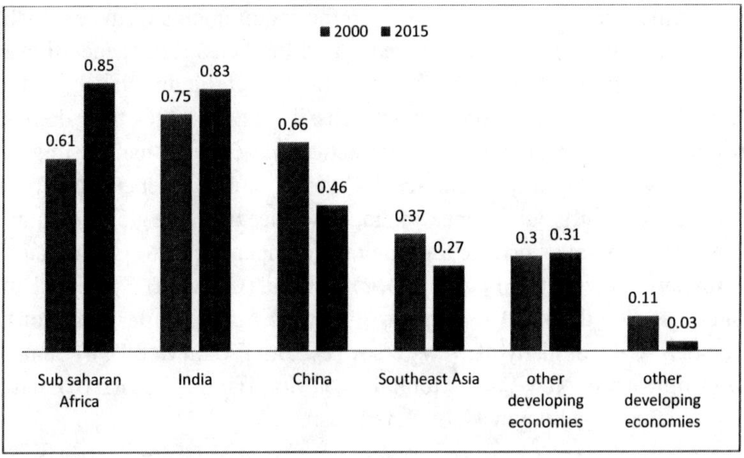

(IEA 2017)

Figure 3.2: People without access to electricity in Billions (Region wise)

Climate Change and Environmental Consideration

Fossil fuels are the main sources of energy as well as major contributors to the global green house gas emission. So globally, energy poverty and climate change impacts are the major challenges for energy sector. Burning of coal and petroleum products is very common worldwide. The natural gas is largely considered as the cleanest, but at the time of cooling, liquefaction, storage, transport and regasification, it produces huge amount of greenhouse gases to the environment. The consequences of climate change like extreme weather conditions, extinction of living beings and effects on human health have made fresh awareness among nations regarding fossil fuel usage. Several nations especially in the European Union have reduced their fossil fuel usages. Renewable electricity, energy efficiency measures, bio-fuel based or electric powered vehicles became popular in European nations. The cost of renewable energy dropped recently owing to the introduction of efficient technologies, high subsidy, increased investments and low interest loans. Nuclear energy which is free from green house gas emission took a major role in all countries in the last decades of twentieth century. But after the Fukushima incident, the growth of nuclear industry has also decreased.

Dependence on the Persian Gulf

The Persian Gulf region satisfies the most part of the energy requirement of the whole world and it was abundantly available from there with cheap price during the earlier decades of oil industry. Oil became an important requirement in the 20th century due to the requirements from sectors like military, transportation, mechanized agriculture, electricity generation and heating of buildings, among others. Earlier, several industrialized nations were largely dependent on imported fossil fuel resources than domestic resources. Because, domestic oil extraction was costlier than the imported oil, as it was in the case of America. As a result, ambitious energy companies settled in the Gulf region for extracting oil. Since then, the global oil market was driven by seven private transnational companies: 1) Anglo-Iranian Oil Company (now British Petroleum), 2) Gulf Oil (Chevron), 3) Royal Dutch Shell, 4) Standard Oil Company of Southern California (Chevron),5) Standard Oil Company of New Jersey (Exxon/ ExxonMobil), 6) Standard Oil Company of New York (Mobil/ ExxonMobil)and 7) Texaco (Chevron). They came to be known as the Seven Sisters.

The Organization of Petroleum Exporting Countries (OPEC) was formed in response to the price policies of the Seven Sisters and highlighted the inalienable right of all countries to exercise permanent sovereignty over their natural resources. They emerged as a major say in the pricing of crude oil in world market. Iran, Iraq, Kuwait, Saudi Arabia and Venezuela were the founding members and now there are 15 countries as members (OPEC 2017). The organisation was formed for the collective bargaining and self defence against the major energy players in the industry from the developed countries. During 1970s, OPEC was contributing around 56% oil to world oil demand. However, the Seven Sisters continued to play a significant role in the production, refining and distribution in the energy sector.

The US actions to support Israel against Egypt in Yom Kippur War in 1973 influenced the OPEC countries to stop oil exporting to the US and its allied countries. The oil embargo with the Soviet influence, these oil exporting nations wanted to exert pressure over those nations which had supplied weapons and aids to Israel. Arab oil embargo quadrupled the price from $3 per barrel to $12 and further leading to nationalization of the oil industries. The Iranian Revolution of 1979 also caused disruptions of oil supplies and the oil price rose to the highest level. Again, the Iran- Iraq war in 1980 distracted the oil production of both the countries. It especially affected the OECD nations, because they were getting cheap oil from the Arab World without any hindrances. The US sanctions on Iran, Iraq and Libya forced the industrialized nations to depend heavily on Saudi Arabia for their oil needs. These developments, including price variations and supply volatility led to the increase of domestic production and energy diversification by major industrialized nations. They started explorations on Alaska, the Gulf of Mexico, Siberia and the North Sea for oil and began new search on alternative resources like coal, natural gas and nuclear energy. They established emergency stocks and joint response mechanisms in OECD member countries.

Impact of the 1973 Oil Crisis

After the oil 1973 crisis, energy security became a top agenda for energy dependent nations, the energy resources became a strong element of state power (Cesnakas 2010, 31-33). Arab oil embargo revealed the significant influence of energy exporting states over other countries and international market. Developed countries dealt with the energy crisis through different ways such as substituting foreign imports with domestic production of alternatives like synthetic aviation fuel, imposing restrictions on non-essential uses of fuels and military control over strategic energy resources and infrastructure abroad (Yergin 2006, 69-82). The newly discovered energy resources from the Central Asia during this time became the field of competition forenergy importing countries. Control over energy resources is an element to obtain the state power. So, history witnessed large amount of military actions in order to get the control over energy resources. The United States' presence in Iran until 1979 and the invasion of Iraq in 1990 are such indicators. Similarly, Russia, Venezuela, Saudi Arabia and Iran used its energy resources as strategic influence over the rest of the world. For instance, Russia suspended the natural gas and oil supply to Belarus and Ukraine in the period 2004 - 2009. However, some energy rich nations like Canada, Mexico, Norway and the Netherlands did not adopt such manoeuvring.

Later, the natural gas industry began to grow as a result of the abundant production from countries like the US, Qatar and Iran. Factors such as less greenhouse gas emitting property, cheap price and the switching policies of several states from coal to gas also promoted the growth of natural gas industry (B.P. 2018).

The US, China, Russia are in the forefront of global resource competition. The US and China are energy starving countries and Russia wants to dominate over the transportation of energy abroad especially in Europe. It is well known that the American conflict with Iran and Iraq has been influenced by the aspirations to get control over Persian Gulf oil. The energy crisis relocates various forces to East Central Europe, Central Asia, North and Central Africa which occupy world's 80% oil and natural gas. The Caspian Sea Basin has emerged as the new source of oil and natural gas. So the US military aid started flowing to the region and established several bases in the Central Asia. China has influence over African countries like Algeria, Angola, Chad, Equatorial Guinea, Nigeria and Sudan. Russia and China together contribute technical and arms assistance to the Central Asian Republics through Shanghai Cooperation Organization (SCO). The Baku-Tbilisi-Ceyhan (BTC) pipeline creates tensions in Georgia due to the US and Russian interventions. Some countries or regions such as Niger Delta region of Nigeria, Darfur in western Sudan, the uranium producing areas of Niger and Zimbabwe, oil rich Cabinda province in Angola and in numerous other areas are suffering from the "resource curse" (Klare 2008, 1-8).

Global Energy Institutions

There are no international legally binding organizations in the energy field, but some organizations are actively engage in energy affairs internationally, regionally and nationally. Most of them consider energy related issues as sector wise, such as oil, renewable and nuclear, etc. The Organization of Petroleum Exporting Countries (OPEC), International Energy Agency (IAE), International Renewable Energy Agency (IRENA), International Energy Charter, Latin American Energy Organization (OLADE), Asia Pacific Economic Cooperation Energy Working Group, African Energy Commission are some of them. All these organizations are designed by states to foster international energy cooperation. There are certain organizations which promote the reduction of greenhouse gas emissions to lessen the human rights violations and environmental security threats.

OPEC

In 1960, the Organization of Petroleum Exporting Countries (OPEC) was established in Baghdad, Iraq with five members, namely Iran, Iraq,

Kuwait, Saudi Arabia and Venezuela. Now there are 14 members and it controls 80% of world's proven oil reserve which is more than 1.2 trillion barrels of crude oil. After the discovery of oil, outside players made profit from the trade and they fixed the price also. So the producing countries joined hands to stabilize the price for the profit of them. They produce more than 40% of daily supply in the global level.

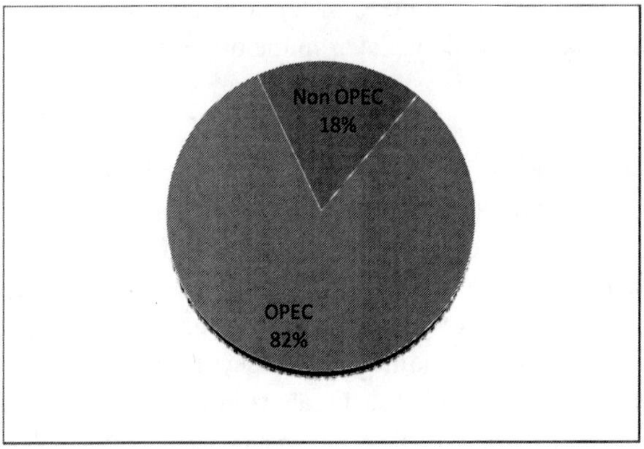

(OPEC, 2018)

Figure 3.3: Share of World crude oil reserves 2017

OPEC used oil as a political and economic weapon in 1973. They announced oil embargo against the UK, Canada, Japan South Africa and the Netherlands as well as against the US, due to their support of Israel in the Palestine issue. The sudden drop down of the US dollar value was also

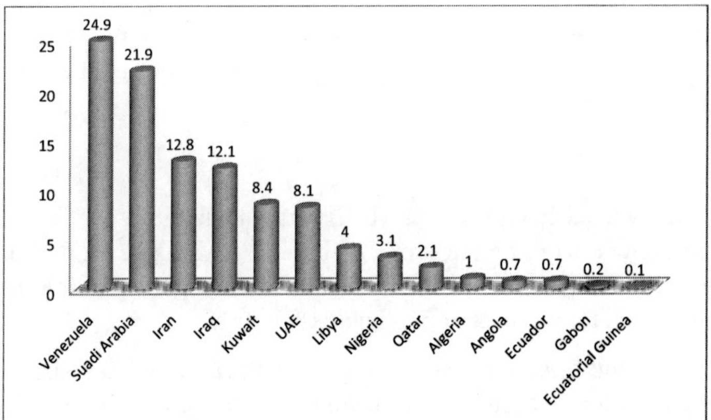

(OPEC, 2018)

Figure 3.4: Proved Crude oil reserve in OPEC

a reason for this move from OPEC. After 1980s, the oil production of non OPEC countries increased and the price fell down to a very low level.

Therefore, OPEC members reduced their production, but the internal disputes among member nations and the production of non OPEC countries balanced the price. OPEC is continuously trying to hold control over the oil market. In 2016, they cut the production. But US shale, gas from Russia and Iran discouraged the policies of Saudi Arabia and OPEC. However, OPEC still remains to be key player in the oil market.

IEA

International Energy Agency (IEA) was established in 1974 with 16 members and now it has a membership of 30 countries. It was formed in response to the 1973 oil crisis and the domination of OPEC in the oil market. Most of the members are from OECD nations with a few exceptions. The organization comprises of industrialized nations and energy consuming nations. Since 1973, it maintains a reserve to meet the emergency requirement. It is a legally binding organization and share their information and technological developments each other (Colgan and Van de Graff 2009, 2-5). The organization is a source of statistical and other information about different energy sectors and promotes alternate energy sources with advanced technologies.

IRENA

Formed in 2009, the International Renewable Energy Agency (IRENA)engages in worldwide promotion of renewable energy. It promotes use of alternate energy sources like solar, wind, ocean, geothermal etc., and acts as a platform of international corporation for sustainable development. IRENA gives advises to nations on various policy measures for a green future.

IEF

International Energy Forum (IEF) was founded in 1991 and has 72 members. It is an open platform for global energy dialogue for its member states. It consists of energy producing and consuming nations. It is also an energy forum for oil trade and its market stability.

OPEC and IEA are not able to cope with the new international energy issues. The energy consuming giants from Asia, the unstable price, lifestyle changes, increasing population, need for sophisticated fuel etc., are quite often outside the purview of IEA and OPEC. So IEF arranges a platform to open up these issues and provides opportunities for producer- producer, consumer – consumer and producer - consumer dialogues (Fattouh & Linde 2011, 7-8).

IAEA

International Atomic Energy Agency (IAEA) is an intergovernmental forum for nuclear energy. It promotes research and developments and supply safeguard to member states. It reports annually to the United Nation General Assembly and check nuclear facility under its control.

Energy Charter Treaty

This international agreement proposes energy security with sustainable development in a more open and competitive market. It provides a stable framework for investment in energy, acknowledging the linkage between energy and environment. It seeks energy trade, transit of energy goods, technological transfer and energy efficiency through international cooperation. It is a multilateral treaty with binding force (Hober 2010,153-90). It is the only binding treaty in the energy sector. It has provisions regarding environmental protection, and dispute resolution and investment protection.

Nuclear and Renewable Energy Developments

Nuclear energy developments started after 1950s and grew rapidly around 1960s, especially in the US. The International Atomic Energy Agency (IAEA) and the European Atomic Energy Community (Euratom) were established in 1957. The IAEA promoted civilian nuclear activities in developing countries with the support of the US. However, in 1980s the concerns of waste disposal, radiation and safety over nuclear energy generation led to the slowdown of the industry. Great disasters that occurred in the Three Mile Island, Chernobyl and Fukushima generated wider concern from time to time regarding the feasibility of nuclear energy industry. Around 31 countries had nuclear reactors in 1991.

The large scale demand of oil due to the industrial and economic growth, the development of Asian economies and their need of energy in a high rate, climate change threats, peak oil crises and concerns over nuclear energy created the energy situation a complex one in international realm. As countries having control over the energy resources can only achieve growth and development, every nation tries to achieve energy security in some way or the other. However, the growing environmental concerns became a determining factor in most of the countries' energy policies. As a result, renewable energy has achieved a pivotal status in global energy engagements in these days.

Renewable energy production has increased in the last years due to the changes in energy policies and cost reduction in favour of expansion of the sector. The International Energy Agency predicts that 2/3 of global renewable energy would come from three countries, namely China, the USA and India by 2022 (Smith 2018). Solar photovoltaic energy usage is increased by 32% in 2017, and total renewable energy usage shows 8.3% annual growth. China is installing around 50% of new capacity additions and India contributes 10%. These new capacity additions are coming from solar power. The Paris Agreement and the need to reduce global temperature below 2° c are the main pushing forces behind the policies of all the nations (IRENA 2018).

India's Energy Engagements

Since 1973, energy security occupies a vital position in every nation's policy making. Among the resources, oil played a major role in the early days of energy engagements. So the energy security debates focus on supply stability and other external factors including the tensions in Persian Gulf region. Inadequacy of domestic production and the increased demand forced India to depend on large scale import. But it became necessary to reassess the energy dealings due to the Gulf war and the high price of oil. In the case of gas, the insufficient pipelines and geographical tensions have been interrupting the easy transport. Maritime security is also a part of energy discussions. The Strait of Hormuz, the Suez Canal and the Bab- al- Mandeb are challenging spots in terms of security. In this light, ensuring the presence of sufficient navy force for the protection of the sea lines is a serious considerations for India.

India has been the fourth largest consumer of crude oil and petroleum products after the United States, China, and Japan and the fourth largest net importer of crude oil and petroleum products in 2015. The country depends heavily on imported crude oil, mostly from the Persian Gulf (EIA 2016). India has to maintain a good energy relation with other nations to meet its huge energy requirement. So, India engages in diplomatic dialogues, trade, infrastructural aid, negotiations etc., with several nations all across the world. The Hydrocarbon Vision 2025 announced in 2000, is a major step in India's energy policy framework. It emphasized the significance of globally competitive energy industry and the need of investments in equity in oil ventures abroad. ONGC Videsh Limited (OVL) keeps investments in Russia, Sudan, Vietnam, Iran, Libya, Syria, Myanmar, Iraq, Australia, Cote d'Ivoire, Egypt, Cuba, Qatar, Nigeria and Brazil. India is also a huge market for energy sources and its technologies.

Now the world energy consumption mainly comes from the two non OECD Asian giants which are India and China. Indian National Oil Companies have equity stakes in overseas oil and gas fields in the Persian Gulf, Latin America, the Caspian Sea region and Africa etc. India is one of the largest market for resource rich as well as technologically advanced countries. Saudi Arabia has been the top oil source for India for a long period. In 2017-18 April to October, Iraq supplied 25.8MT of oil and overtook Saudi Arabia which accounted 21.9 MT. India depends 80% on import for its oil demands. Around 58% of India's crude oil came from the Persian Gulf in 2015. India imported 202.851MMT crude oil in 2015-16(Ministry of Petroleum and Natural Gas 2017). Coal, Natural Gas and Nuclear resources are also mainly coming from abroad. The increasing energy consumption and demand are the thriving force behind the energy searches of India.

The economic development after 1990s increased India's energy dependence. After the 1973 oil crisis, energy security became a significant agenda in India's energy diplomacy. India followed 'resource nationalism'. During 1990s, the search for 'equity oil' gained a place in India's energy diplomacy. The Gulf War and the fluctuation of price became a rising concern for India. The dependence on hydrocarbon resource influenced the energy diplomacy of India and it emphasized overseas accumulation of energy sources. Countries like Cuba, Sudan, Kazakhstan, Libya, Iran and Ivory Coast are some examples for the equity oil searches. India's self-reliance of petroleum production was only 9% in 1947-48 and reached 56% 1990-91. But in 2007-08 it had only 31% self-reliance and was importing about 70% petroleum and petroleum products (Singh 2010, 20-25). Now it imports 4.37 million barrels per day (bpd) and has became the third largest oil consumer in the world.

The economic reforms since 1991 have led to the liberation of Indian capital and encouraged Indian business to venture abroad and take a bold global view of their operations. India's growing dependence on the rest of the world is not limited to oil and natural gas. It depends on import of coal as well as uranium for its energy needs. If an assured supply of these vital resources becomes an important national security objective for India, the nature of India's political ties with the resource rich developing nations is bound to alter (Mohan 2009, 130-31).

Iraq achieved the top supplier position in 2017. Saudi Arabia fell down to second ranking. Iran is the third largest oil supplier by replacing

Venezuela. Persian Gulf is the largest oil supplying region with 63% of its import share. Africa's oil supply increased and Latin America's declined. India started oil shipments from the U.S also (Verma 2018). However Saudi Arabia is the key supplier and Nigeria's contribution is also high in last decades. India imports from Africa, Europe, Australia, the U.S, South East Asia and Latin America. But Persian Gulf is still the major supplier for India. Considering the other regions, the cost of production and transport of the Persian Gulf oil are comparatively less. So within the 70% of oil import dependence, the Persian Gulf contributes 70% import share. However, the instability of the region, peak oil, price fluctuations, need for diversification of energy source etc., compels India to seek energy relationship with other regions.

Central Asia and the Caspian Sea region are the new energy partners for India, due to its vast sources of energy. It occupies 4% of the total oil reserves and 5% of total gas reserves. However, the development of oil fields in this region is very expensive compared with the other West Asian countries. And the resource rich region is land locked and it is difficult to reach. Russia's strategic involvement and Iran's influences are another issues behind the supply disruptions from this region.

India engages in diversifying its energy source through energy diplomacy with other regions. Our relationship with neighbours, especially Bhutan and Nepal enables to get hydropower to the nation. India also takes advantage of the relationship with Myanmar and Afghanistan for the aim of energy security. Malaysia and Indonesia also have crucial role in India's energy requirement. However, comparing to different states and regions, the Persian Gulf is still the major contributor to the energy basket of India.

Table 3.1: Import dependence of oil

Countries	***Imported oil in MT***
Saudi Arabia	40.4
Iraq	26.9
Venezuela	23.6
Nigeria	23.4
UAE	15.7
Iran	12.7

(EIA, 2017)

In 2015-16 India imported 202MMT crude oil, 16.58MMT LNG and 28.30 MMT petroleum products and exported 60.54MMT petroleum products particularly from Gujarat (Minstry of Petroleum and Natural Gas

2016). Essar Oil and RIL are in the exporting field which ships motor gasoline, gasoil, jet oil and naphtha to the UAE, the US, the Netherlands and Saudi Arabia etc.

Import Dependence of Crude Oil

India is the fourth largest LNG importer and sixteenth largest gas consumer. Petronet is the major importer of LNG supplies to India. It signed an agreement of 8.5 MTPA LNG from Qatar under a long term contract. It started from 2004. In 2015, Qatar was the largest exporter of LNG to India which contributed 60% of total LNG imports. Nigeria, Egypt and Yemen are also suppliers of LNG to India. Petronet planned to make regasification terminals at Sri Lanka, Bangladesh, the Andaman &Nicobar Islands and Mauritius (Petronet 2017). Saudi Arabia, Oman and the UAE are the other nations which provide LNG, but the US and China hold major share in Saudi gas fields (ChaturvedI 2013). India has agreements with Australia's Gorgon LNG terminal, Sabine Pass, Cove Point and Main Pass in the US and Indian Oil Company has invested in natural gas projects in Canada and Mozambique (EIA 2016).

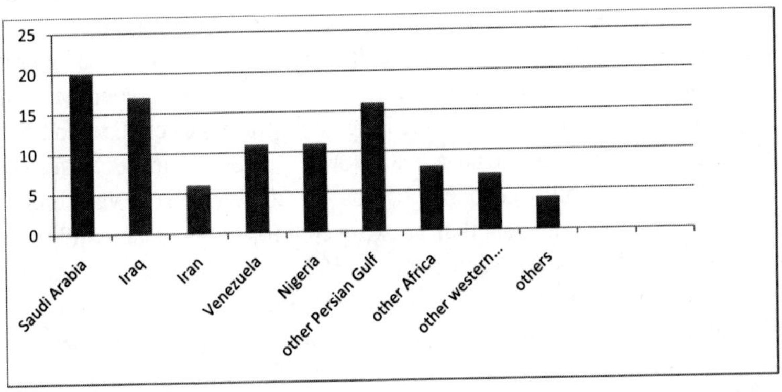

(EIA 2016)

Figure 3.5: India Crude Oil Import dependence

Coal

Coal is the primary energy source of India and it meets 55% of energy demand from coal and its related products. Even though there is a need to reduce coal consumption, India's energy scenario shows considerable dependence on coal. India has one of the largest coal reserve, but it imports good quality coal to fulfil the growing industrial requirements.

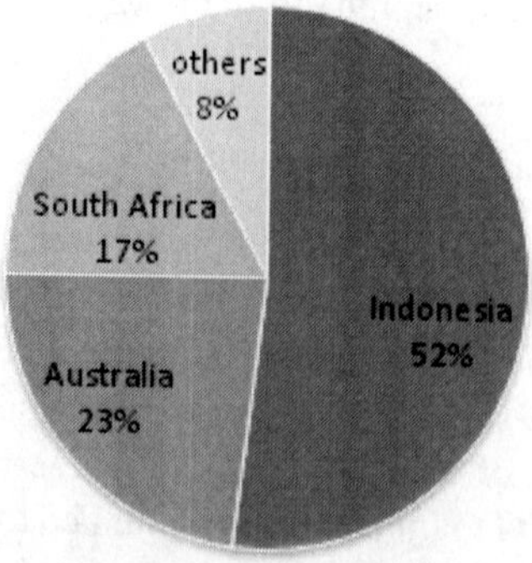

(EIA 2017)

Figure 3.6: India's Coal Import

There is a possibility to depend on coal for the coming next few years due to the accessibility as well as affordability of coal and the rising energy demand of India. In installed power capacity, the coal constitutes 57.3% in India. Countries like China, India, the United States, Australia, Indonesia, Russia, South Africa and Germany are the major producers of coal. Even though China and India occupy the first and second places respectively in terms of production, they are also the biggest importers of coal around the world. Australia and Indonesia are the top exporters in the coal sector. India imported 217 million tonnes of coal in 2017-18 fiscal year and it constituted more thermal coal than cocking coal for the huge demand from power sector. India's power sector depends 57.3% on thermal coal and the cheap availability contributes to the large scale import share. The domestic coal production covers only 688.4 MT. But India's steel, power and cement industries demand huge quantity of coal and therefore the import is increased by 8.1% in the fiscal year 2017-18. The figure 3.7 clearly explains India's coal import dependence. There was reduction of coal import during 2015-17, but in 2017-18 the coal import increased due to several reasons. The quality, reliability and affordability are the main reasons behind the import dependence. Indonesia (52%), Australia (23%) and South Africa (17%) are the major coal exporting countries to India.

The demand for thermal coal comes mainly from power sector as well as the cement sector and the coking coal is the main component in the steel sector. India has not sufficient cocking coal reserve and therefore its import accounts 13% increase in 2017-18. The poor transportation facility,

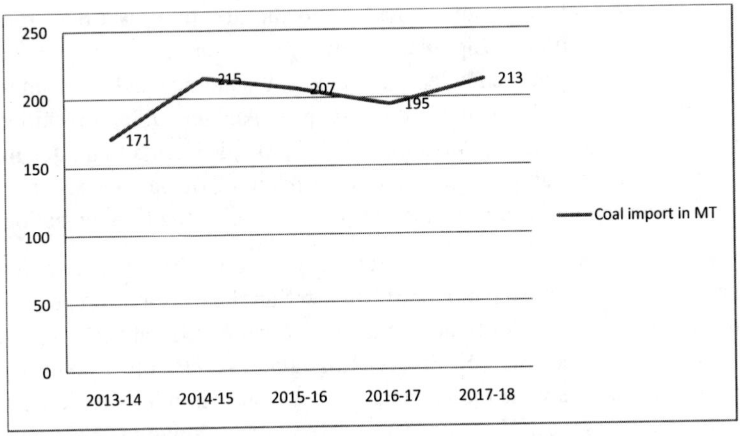

(Ministry of Coal 2018)

Figure 3.7: Coal Import in MT

especially rail system, acts as a hindrance in the domestic coal supply. India has considerable coal reserve, but it is mainly thermal coal and the sulphur content is very high in it. Moreover, the consumers can freely import coal and they have the opportunity to buy affordable and good quality coal. A growth of 8.1% in the Financial Year 2017-18, indicates India's growing interest in coal import.

Nuclear Engagements

India's developments in nuclear programme solely depended on imported fuel, heavy water and technological assistance. Eisenhower's Atoms for Peace initiative helped India in its growth of nuclear developments. The US provided a training programme for Indian scientists in 1955 and 1974 at the US nuclear energy research projects. Canada provided 40 MW Canada-India Reactor (CIR) and the US supplied heavy water for the 1956 the Canada-India Reactor Utility Services (CIRUS). The reactors of Rajasthan Atomic Power Plant (RAPP) and Madras Atomic Power Plant (MAPP) are Canadian Deuterium Uranium (CANDU) type reactors. The US also granted assistance in Trombay reprocessing facility and Tarapur reactors. Canada had not imposed any restrictions or safeguards on the nuclear dealings with India. The nuclear test conducted by India was a shock to the international arena and the fuel used in the test was from Canadian assisted CIRUS reactor. In 1974, the US and Canada withdrew from all nuclear engagements with India. By the time, Russia agreed to manage the crisis and supplied fuel to the reactors in Rajasthan. Russia once provided fuel to Tarapur reactors and the negative reactions from NSG stopped thc future shipments. However, Russia acts as 'sovereign guarantor' for the lifetime nuclear fuel supply, technology and freedom to reprocess the spent fuel. The nuclear tests provoked the US and its allied countries such as Canada, Australia, New Zealand, German and Japan. They recalled their ambassadors and suspended all financial assistance. France supported India during this time and gave fuel to the Tarapur station.

Since 1974 India had experienced nuclear isolation from resource rich countries. India was not a member of Nuclear Suppliers Group and in 2008 NSG provided a waiver for India to trade with other NSG members without signing NPT. Besides the US, France, Russia and several other countries agreed to cooperate with India. Japan, Argentina, Namibia, Kazakhstan, Canada, South Korea, Vietnam, Czech Republic, Mongolia, Australia, Bangladesh and Sri Lanka (Department of Atomic Energy (DAE), 2018) followed suit.

West Asia and the Persian Gulf

India's dependence on the Persian Gulf for its crude oil is an enduring one and has increased from 58 % in 2014-15 to 63.5% in the April-October period of 217-18. India had imported 109.9 MT out of 189.4 MT of total crude imports in 2014-15 from the region (*The Economic Times* 2017). Persian Gulf is a guaranteed energy resource centre for India. The migrant labour, trade and energy engagements created the Arab Gulf a strategic region for India. Even though there are certain threats and instabilities for the supply of energy and other engagements, the region is significant in many ways. Due to problems on access of energy from the Caspian Basin, Central Asia and Russia, and Iraq, many countries need to rely upon the Persian Gulf to fill their energy baggage. India maintains strong relation with the Gulf States of Saudi Arabia, Qatar, Bahrain, the United Arab Emirates and Oman. The US, Russia and China also engage in business in this region. The relation of India with the GCC countries is based primarily on energy access. From 1990 to 2012, India became the third largest consumer of energy in the world. India is more dependent on Arab Gulf for energy needs than any other countries (Pethiyagoda 2017). In coming decades, oil and natural gas remain to be the significant part of India's energy mix. Saudi Arabia exported 795,000 barrels per day to India from January to April 2015, indicating an increase of around 4.6 percent over the same period in 2014. India's Link West Policy signifies the growing energy relationship with the West Asian region.

Iran

Iran has the largest deposits of proved oil and natural gas reserves in the world. Iran is one among the world's top 10 oil producers and top 5 natural gas producers. Iran produced almost 3.4 million barrels per day (b/d) of petroleum and other liquids in 2014 and an estimated 5.7 trillion cubic feet (Tcf) of dry natural gas in 2013. Iran is the second largest oil exporter after Saudi Arabia and holds the world's second largest reserves of natural gas after Russia. Even though there are abundant proved resources, Iran can not tap it because of the international sanctions. The sanctions imposed by the US and the EU in 2011 and 2012 led to the harsh decline in Iran's upstream projects and is resulting in a near 1.0-million b/d drop in crude oil. Iran's oil and natural gas export revenue was $118 billion in the 2011-12 fiscal year and dropped by 47% i.e., $63 billion in 2012-13 fiscal year. The same is the case in the natural gas sector. The production growth rate is very low in Iran during the sanction periods. So, Iran's largest upstream project 'South Pars' which is located offshore in the Persian Gulf, holds almost 40% of Iran's proved natural gas reserves d is run by Iranian oil companies. The Iranian nuclear programme was began with the help of the US in 1950s. After the 1979 Iranian revolution, the US imposed certain sanctions and the UN imposed further sanctions in 2006 and it affected the economy, especially in the energy field of Iran. A Joint Plan of Action (JPOA) was established between Iran and the five permanent members of the United Nations Security Council and started its implementation in January 2014. Iran agreed to drop down or freeze some of its nuclear activities during negotiations in exchange for some sanctions relief but even now most of the companies are trying to keep away from Iran due to fear of isolation from western countries. Iran maintained its energy deals in the midst of sanctions from America with the help of countries like Brazil, China and India (Bansal 2014,8-14).

Iran is significant for India by its abundant oil and natural gas reserves. India maintains the relation in a strategic way because of its access to the Central Asia and Afghanistan. It is the shortest route for the Caspian region and Caucasus region. The declining trade between the two countries during the sanction period got a momentum since the Joint Comprehensive Plan of Action (JCPA), 2015 and the resulting easing of sanctions from western nations. According to Pant (2008, 124) "While India and Iran participate in the global energy market as buyer and seller, they share strategic concern regarding the emerging dynamics of global hydrocarbon regime. Hence their energy relations have to be conceived beyond the limited parameter of commercial exchange."

Indian investments in Iran helped to develop the gas reserves. The low external investments due to the sanctions affected oil and gas production in Iran. Though Iran was India's second biggest supplier of crude oil after Saudi Arabia till 2010-11, western sanctions over its suspected nuclear programme lowered it to the seventh position. Now, Iran is the third largest supplier to India with 27.2 MT oil in 2016-17 financial year and selling 12.5 MT oil during the period of April -October of 2017-18 (Economic Times 2017).

Table 3.2: India's import of oil from Iran

Financial Year	*Import of Oil in MT*
2008-09	21.89
2009-10	21.19
2010-11	18.49
2011-12	17.44
2013-14	11.00
2014-15	10.95
2015-16	12.70
2016-17	27.20

(EIA 2018)

Iran produces 800 million cubic meters of gas per day. But it exports only 40 mcm/d. Iran-Pakistan-India (IPI) pipeline was an ambitious project from the part of India. But it could not work out due to the geographical complexities and political strains. India had almost abandoned the IPI pipeline in 2008 due to the international sanctions against Iran over its suspected nuclear programme (Bansal 2014). So India planned to look into the feasibility of another option, namely the Iran-Oman-India pipeline. South Asia Gas Enterprise Private Ltd (SAGE) is the consortium behind this 1300 km undersea pipeline, which can transfer Turkmenistan and Qatar gas through this pipeline. However, the US intervention is preventing the progress of the pipeline (Jangir 2012, 1-6).

Iraq

Iraq has the fifth largest crude oil reserves in the world and it is OPEC's second largest crude oil producer after Saudi Arabia. After years of sanctions and wars, Iraq is again in the process of developing oil and natural gas production. Iraq's crude oil production grew from 1.5 million barrels per day (b/d) to 4.1 million b/d in 2015. The decrease in crude oil prices, ISIS influence, Kurdistan issues and political unrest etc., are affecting the Iraq oil development.

The United States

The United States and India have long strategic partnership. The recent developments ensure collaboration in energy research and export of the US clean energy technology to India. In 2009, the Partnership to Advance Clean Energy (PACE) was started by India and the US to support the clean energy technology. In 2005, the US and India initiated an Energy Dialogue. It deals with areas of coal, oil and gas, nuclear and renewable resources, electric power generation and energy efficiency. For tracking the progress, the US-India Energy Dialogue is convened yearly. The US-India Clean Energy Finance (USICEF) initiative's support was $20 million and it was collected from different foundations and Indian Government. This supports the clean energy projects and it may help the project developers to promote their business in this field. The Overseas Private Investment Corporation (OPIC)of the US Government assists the long term financing. However, according to the US representation in the WTO, India's solar program was discriminatory and the U.S. solar exports to India had fallen by 90 percent from 2011. In the US complaint, finally the WTO court came out with the verdict that India had broken the trade rules by requiring solar power developers to use Indian made cells and modules and such "local content" requirements are banned because they discriminate in favour of domestic firms against foreign competitors (Miles 2017).

The Joint Clean Energy Research and Development Centre (JCERDC), is a collaboration between the USA and India to promote joint clean energy research in the areas of solar energy, second generation bio-fuels and energy efficiency of buildings. The India-US Energy Dialogue has provided a platform to collaborate on energy and promoting greater technological innovation, scientific collaboration, trade, research and development, deploying environment friendly technologies and products, and promoting sound regulatory frameworks to deliver energy solutions for sustainable growth (Planning Commission 2014).

In the field of nuclear energy, the US aided the nuclear initiatives of India as part of the 'Atoms for Peace' programme. America built reactors in India and allowed the scientist to study in the US laboratories. But in 1968, India refused to sign the NPT agreement and dared to test the first nuclear bomb in 1974. Then onwards, the US isolated India and imposed sanctions for 30 years. However, later the US adopted a friendly relation with India, resulting in allowing the NSG waiver. Now, even though India is a non signatory, it can trade with other NSG members. The civil nuclear deal permits trade in nuclear material, nuclear reactors and nuclear raw materials. However, much trade has not happened due to liability issues and other matters. During the visit of Prime Minister Narendra Modi in 2016, the US announced the establishment of six nuclear reactors in India by the US firm Westinghouse. The project was delayed due to Westinghouse's financial difficulties and Japan's procedural issues in ratifying the deal with India (*The Hindu* 2017).

Canada

India maintains close relations with Canada over hydrocarbons, nuclear energy and clean technologies for a long time. Canada is a resource rich country, especially in terms of natural gas, coal, shale gas, uranium and oil. It has the third largest proven oil reserve. Also, it is the second largest producer and exporter of uranium in the world. India imports coking coal which is largely used by steel industry as India's coal contains large sulphur contents. As per the National Steel Policy 2017, the coking coal requirement will increase from the current level of around 60 million tonnes per annum (MTPA) to 160 MTPA. India imports around 3 million tonne of coal from Canada (*The Times of India* 2017). India's largest steelmaker, the Steel Authority of India(SAIL) has shifted their coal import from Australia to Canada and South Africa. There are collaborative research held on shale gas, oil sands and natural gas. Indian companies are looking towards its oil sand especially on Northern Alberta.

Canada has abundant uranium resource. The Nuclear Cooperation Agreement was signed in June 2010 and a Joint Committee on Civil Nuclear Cooperation was constituted in 2013. The Department of Atomic Energy signed a $350 million contract with Cameco Corporation, based in Canada to purchase 7 million pounds of uranium. In 2013, the two countries established an Energy Dialogue promoting collaboration and joint efforts in energy sector. The Canada-India Energy Dialogue is annually conducted and discusses about the prospects of cooperation on renewable energy, petroleum and natural gas as well as electricity between the two countries.

Europe

In EU- India relations, energy sector especially renewable energy and energy efficiency occupies a significant position. The EU and India have held an energy dialogue since 2005 and meets once a year. The EU supports the Facilitating Offshore Wind in India (FOWIND) Project with € 4 mn for resource mapping, policy guidance and capacity building measures (EESA 2016). In 2015, India adopted an offshore wind energy policy and planned to build the projects in Gujarat and Tamil Nadu. Gujarat has the port and infrastructural facilities, but Tamil Nadu possesses the wind energy capacity more than that of Gujarat. The state acquired the First Offshore Wind Farm Project in India (FOWPI), which is funded by the EU. It was designed to build in sea bed area located near the Gulf of Khambhat in Gujarat with a tentative capacity of 200 M.Th. EU has an experienced wind industry and the FOWPI includes all technical specifications and design document (FOWPI 2017). The EU provided €1,8 mn for the project. The EU in collaboration with the Bureau of Energy Efficiency, implemented in the states of Maharashtra, Madhya Pradesh, Bihar and Odisha energy efficiency initiatives in commercial buildings. It provides technical assistance to set up the legislation and procedures for implementation of the Energy Conservation Building Code schemes and certification mechanism and a monitoring and verification framework (European External Service Action 2016). The EU assisted India's Solar Park Programme and gave an assistance of worth € 1.66 million to support integration of solar energy into the electricity grid. Indo European Union Sustainable Development (I.E.S.D.) has undertaken various development programmes in India. It includes development of a 100 MW plant in Uttarakhand, development of a 100 MW Solar Park in Tamil Nadu and signing of an agreement for the construction of another 1000 MW photovoltaic plant in Odisha (IESD 2017). The EU is associated with the Ministry of New and Renewable Energy and the National Institute for Solar Energy (NISE) for assisting the operations and maintenance of solar parks and promoting smart grid cooperation as well as established a Roof-Top solar cell in the Ministry of New and Renewable Energy. The EU is also supporting another 3 MW Solar Thermal-Biomass hybrid power plant in Bihar.

The EU and India actively collaborate on the International Solar Alliance (ISA). India is a founding member as well as a major contributor to the target achievement of ISA which is 1 TW of solar electricity by 2030. India agreed of 175 GW of electricity from renewable including 100 GW from solar by 2022. The International Solar Alliance was opened by Prime Minister Narendra Modi and then French President Francois Hollande at the UN Climate Change Conference in Paris on November 30 2015. It is a collaboration between solar rich countries. Its target by 2030 is 1TW of solar energy (Raghavan 2018). The EU offered digital platform as well as support in technical studies for the solar parks with International Solar Alliance (ISA) secretariat.

The EU-India Climate Change Dialogue and Partnership was announced during 2016 for clean energy and to address the climate change related threats. So the EU contributes to energy efficiency in buildings, development of renewable energy sources including solar and offshore wind, smart grids, energy research and innovation (Sachdeva 2015). The EU-India Agenda for Action-2020 determined and committed towards an economic model with low primary energy resource consumption. It enhances the energy cooperation on renewable energy, energy efficiency, smart grids, clean coal technology, energy security and energy research. The cooperation between EU and India enhances the biofuel energy sector. The European Union is a significant factor in the renewable energy realm of India.

Caspian Sea

India considers Central Asian states as 'near abroad'. Recognizing the importance of this region, the then Prime Minister, Vajpayee identified the need of new silk route and promotion of "Connect Central Asia Policy"in 2002. Central Asian states such as Kazakhstan, Kyrgyzstan, Turkmenistan, Tajikistan, and Uzbekistan are rich in energy resources. Turkmenistan has the highest gas reserves in this region and fourth position in the world. Uzbekistan and Kazakhstan possess the second and third highest gas reserves in this region. Kazakhstan is 12th in global oil deposits. ONGC has stakes in Alibekmola and Kurmangazy oilfields in Kazakh owned areas of the Caspian Sea. Tajikistan and Kyrgyzstan are rich in hydropower capacity. Kazakhstan has oil as well as uranium resources. India is planning to invest in the exploration and production in Kazakhstan oil and gas fields. Uzbekistan also possesses uranium. The entry as a full member country in Shanghai Cooperation Organisation (SCO) by India enhances the energy cooperation between the two countries. Iran's Chabahar port link supports the energy trade cooperation of South Asia and Central Asia. It opened up new trade route and strengthened the relationship towards Central Asia Energy hub. The port provides opportunity to enter the land locked region through water. The route provides hopes to the development of TAPI pipeline. India has investments in training, designing, construction, exploration and production of oil and gas fields of Turkmenistan. The region can be a significant clean energy provider for the India's energy thirst. Caspian sea is an important source for hydrocarbon resource for India. The region has proven gas reserves estimated to be 243-248 trillion cubic feet (tcf). The gas rich Caspian states are potential supply sources for Asian energy markets.

Caucasus Region

It is located between black sea and Caspian Sea and home to Caucasus Mountain. It includes Georgia, Azerbaijan, Armenia and Russia. ONGC

Videsh Ltd and its consortium have investments in the Azeri, Chirag and the deep water portion of Gunashli fields (ACG) in the Azerbaijan sector of the Caspian Sea till 2049. Azerbaijan is a dependable oil and natural gas provider for India. ONGC is an equity partner for Azerbaijan. ACG oil fields produce approximately 585,000 barrels crude oil. It is transported through the Baku-Tbilisi-Ceyhan Pipeline (BTC Pipeline) to Mediterranean coast of Turkey. From Turkey it is shipped to other parts of the world. OVL has share in BTC pipeline and stakes with SOCAR which is Azerbaijan's state energy company (Business Line 2017). India and Azerbaijan have agreed for cooperation in the future renewable energy field. GAIL has signed MoU with SOCAR for exploring petrochemical products. As far as Georgia is concerned, the Indian company, Jindal Petroleum Georgia Limited, is producing oil from Sartichala area of Samgori field. The company has production and exploration license and has five oil blocks in Georgia.

Australia

India and Australia engage in energy security issues for a long period of time. Australia provides Uranium, natural gas and renewable energy technologies to India. India Australia Energy Security Dialogues were held in New Delhi and Brisbane in 2013 and 2014 respectively. Indian coal experts are being trained at SIMTARS, Australia. There is a proposal to build a virtual reality training centre at ISM, Dhanbad in Jharkhand in association with SIMTARS, CIL and NTPC. Australian institutions and ISM, Dhanbad are engaging in promoting operations in the areas of R&D, clean coal technology, energy efficiency, smart grid and mining technology. It is also planning a close collaboration in the field of coal gasification (CBM/CMM) in India. Australia is the eleventh largest resource of Natural Gas. India is importing natural gas from Australia's Gorgon Project. Australian expertise in solar roof top and wave energy will be helpful for India. The grid integration of renewable energy is also a matter of consideration between the two nations (Ministry of Power 2016). The Uranium supply deal was signed in 2014 and supply started since 2017. Australia is the third largest uranium exporter at global level. As India produces only 20% of its metallurgical coal for its steel industry and infrastructural needs, India imports 80% of its metallurgical coal from Australia.

Russia

It is the world largest producer of crude oil and the second largest producer of natural gas. Russia's proven oil resources were 109.5 billion barrels and produced 554 million tonnes of oil in 2016. Russia has the second largest shale gas resources in the world with 74.6 billion barrels, while the USA has 78.2 billion and China has 32.2 billion barrels. Russia has significant coal and uranium resources as well (ITE 2017). The hydrocarbon oil and gas are located in Volga Urals, West Siberia, East Siberia and Sakhalin Region. Sakhalin region is one of the highest natural gas reservoirs and it has Uranium potential as well (EIA 2015). Russia since its Soviet era was a friendly partner for India in terms of energy. Russia has provided great assistance in India's oil and gas exploration, construction of hydroelectric plants and coal mining industry. Both the countries have jointly owned shares in several oil rich regions.

India has strong and long term cooperation with Russia in its energy sector. The Soviet association helped India in its hydropower, nuclear energy, thermal projects, petroleum drilling as well as infrastructure facilities of power sector. During the period of isolation of nuclear suppliers group, Russia provided adequate nuclear raw materials and technological expertise to India. India signed a nuclear deal with Russia in 1988. Russia manages the technical expertise for 12 nuclear power plants in India. Since NSG sanction, Russia is the major player in India's nuclear energy field. Kudankulam Nuclear Power Plant (6000 MW) is using the water-water energy reactors (*Voda Voda Energo Reactors* or VVER).

The Indian investment in Sakhalin 1 project (2001) is the largest foreign investment by the nation. Indian Oil Corporation (IOCL), Oil India Limited (OIL), ONGC and Bharat Petro Resources Limited (BPRL) also have assets in Russia's oil and gas sector. India Oil Corporation Limited, Oil India Limited and Bharat Petroleum Corporation Limited together formed a consortium and it 23.9 per cent stake in JSC Vankorneft and 29.9 percent stake in LLC Taas-Yuryakh Neftegazodobycha. Vankorneft is for the development of Vankor field located in Eastern Siberia. Tass - Yuryakh oil field produces 20000 barrels of oil per day (Telegraph 2016). Russia is critical for India's natural gas aspirations and Iran, Central Asia and Pakistan would be part of this engagement. The high import bill on India's energy forced to build new pipeline to get access of gas. Rosneft Oil Company, the national oil company of Russia has acquired 98% stakes in Essar Oil Limited which is the second largest private oil refiner in India. The deal enables Russia to involve in the oil retail market in India (*Business Line* 2017).

Tata power purchased mining license in Far East Russia. It has high quality coal reserves. ONGC Videsh Limited (OVL) has 20% stake in Sakhalin 1 project. It can buy oil and gas from here. OVL has control over the exploration of the resources from this region. India's energy firms have interest in Sakhalin lll project, gas liquefactions and downstream petroleum units in Russia. Russian oil companies have investments in upstream and downstream oil and gas projects in India. Russia and India jointly agreed to build a nuclear power plant in Bangladesh. After Saudi Arabia, Russia is the largest crude oil producer in global level. ONGC/OVL invested $2.7 billion in Sakhalin Island. The Sakhalin-I project has equity stakes of Exxon-Mobil (30%), Japanese SODECO (30%), Russian Rosneft (20%) and OVL (20%). It is the most risky energy project that has been established by Russia in its far east. It has abundant LNG and oil resource. Rosneft is interested in offshore exploration program with Reliance Industries in East Siberia and North Russia. OVL is joining hands with Russian firm Rosneft for exploring and developing the Vankor oilfield in East Siberia. Joint bidding for Trebs and Titov oil fields in the Timan Pechora Basin in Nenets Autonomous Okrug region of North Russia is under discussion. Russia's technological advancement and diminishing oil reserves of old fields influence its attention towards the new fields such as Arctic Region, East Siberia and Sakhalin Island.

Africa

India invested and bought 25% stake in Sudan's Greater Nile Project blocks 1, 2 and 4 and agreed to build a 1,500-kilometre pipeline to Port Sudan in Red Sea. China is also a partner in this project with 40% stakes. The Canadian company Talisman Energy held stakes in the Sudan oil field till 2003. But it left the country because of civil wars and human rights violations in the region. In this time, OVL acquired the shares from the Canadian company. The war occurred between the Muslim government of the north and the mostly Christian Sudanese People's Liberation Army (SPLA) of the south. The people living in the surrounding areas were forcefully evacuated amidst bombings and killings. The oil fields were occupied by warring factions and they destructed the harvest and livestock of the surrounding areas. The oil companies also have their role in the human rights violations of this area. Oil wealth has been used to purchase arms and ammunition which we reemployed against its own citizens (Human RightsWatch 2003). The India's oil companies handed over the pipelines to the Sudan government in 2005. The blocks together produced 50000 barrels per day. In 2011, Sudan and South Sudan were separated and most of the shares were under the South Sudan government. Blocks 2A, 2B and 4N are with Sudan, while blocks 1A, 1B and 4S are with South Sudan. Block 5 is in South Sudan and is producing 16000 bpd. Block 2B produced

28000 bpd and block 4 is in the exploration stage. Block 2B was expired in 2016 and Sudan government wanted to increase the royalties and tax for renewing the contract. In the bargaining, Sudan government declined to pay around $300 million to the OVL. India built its oil pipeline by its state owned companies such as OVL (90%) and OIL (10%)(OVL also 2017). Despite the conflicts and unresolved issues, India is continuously producing oil from the two nation's oil fields.

Table 3.3: Proved reserves and production of oil in Africa 2017

Country	*Proved reserves of oil (thousand million barrels)*	*Production of oil Thousand barrels/day*
Algeria	12.2	1579
Angola	11.6	1807
Chad	1.5	73
Republic of Congo	1.6	238
Egypt	3.5	691
Equatorial Guinea	1.1	280
Gabon	2.0	227
Libya	48.4	426
Nigeria	37.1	2503
South Sudan	3.5	118
Sudan	1.5	104
Tunisia	0.4	63
Other African Nation	3.7	233
Total	128.0	7892 Thousand Barrel per day

(BP 2017)

Table 3.4: Natural Gas Proved Reserves

Country	*Trillion cubic meters*	*Billion cubic meters*
Algeria	4.5	91.3
Egypt	1.8	41.8
Libya	5.3	10.1
Nigeria	5.3	44.9
Other African Countries	1.1	20.2
Total	14.3	208.3

(BP 2017)

India imports coal from South Africa, Mozambique, Egypt, and Algeria. Increasing demand of energy leads India to diversity its sources and search for oil reserve assets abroad. South Africa has huge reserves of cocking coal. Coal Videsh of India has control over coal mines in South Africa. Coal India Africana Limitada (CIAL) acquired assets in Mozambique earlier but it had less presence of coal content. However, India did not give up the projects in Mozambique and now it is has commissioned other projects. India imports its 7.5% of oil from African nations, mainly from Nigeria and Angola. Now the natural gas imports also is in a growing stage. Nigeria and Equatorial Guinea contribute gas to India. India exports refined petroleum products to Africa.

Madagascar was a participant of international solar alliance. Another initiative of in solar energy was seven elderly women from Madagascar village trained by Barefoot Cottage for 6 months in India and installed solar equipment in their villages. They were using kerosene and unsustainable energy sources earlier. Now nearly 200 families acquired solar equipment.

In Mozambique, ONGC Videsh Ltd., holds 16% stake in Rovuma gas field. It is the second largest coal reserve in Africa. Private companies from India are operating in Tete province of Mozambique which is abundant in coal reserve. These companies operate power plants there and sells electricity to Mozambique Electricity Utility Company. India provides assistance to solar initiatives of Mozambique.

OVL and Essar have assets in Nigeria. It is the world's sixth largest producer of oil. It has 37.1 million barrels of oil reserves and 5.3 cubic trillion meters gas reserves. The crude oil of Nigeria is high value and low sulphur content (Sing 2017). Reliance, Essar, BHEL of India have investments in Nigeria's energy sector. Egypt and Nigeria had been major crude oil supplier earlier. But now they import oil from several other African countries. Madagascar, Niger, Namibia, South Africa, Gabon and Malawi supplies uranium to India. Geographical locations and quality of coal and oil influence foreign nations to explore here.

Latin America

Latin America possesses one fifth of the global oil reserves. Venezuela, Brazil, Cuba and Brazil are main countries which have cordial relations with India in Latin America. Venezuela possesses 300.9 thousand million barrels of oil. It is one of the major trade partners of India in the case of energy. The Orinoco River of Venezuela has the largest oil reserves in the world. It accounts around 270 billion barrels of oil. India's OVL has 40% stake in this field with 22,000-23,000 BPD and now the Venezuela Oil Company has offered an additional 9% stake. Orinoco's oil is often referred as 'oil sands' or 'extra heavy oil' because it has no bitumen content. Venezuela holds 85% of the Latin American crude reserves. Oil sand in this region is similar to those in Alberta Canada. However, the tar sands here is less vicious and less costly for processing than in Canada. Venezuela has 5.7 trillion cubic meters natural gas and hold eighth position in the world. Brazil has only 4 trillion cubic meters of natural gas, in which 12.6 thousand million barrels belongs to Tupi and Jupiter oil field.

The Indian companies such as United Phosphors Limited (UPL) and Suzlon Energy have investments in Argentina, Brazil and Colombia in the power sector. India imports 20% of its oil from Brazil, Colombia, Mexico and Venezuela (Desai 2015). During the Hugo Chavez's period, ONGC Videsh Ltd (OVL) and Petróleos de Venezuela (PDVSA) jointly operated in San Cristobal field with a production capacity of 30,000 bpd. OVL, Indian Oil and Oil India Ltd have a combined share of 18 percent in the Carabobo oilfield, with a production capacity of 400,000 barrels per day. Reliance Industries and Essar also import oil from Venezuela.

Asia Pacific

Asia Pacific region is relatively significant in terms of energy for India. The coal import, renewable energy, natural gas pipelines, strategic oil transport routes, the growing Chinese influence etc., are influencing the regional importance of energy. Malacca Strait is a strategic point for India, because it is the major oil and gas trade route for India. The strait accounts around 25% of world trade and is notorious for being a home of piracy, smuggling, maritime terrorism and several other illegal activities. India maintains strategic relations with Strait of Malacca's littoral states such as Malaysia, Singapore and Indonesia. The South China Sea is a disputed area and China claims all the oil resources in the sea as their own. But Vietnama Philippines, Malaysia, Brunei and Taiwan are opposed to the claim. Vietnam has invited India to invest in the South China Sea and China has expressed strong disagreements about it. The South China Sea is a strategic route for India from the Indian Ocean and the Malacca Strait to the East China Sea. India's 50% of trade passes through this strategic location and the region holds one billion barrels of oil and 190 trillion cubic feet of natural gas (EIA 2013). India has interest in this resource rich area for its vast energy requirement. India and the ASEAN have strong relationship in various fields, especially on energy. The first Ministerial Meeting on cooperation in Renewable Energy between India and ASEAN was held in 2012. The US-Asia-Pacific Comprehensive Energy Partnership (USACEP)is another major initiative in energy in this region. Renewable energy, human resource development, technical cooperation, natural gas cooperation and capacity building programmes are the major themes in this sector.

India and Indonesia maintains a significant relation in the field of energy. India Indonesia Energy Forum was held in Jakarta in 2017. Indonesia has a large coal reserve and India is the third largest importer of coal from Indonesia. The coal imports constitute $3.5 billion in 2016. Indian coal companies have investments in Indonesian coal mines (Ministry of Mines 2018). Also, Indonesia is a crude oil supplier to India. India has close collaboration with the country in areas of exploration of oil, gas and coal, gasification of oil, technical expertise and sharing experience in the field of renewable energy. Tata Power has collaboration with PT Bumi Resources of Indonesia. In addition, Reliance Power, GMR Energy and ESSAR Group have stakes in coal mine of Indonesia.

The Philippines and India signed a Memorandum of Agreement on Enhanced Cooperation in the Field of Renewable Energy in 2007. It focuses the research and development, technical expertise sharing and training in renewable energy sector. In 2011, India and South Korea signed a nuclear energy cooperation agreement and started the nuclear energy developments.

India has relations with Vietnam in oil and gas exploration, nuclear energy and as an ASEAN regional connectivity link etc. India's ONGC has two blocks in South China Sea. Since 1989 ONGC Videsh Ltd. has oil trade with Petro Vietnam.

The Bay of Bengal Initiative for Multi-Sectoral Technical and Economic Cooperation (BIMSTEC) initiated a natural gas grid such as BIMSTEC gas pipeline for countries like India, Myanmar, Thailand and Bangladesh. It proposed a hydro power connectivity between Nepal, Bhutan, India and Bangladesh. It is a link between South Asia and South East Asia. It established as an energy information centre and conducts various workshops and training programmes. BIMSTEC is the major motivating force behind the regional integrated electricity grid.

China

China is the biggest energy consumer in Asia and India is one of the largest growth market for energy. Both countries accounted for two thirds of worlds rising energy use. In 1950s, China had only 3.73 million tonnes of oil production. Invention of Daqing oil field produced enough oil for China till 1970s. However, after 1970s the expansion of Chinese economy led to the decline of self sufficiency of energy. Yet, China exported coal and oil to other countries. China began its import of oil in 1983 and became a net importer of oil products in 1993, and a net importer of crude oil in 1996. China's oil companies were interested in overseas energy assets since

1993. China has investments in all major energy rich regions. Now the two energy markets of India and China influence on crude oil pricing. China's coal and Natural Gas demand is also in a rising state. Sometimes the two countries are in a competitive mode. In Africa, China's investment is considerably huge, but in various fields acquiring stakes became competitive for both countries. The Caspian Sea region is another energy resource centre which holds China's leading role.

Arctic Region

The Arctic Region comprises 90 billion barrels of undiscovered oils and 1670 trillion cubic feet of natural gas. The melting of the ice provides the ease of access to the unexplored resources. After the oil shock of 1973, the United States showed interest in this region and Trans Alaska Pipeline transports oil to the United States System. Still there is vast untapped oil and natural gas reserved under the Arctic Ocean. The United Nations Convention on the Law of the Sea (UNCLOS) restricted the exploration in this region to certain countries (American Security Project 2017). The neighbouring countries of the region are the US, Canada, Russia, Norway and Denmark and they have the major accessibility and opportunities in this region. Finland, Sweden and Iceland have also options to engage in the region. However, other countries can only cooperate with these countries. India also has this limitation. India invested in Sakhalin-1 project which is situated in North Pacific Ocean. Now India is an observing member of Arctic council. Indian oil companies have interest in the Arctic Ocean, Siberia and Far East Russia. India wants to buy LNG from Russia Yamal gas project which is situated in Arctic Siberia and has hydrocarbon resources. Russia and China have investments there. They hope for the Asian Market via the Northern Sea. Since the climate condition is very harsh, Russia launches icebreaking LNG carriers. The new and shortest route through the Northern Sea instead of Suez Canal will change the South Korea as an oil storage hub. So India can achieve LNG with tariff concession for storage and transportation. Arctic Region is a storage spot for India due to its vast energy resources and changing climatic conditions. The Northern Sea route is also a significant route for India. LNG instead of oil will be the future energy resource with less emission. So India's invention in Arctic affairs will be significant for India's energy landscape.

South Asia

South Asia is a peculiar region with regional tensions and diversities and at the same time carrying the same cultural remnants. The track record of regional cooperation is not much constructive, compared with other regions. Even so, as far as energy is concerned, there are certain prospects to unite the region. Firstly, India can act as a regional integrator in terms of energy due to its geographical location, financial viability and political strength. Secondly, Afghanistan is a regional energy corridor to link the Central Asia with the South and South East Asia. Thirdly, Nepal and Bhutan have abundant water resources and it can be utilized for India, Bangladesh and Myanmar. Finally, Pakistan is also an energy hungry nation. Being so, healthy regional cooperation can facilitate the natural gas transport.

Nepal

The estimated hydro power potential of Nepal is 83000MW. It has only 698 MW installed hydro power capacity in which 473MW is connected to the public transmission grid and 167 MW is under private generation capacity. There are 1250 MW hydropower projects under construction. Nepal has the lowest per capita energy consumption in South Asia and suffers with power crisis (Ebinger 2013). The country can overcome the power crisis by the efficient usage of hydropower potential. India has a major role in Nepal's hydro power sector and it provides financial as well as technical aid to build up the hydro power plants. Nepal and India imports electricity each other. During the time dry season, Nepal which is mostly hydropower dependent, heavily relies upon power import from India to meet its needs. India and Nepal plan to build new transmission lines through the two countries. There are around 30 hydropower projects functioning with the help of Indian companies and joint ventures. Nepal has abundant inland water resources such as 6000 rivers and tributaries. It can meet the energy demands of South Asian power hungry neighbours such as India and Bangladesh. Hydropower is the major energy resource available in Nepal, but the potential has not been fully exploited. The renewable power trade will enhance India's clean energy developments and simultaneously it will benefit Nepal through the earnings.

Sri Lanka

Sri Lanka signed an agreement with India in 2017 to build an LNG plant in Colombo and a solar power plant in Sampur in Trincomalee. The Indo Sri Lanka relationship increased the natural gas usage of this island nation. Indian Oil Corporation operates in Lanka also. In renewable energy sector, India made its presence through the deployment of wind and solar installations. India's NTPC has one LNG plant at Sampur with 500 MW. India and Sri Lanka are planning to build a transmission line under the sea which will be executed by the Power Grid Corporation, India's largest electricity transmission firm.

Mauritius has recently become a petroleum storage hub and India plans to build the storage facility. With establishing such an outreach, India hopes to transfer its petroleum products to Mauritius and selling it from there.

Bhutan

Bhutan has around 30000MW hydropower potential and India supports Bhutan's hydropower plant by technical and financial assistance over the years. Chuka, Kurichhu and Tala are some major hydropower projects constructed in Bhutanwith Indian cooperation. Similarly, Punatsangchu1 (1200 MW), Punatsangchu II (1020 MW) and Mangdechhu (720 MW) are under construction. Kholongchhu (600MW), Bunakha (180 MW), Wangchu (570 MW) and Chankarchu (770 MW) are the four projects signed under the Indo Bhutan joint venture. In 2014, Prime Minister Narendra Modi visited Bhutan and laid the foundation stone of the 600MW Kholongchu Hydro-electric project. India has also agreed to develop 10,000 MWs of hydropower in Bhutan, for export of surplus power to India by 2020.

Hydropower is the key area of Bhutanese economy. It constitutes 40% of Bhutan's domestic revenue. The hydropower projects constitute a major factor in cementing the strong Indo Bhutanties. However, the growing Chinese influence and the Doklam issue are major concerns for India in this front.

Bangladesh, Bhutan, India and Nepal (BBIN) are arranged in an agreement to achieve energy security. Nepal and Bhutan have abundant source of hydroelectricity. India has financial resources as well as technological expertise.

Notun Projonmo-Nayi Disha (New Beginning-New Direction) which was the joint declaration by Bangladesh and India collaboration in terms of energy grid especially hydro -electricity. There are various agreements regarding electricity transmission and Bangladesh is benefitted by 500MW electricity since 2011. The Power Grid Corporation of India Ltd. (POWERGRID)and Power Grid Company of Bangladesh Ltd. (PGCB)are jointly working. There is a 400 KV line between India and Bangladesh. Palatana project of Tripura provides 100 MW. In 2010, the two countries jointly built a thermal power plant in Bangladesh at Rampal. Adani Power Group and Reliance are interested in Bangladesh power sector especially in coal and natural gas power plants. Grid connection and power transmission are significant for the fulfilment of energy requirement of the country. Bhutan and Nepal can export electricity to Bangladesh through India (Patnaik 2015). India and Bangladesh have a cordial relation in the case of nuclear energy. The two countries have agreed to build a nuclear power plant in Roopar, Bangladesh which is the first nuclear initiative in Bangladesh. India will train the personnel, supply equipment and help in construction and installation works of the plant. Bangladesh has 6.3 trillion cubic feet natural gas reserves(BP Statistical Review 2017) and produces 26.6 billion cubic meters in 2017. Myanmar has an estimated gas reserves of 41.3 trillion cubic feet and 18 billion cubic meters production in 2017. So there is a need to develop the proposed Myanmar Bangladesh and India Pipeline. Bangladesh is a critical factor in South Asia's energy aspiration including South Asia energy grid and link towards South East Asian nations.

Regional cooperation is necessary for the efficient allocation of resources (Bose 2007). Regional tensions between countries especially India and Pakistan, the Chinese influence, lack of political will of authorities, continued mistrust between nations, regional insurgencies and influence of the US are challenges in this area.

Multilateral Natural Gas Pipelines

Natural Gas acts as an alternative to conventional energy sources due to climate challenges and environmental pollution. So South Asian and South East Asian nations took initiatives in natural gas pipelines. But the regional tensions still resist the gas cooperation in this region.

Iran-Pakistan-India (IPI) Pipeline

Iran has huge reserves of gas and the pipeline can ensure the natural gas needs of India and Pakistan. Both the countries are energy starving but the dispute between them is the major hindrance to achieve the resource. Transit fees and tensions in the pipeline route made the project almost discarded. The US also played in the midst of this, because it is not interested in the Iran India partnership. But Iran is a major energy partner of India for several years. It is the strain in India Pakistan relationship which prevented further developments of the IPI project.

Turkmenistan-Afghanistan-Pakistan-India (TAPI) Gas Pipeline

The negotiation for TAPI Pipeline, also known as Trans-Afghanistan Pipeline, was started in 1990 and originally it was Turkmenistan, Afghanistan and Pakistan (TAP) pipeline. India joined the project in 2003 and an Inter-Governmental Agreement (IGA) was signed in 2014.

Turkmengaz, Afghan Gas Enterprise (AGE), Inter State Gas System (ISGS) and GAIL are the companies involved in this project. Russia and China have strong influence in Turkmenistan which is rich in hydrocarbon resources. The estimated cost of Trans-Afghanistan Pipeline is $15 billion. If the project is accomplished, that would connect Central Asia with South Asia. The Galkynysh Gas Field in Turkmenistan has 16 trillion cubic feet and is being funded by the Asian Development Bank. The 1,814 km pipeline covers 214 km in Turkmenistan, 774 km in Afghanistan, 826 km in Pakistan and arrives at Fazilka, in India-Pakistan border. It will deliver 33 billion Cubic Meter gas to the three nations.

Myanmar-Bangladesh - India Gas Pipeline

The South Asia and the Myanmar relation in the natural gas enable the West Bengal and North Eastern states of India secure in terms of energy. The proposed route extends 900 km and transports gas from the Shwe field off the Bay of Bengal through Rakhine region in the southern Myanmar, to the state of Tripura and enters into Dhaka and then reaches at West Bengal. Bangladesh energy policies and the regional influences delayed the project and now the three governments reconsider prospects of the pipeline.

Oman-India Gas Pipeline

It is a subsea natural gas pipeline which has connection with Oman as well as Iran. It starts from Chabahar Port of Iran and ends at Gujarat and can avoid the geopolitical risks. Oman can export the gas from Iran from their plants. Iran and Oman signed the agreement in 2013 to supply gas to Oman via undersea over 25 years. But the continuing sanctions of the US against Iran still acts as a threat to the project and several environmental risks are behind the undersea pipeline.

India's Energy Security: The Role of Import Diversification

India's energy landscape is a mix of coal, natural gas, oil, hydro and nuclear power, wind, solar and bio-energy. India's import dependence for its energy needs is critical in its energy security. Traditionally India depends mostly on the Persian Gulf oil and it could not ensure the increasing energy demand of the country. So, nowadays India shifted its approach and turned every nook and corner in the world for different and adequate supply of energy. Invention of Natural Gas and its less emission of CO_2 changed India's conventional oil dependence. The fluctuating price and regional instabilities are affecting the oil and natural gas import. Price is volatile for oil in international market. Natural gas is traded in regional markets and the price varies in different regions. Regional instabilities of oil rich regions such as the Persian Gulf region and the transit route of natural gas pipeline are security threats for the energy needs of the country. Saudi Arabia, Iran, Iraq and Kuwait are the main crude suppliers for India. Qatar and Nigeria are the main gas suppliers. India was enforced to diversify its oil imports due to the heavy dependence and as well as the political instabilities of the region. So, India made deals with the US and Australia for its continuous oil supply. India wants natural gas also from these two countries and some African countries. Natural Gas is a secure source for India by its less environmental threats. But the gas pipelines routes abroad are not friendly with India and domestic north eastern routes also not safe for continuous supply. So most of the imports are coming via LNG cargoes from Qatar, Australia and Trinidad and Tobago. Shale gas revolution after the development of hydraulic fracturing is also a new innovation to contribute to the diversification of energy supply. The Indo US nuclear deal is also a significant step in the diversification of energy import. Russia, Canada, Kazakhstan etc., provide uranium for India's energy basket. India has signed agreement with several countries for the availability of nuclear technologies and resources. However, as a consequence of Fukushima disaster, instead of nuclear energy, renewable energy has become more appealing and preferable. In fact, India is huge market for renewable energy. The modern equipment for solar and wind power are more efficient and cost effective. Government policies, incentives, infrastructure development and investment promotions of current energy scenario are a good platform for energy diversification.

Scramble for Energy Resources Abroad: India's Quest

The energy resources are the most needed factor behind the economic well being of Indian economy. So, India wants to acquire influence in foreign energy assets or equity stakes in oil and gas fields. It started in 1990s by ONGC-Videsh (OVL) and Indian Oil Corporation Limited (IOCL). China is a major challenger for India in the field of hunt for global energy resources. India is far behind in the amount of investments comparing with China in the search for energy. China is using military and financial tools to secure oil fields. However, the new private companies from India achieved significant breakthrough in Africa with the help of the Government. Russia also prefers energy investments from India. The joint venture in Siberia and investments in Sakhalin-1 and Reliance Industries' shares in refineries are the major developments in the exploration of oil from the region. In 2009, OVL invested $2.1 billion in Imperial Energy's assets in Russia. It has investments with Imperial Energy in Vietnamese oil field as well as Vietnamese oil block in the South China Sea. In Vietnam, Indian companies sell their gas to the electricity grid of their country.

India has assets in 15 countries for oil and gas. Vietnam, Sudan, Russia, Egypt, Iraq, Iran, Myanmar, Libya, Cuba, Brazil, Nigeria, Colombia, Spain and Syria are among them. The recent developments such as NSG waiver helped India to import nuclear fuel and technologies from various countries. In Brazil, India blocked Chinese Sinochem Group from acquiring the share of Brazilian Oil field. During the 10th Five Year Plan, India opted to invest $2.85 billion abroad, such as Iraq, Iran, Algeria and Venezuela. Also, OVL bought 25% share of Great Nile Project in Sudan. India's realist explorations in African energy rich regions expanded during this period. But the division of Sudan made so many security issues before the energy opportunities of India. In Vietnam, OVL is selling the gas for electricity generation from its own assets. Sakhalin-I in Russia's Far East is the first foreign investment by OVL. India had investments in Al-Furat project with 85000 bpd production per day and Deirezzour region of Syria. But the ISIS issue and the US and the EU sanctions cut down the production and import. OVL has also shares in llanos basin of Colombia. ONGC, also plans further field developments in Vietnam. India spent a considerable amount of investments in countries with human rights violations and civil wars. In these countries, sometimes India was compelled to stand against human rights in certain circumstances. Sudan, Iran and Myanmar are some examples. Reliance Industries has share in the shale gas field in the US. It is the largest foreign share in this field. It has stakes in Kurdistan, Yemen, Iraq, Venezuela, Peru, Oman, Myanmar, Columbia, East Timor and Australia. OVL, Indian Oil Corporation (IOC), Oil India (OIL) and Bharat Petro Resources (BPRL), HPCL joined together as a consortium and stakes in Russia's Vankor Cluster oil fields in the Arctic region. Indian oil companies have investments in all the continents in the world. It enables them to expertise and access modern technologies.

India is the fourth largest energy consumer and it heavily depends on crude oil and coal. The energy engagements with foreign nations are significant due to its huge import dependence. India's transport and industries are run by the assistance of foreign nations. But it contributes insecurities to the environment, human beings and societies etc. Now renewable energy became viable resource for even developing nations. In the case of renewable energy also we need technological ad financial assistance from other nations. The international, regional, multilateral or unilateral relations are necessary for the growth of the clean energy future.

Reference

ASP (United States American Security Project). 2017. *Fact Sheet: Climate Change and Energy Security in Alaska.* Washington, DC: ASP.

B P (British Petroleum). 2017. *B P Stistical Review of World Energy 2017*, https://www.bp.com/content/dam/bp-country/de ch/PDF/bp-statistical-review-of-world-energy-2017-full-report.pdf .

Bansal, Alok. 2014. "US Iran Relations and their Impact on India." *Scholar Warrrior.* 8-14.http://www.claws.in/images/journals_doc/78081265_AlokBansal.pdf.

Barton, Barry, Catherine Redgwell, Anita Ronney, and Donald N Zillman. 2004. *Energy Security: Managing Risk in a Dynamic Legal and Regulatory Environment.* New York: Oxford University Press.

Bose, Srinjoy. 2007. *Energy Politics: India-Bangladesh-Myanmar Relations. Institute* of *Peace* and *Conflict Studies* (IPCS) Special Report 45 (July). http://www.burmalibrary.org/docs09/IPCS-Special-Report-India-Myanmar.pdf

BP (British Petroleum). 2018. *B P Energy Outlook.* B.P Energy Economics. https://www.bp.com/content/dam/bp/business-sites/en/global/corporate/pdfs/energy-economics/energy-outlook/bp-energy-outlook-2018.pdf.

BP (British Petroleum). 2018. *B P Energy Outlook.* B.P Energy Economics. https://www.bp.com/content/dam/bp/business-sites/en/global/corporate/pdfs/energy-economics/energy-outlook/bp-energy-outlook-2018.pdf.

Business Line. 2017. "Essar to announce Rosneft deal closer today." August 20, 2017.

Business Line. 2017. "OVL gets extension till 2049 for Azeri-Chirag-Deepwater project." September 18, 2017.

Cesnakas, Giedrius. 2010. "Energy Resources in Foreign Policy: A Theoretical Approach." *Baltic Journal of Law and Politics* 3(1): 30-52.

Chaturvedi, A.K. 2013. *Role of Pakistan in India's Energy Security: An Issue Brief.* New Delhi: Vij Books India Pvt Ltd.

Colgan, Jeff and Thijs Van de Graaf. 2013. "Mechanisms of informal governance: Evidence from the IEA." *Journal of International Relations and Development.* http://thijsvandegraaf.be/wp-content/uploads/2012/04/Colgan-Graaf-JIRD-July-8.pdf.

DAE (Department of Atomic Energy). n.d. "Important Agreements" DAE, Government of India.Accessed November 2, 2018.http://www.dae.nic.in/?q=node/75.

Desai, Ronak. D. 2015. "A New Era for India Latin America Relations." *Forbes,* June 25, 2015. https://www.forbes.com/sites/ronakdesai/2015/06/25/a-new-era-for-india-latin-america-relations/.

Ebinger, Charles. K. 2012. *Energy and Security in South Asia: Cooperation or Conflict?* Washington DC: The Brookings Institution.

EEAS (European External Action Service). 2016. "India-European Union Partnerships for Sustainability, Clean Energy &Climate Action". Accessed November 31, 2018. https://eeas.europa.eu/sites/eeas/files/india-eu partnerships for sustainability clean energy and climate action.pdf.

EIA (United States Energy Information Administration). 2015. *Russia's Key Energy Statitics.* Washington, D.C: EIA.

EIA (United States Energy Information Administration). 2016. *Country Analysis Brief: India.* Washington D.C: EIA.

EIA (United States Energy Information Administration). 2017. *Beyond China and India, Energy Consumption in non- OECD Asia Continues to Grow.* US: EIA. https://www.eia.gov/todayinenergy/detail.php?id=32972.

EIA (US Energy Information Administration). 2016. *Annual Energy Outlook 2016 with Projections to 2040.* Washington D.C: EIA. https://www.eia.gov/outlooks/aeo/pdf/0383(2016).pdf.

EIA (US Energy Information Administration). 2016. *World Shale Resource Assessment..* Washington D.C: EIA. https://www.eia.gov/analysis/studies/worldshalegas/.

Fattouh, Bassam and Coby van der Linde. 2011. *The International Energy Forum: Twenty Years of Producer-Consumer Dialogue in a Changing World.* Riyadh: International Energy Forum.

FOWPI (First Offshore Wind Farm Project in India). 2017. "Oveview. "Gurugram: FOWPI.Accessed November 30, 2018.https://www.fowpi.in/.

Hober, Kaj. 2010. "Investment Arbitration and the Energy Charter Treaty."*Journal of International Dispute Settlement 1(1):153-90.*

Human Rights Watch. 2003. "Sudan, Oil, and Human Rights." https://www.hrw.org/reports/2003/sudan1103/sudanprint.pdf.

IEA (International Energy Agency). 2017. *Energy Access Outlook 2017.https://www.iea.org/access2017/.*

IESD (Indo European Sustainable Development). 2017. "Diplomatic Mission for the Indian Photovoltaic Market Development." New Delhi: IESD. http://www.iesd.eu/news/i-e-s-d-partecipated-in-the-diplomatic-mission-for-the-indian-photovoltaic-market-development/.

Indo-US Science & Technology Forum. (2014). "Here comes the Sun." *Connect* 6 (1): 4-9. Solar Energy Research Institute for India and US.

IRENA (International Renewable Energy Agency). 2018. *Renewable Capacity Statistics 2018.*Abu Dhabi: IRENA. https://www.irena.org/publications/2018/Mar/Renewable-Capacity-Statistics-2018.

IRENA (International Renewable Energy Agency). 2018. *Renewable Energy Policies in a Time of Transition*. Abu Dhabi: IRENA.

ITE Group. 2017. *Russian Energy in 2016: Russia: The Figure*. ITE Oil and Gas. http://www.oilgas-events.com/market-insights/MIOGE-Preview/Russia-Oil-Gas-Statistics.

Jagniti, Sharinee. 2012. *India's Africa Policy: Towards a More Coherent Engagement.* Nanyang Avenue, Singapore: S Rajaratnam School of International Studies.

Jangir, Sunil Kumar. 2012. "Indo Us Nuclear Deal and 123 Agreement." *International Journal of Scientific and Research Publications 2* (10): 1-6.

Klare, Michael. T. 2008. "The New Geopolitics of Energy." *The Nation*, May 19, 2008.

Miles, Tom. 2017. "U.S. takes India back to WTO in solar power dispute." *Reuters,* December 20. 2017.

Ministry of Coal. 2018. *Provisional Coal Statistics 2017-18*. Government of India. http://www.coalcontroller.gov.in/writereaddata/files/download/provisionalcoalstat/ProvisionalCoalStat2017-18.pdf.

Ministry of Coal. 2018. *Production, Supply and Import of Coal.* New Delhi: Press Information Bureau, Government of India.http://pib.nic.in/newsite/PrintRelease.aspx?relid=186616.

Ministry of Mines. 2018. Indian Minerals Yearbook 2017, Coal and Lignite. Nagpur: Government of India.

Ministry of Petroleum and Natural Gas. 2017. *Indian Petroleum & Natural Gas Statistics 2015-16*. New Delhi: Economic and Statistics Division, Government of India. http://petroleum.nic.in/more/indian-png-statistics.

Ministry of Power. 2016. Energy Cooperation to be the Defining Feature of India-Australia Relationship. http://pib.nic.in/newsite/PrintRelease.aspx?relid=136293

Ministry of Power. 2017. 1st 'India Indonesia Energy Forum' held in Jakarta. http://pib.nic.in/newsite/PrintRelease.aspx?relid=161220.

MNRE (Ministry of New and Renewable Energy). 2017. *Year End Review 2017*. New Delhi: Press Information Bureau, MNRE, Government of India.

MNRE (Ministry of New and Renewable Energy). *2018.* Year End Review 2018. New Delhi: Press Information Bureau, MNRE, Government of India.

Myers, Henry R. 1975. "Federal Decision Making and the Trans-Alaska Pipeline."*Ecology Law Quarterly* 4(4): 915-61.

OPEC (Organization of the Petroleum Exporting Countries). 2017.OPEC Share of World Crude Oil Reserves 2017, OPEC.https://www.opec.org/opec_web/en/data_graphs/330.htm

OPEC (Organization of the Petroleum Exporting Countries). n.d. *Member Countries,* OPEC. https://www.opec.org/opec web/en/about us/25.htm.

Pattanaik, Smruti S. n.d.*Nepal-Bhutan Bilateral Talks and Repatriation of Bhutanese Refugees*. New Delhi: The Institute for Defence Studies and Analyses, (IDSA). https://www.idsa-india.org/an-jan9-11.html.

Pethiyagoda, Kadira. 2017. *India-GCC Relations: Delhi's Strategic Opportunity.* Brookings Doha Center Analysis Paper. Washington D. C: The Brooking Institution.

Petronet. 2017. "Corporate Profile." https://www.petronetlng.com/PDF/AR2016-17.pdf

Planning Commission. 2014. *India-US Energy Dialogue.* Press Information Bureau, Government of India. http://pib.nic.in/newsite/PrintRelease.aspx?relid=104569.

Raghavan, Sharad T.C.A. 2018. "What is International Solar Alliance." *The Hindu,* March 12, 2018.

RIS (Research and Information System for Developing Countries).2013. *A Dialogue on India-Canada Economic Cooperation.*In the Proceedings of India Canada Cooperation Dialogue. February 12-13. New Delhi: RIS.

Sachdeva, Gulshan. (2015). Indian Energy Security and the Role of Renewables: Possibility of Cooperation with the EU. In *India's Emerging Energy Relations: Issues and Challenges,* edited by Girijesh Pant (47-64). New Delhi: Springer.

Singh, Bhupendra Kumar. 2010. *India's Energy Security: Changing Dynamics.* New Delhi: Pentagon Press.

Smith, Rob. 2018."Three countries are leading the renewable energy revolution." *World Economic Forum*. https://www.weforum.org/agenda/2018/02/countries-behind-global-renewable-energy-growth/.

The Economic Times. 2017. "Iraq replaces Saudi Arabia as India's lead oil supplier." December 18, 2017.

The Hindu. 2017. "Powered by a pause: delay in Indo-U.S. nuclear deal." March 28, 2017.

The Telegraph. 2016. "OVL also bought 11% Stake in Venkor Field."September 29, 2016.

The Telegraph. 2017. "OVL suffers Sudan setback." May 3, 2017.

The Times of India. 2017. "Coal import from Canada may rise as steelmaking makes headway." July 19, 2017.

Verma, Nidhi. 2018. "India's Oil imports in 2017 surged into a record 4.4 million barrels per day." *The Economic Times,* January 17, 2018.

World Bank. 2018. "Understanding Poverty, Overview." https://www.worldbank.org/en/topic/energy/overview.

Yergin, Daniel. (2006). "Ensuring Energy Security." *Foreign Affairs* 85 (2): 69 – 82.

Chapter - IV

India's Energy Sector: Challenges and Constraints Towards A Sustainable Future

Introduction

Clean and modern use of energy is the prime factor behind the economic as well as societal development of every nation. As a large country with huge population, India needs its own strategies and policies to curb its energy intentions. The country's demographic patterns, economic growth, urbanization, industrial development and growing transport sector etc., influence India's energy ambitions. India wants to fulfil its 1.3 billon people's energy aspirations, especially the heavy demand from 30% of urban population, by their lifestyle changes and the energy needs of the majority of poor people. Every nation considers energy as its strategic element but it varies in different context which is relating with nation, society, culture, time period etc.

India is the 6th largest in terms of global population, but it has only 5.7% of total coal reserves and 4% of hydrocarbon resource. The country accounts 30% of global energy demand growth and its share of energy usage is expected to rise to 11% by 2040 (IEA 2017). And its import dependence may rise up to 36-55% by 2040 from 31% in 2012. Even though India has adopted alternative measures to satisfy its energy needs, still it depends on more than 70% on fossil fuels. India's Draft National Energy Policy, 2017 declared its four objectives as access at affordable prices, improved security and independence, greater sustainability and economic growth. But there is huge population under energy poverty consisting of those who have no access of energy or using unsustainable energy sources. The import dependence still makes insecurities in the supply side and the renewable energy contribution is only 6% in the energy mix of the country. The growing transport sector, industrial as well as residential and commercial building needs with its lack of energy efficiency is causing considerable hindrances to achieve sustainable energy scenario. The dependency on fossil fuels and the threats from energy infrastructure lead to human and social insecurity. So, energy security implies energy insecurity as well. This is more applicable in the case of the rural people, as they are very susceptible, marginalized and lack access to proper safety measures or resources. Majority of rural households depend on traditional fuels like fuel wood to meet most of their energy requirements, supplemented by small amounts of kerosene and electricity for lighting. Oil and other fossil fuel depletion, reliance on foreign source of energy, geopolitical reasons, and economic efficiency vs population growth, environmental issues like climate change are also a few challenges in this energy landscape. Environmental and socio economic perspectives are lagging in the India's energy scenario. During the time of extraction, conversion, transformation or use of the energy cause challenges to environmental and societal security.

In the initial stages, need was limited to biological energy in the form of food, which extended to wood when the use of fire was discovered; then to fossil fuels which made industrial revolution and urbanization. These together promoted transportations which used fossil fuels. The newer materialistic culture also promotes energy hungry approach. However, the pressure from this over usage on the environment wants cleaner energy. Still the underdeveloped world mostly depends on poor resources. Not only environmental problems, but also there are a lot of issues relating with the implementation of major energy projects. Displacement, livelihood, deforestation, health concerns etc., are some among them. India faces challenges in meeting lifeline energy needs of all citizens to address social development, health and safety of the energy poor.

Issues of India's Energy Mix

India's energy mix highly relies on fossil fuels including coal and other petroleum products. The energy mix in 2018 consists of Coal (57%), oil (29%), Gas (6%), Nuclear (1%), Hydro (4%), Renewables including bio fuel (2%) (B P 2018). The only source which is comparatively clean in this mix with larger share is natural gas. But, that also contributes only 6% of total energy mix. Renewable power and hydro electricity together occupies 6%, but it consists of solar, wind, biomass and other alternatives. It is far behind the usage of hydrocarbons. The abundant availability and the affordability led to the increasing usage of coal and the feasibility and non availability of efficient alternative cause for dependence of oil in transportation sector. In petroleum products, India consumes Diesel (41%),

Petrol (12%), LPG (11%), Petroleum Coke (10%), Naphtha (7%) and others (19%). Transport sector is the major consumer of diesel, accounting for 70% of the total diesel sales and agriculture is the next end use sector which consists of tractors with highest consumption. Petrol, also around 100%, is consumed by transport sector. Even though the price variations affect oil sector, it is purchasable and accessible for consumers (Barton et al. 2004). The consumption of coal has increased 1.29 % from 462.35 MT to 832.46 MT between 2015 and 2016. Many industrialized nations are not supporting the coal consumption because of its CO_2 and SO_2 emission to the environment. But India's energy profile is dominated by coal with 412 mtoe in 2016 and 955 mtoe in 2040 as the demand growth goes to 132%.

Though the policies of government promote renewable energy sources, hydrocarbon sector and its development is always encouraged. Indian Oil Corporation and other distributing agencies have planned to increase the retail facility and the central government has postponed the date to curtail the polluting emissions of power plants. In the coal sector, the privatization policy also encourages more production of this cheap resource with efficient technologies.

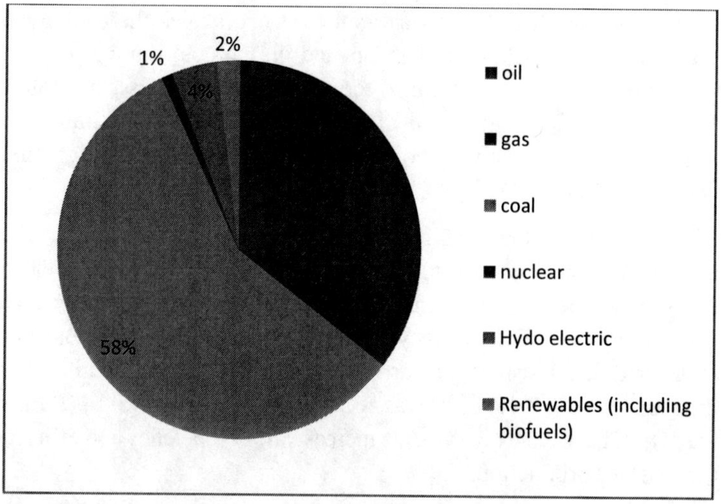

(B P 2018)

Figure 4.1: India's Energy Mix

Coal

India's coal demand has risen by 1/3 during the last five years and the thermal power plant constitutes 70% of India's electricity sector. Its vast domestic reserves and the feasibility make the resource as a major energy provider. But still India faces a lack of production to meet its actual requirement. Due to the increase in demand and consumption, the country depends more on import. Quality of coal is another reason for huge reliance on import.

Table 4.1: Coal Demand 2012-2017

Year	*Million tonnes*
2012	683
2013	761
2014	779
2015	867
2016	874
2017	894

(CIL 2018)

The new policy of the government is to reduce the import with the increase in domestic production. The policy for supporting indigenous coal production leads to the development of the sector which is against the countries climate change goals as well as it challenges the ecology and human health. The policy of 2018 opened up the coal mining to private players. It enhances the coal sector in terms of competitiveness, international and efficient technologies and clean methods. The unavailability of immediate viable alternative energy is the main reason behind the continues heavy usage of coal.

India needs developments in its economic as well as industrial spheres. Coal sector vies the new opportunities like the growing power sector, electric vehicles, private investments and the industrial needs of the country. So the sector shows the growing tendency with efficient technologies, better storage facilities and fast transportation arrangements. The coal production is 567 million tonne in 2017-18, but it was 462 million tonne in 2013-14 (*Business Line* 2018). The private investments increase the competency and efficiency of the massive production.

Inefficient and older mines of the country provide unsafe conditions to the mine workers, especially women and children. Several mine workers are the residents of nearby areas and others are migrants from neighbouring states and regions. They have no other option for their daily bread. Largely mines are constructed as rat holes[2] followed by digging vertical holes. In Jaintia Hills, Meghalaya these rat holes are common. The children's physical structure is more suitable for these holes. In vulnerable working conditions with little oxygen and no ventilation inside the mines, the children from age eight onwards are working there for long hours. Injuries and deaths are common in these mines (Guha 2014). Around 5000 illegal rat hole mines are working in Meghalaya itself. In December 2018, 13 miners were found dead in the rat hole mine in East Jaintia Hills. Child labour is common in mines of Meghalaya, Jharkhand and Odisha. Opencast coal mines[3] are widely used in India. It destroys large scale surface area. As most of them are situated in forests, it causes deforestations, soil erosion, water contamination etc. Washing is required for getting clean coal which requires abundant water. Underground mining affects the level of water body in the nearby area. The water and air get polluted due to fluoride, manganese, nickel, sulphate, carbon dioxide and nitrogen dioxide. Coal mining changes the land use pattern and displaces several people. Water scarcity, pollution, agricultural loss and ecological imbalance are the result of mining. Combustion of coal produces a large part of carbon dioxide, methane and some radioactive elements which cause heart and lung diseases. Unauthorized mine such as rat hole mines are dangerous, but thousands of local, migrant and child labourers work there (Lahiri-Dutt 2007). Due to economic advantage, the villages are never bothered about environmental and health impacts. People use coal for cooking purpose which leads to indoor pollution. During the time of land acquisition, the inhabitants are evacuated. They are deprived of their agricultural land for their livelihood and the huge removal of topsoil would barren the land. Thus the various stages of coal mining process causes local and global impact. The local people and ecosystem are suffered with pollution which has adverse impact upon human health, natural vegetation and water security. The coal bed methane has a direct impact upon global warming and climate change.

Thermal power plant based on lignite and coal is the most vulnerable carbon emitting source of India. During the time of independence, the industrial needs and technological inadequacy forced to utilize this cheap and accessible resource. But in the present global warming scenario, the usage of coal is a threat to humanity. Thermal power plants are producing Sulphur Dioxide (SO_2), Particulate Matter (PM) and fly ash to the environment in a hazardous manner. The Supreme Court also condemned the Central Government and Ministry of Power for not taking actions to reduce the emissions. In September 2018, the court provided a deadline that within 28 months emission standards are to be implemented (*Business Standard* 2018). Most of the power plants are situated in densely populated area with 400 km/km^2.

Oil sector

The oil and gas sector is the most influential and the core industry in Indian economy which has influence over other sectors as well (IBEF 2018). Even narrow price fluctuations of oil and gas affect value of money, trade deficit, transportation cost, interest rate and price of goods and services etc. The sector includes production, import, refining, distribution, marketing, export, and conservation of petroleum products. The crude oil production was 36.01 Million Metric Tonnes (MMT) in 2016-17 and ONGC produced 70.8% of it (Ministry of Petroleum and Natural Gas 2017). India needs 73% of oil and 20% of natural gas via import (B P 2018). India has only 0.7% of the world's proven oil reserves and accounts 3.9% of the global oil consumption. India is heavily dependent on oil import which is largely from the West Asia and Africa. There is often insecurities in supply due to the geopolitical instabilities of these regions. This geopolitical risk influences the market price of crude oil and now the hike of petroleum products and the depreciation of Indian Rupee together critically affect the Indian economy. The domestic production has increased after the introduction of the New Exploration and Licensing Policy and the subsequent entry of Multi National Corporations, reducing the unexplored sedimentary area of 50% in 1996 to 15% in 2009.

In refining capacity, the country had limited capacity compared with the actual requirement. But it is the second largest refiner in Asia with 247 MMT capacity. It needs 600 MMT by 2040 for covering the increasing demand domestically and for exporting purpose. As a developing nation, its refining equipment also faces some shortcomings and needs technological advancement such as automation, digitization, robotics, electric vehicles and artificial intelligence etc., in this sector (*The Economic Times* 2018). There are Strategic Petroleum Reserve (SPR) facilities at Visakhapatnam in Andhra Pradesh, and Mangalore and Padur in Karnataka. The reserves can manage the petroleum requirements for 10 days in times of emergency situations. However, the lack of enough resource and the geopolitical instabilities forces India to maintain more storage facilities and other options.

The extraction, processing and combustion create large scale GHG emissions to the environment. Extreme weather events, rising oceans and record setting temperatures are the result of global warming. The hydrocarbons which is the compound of hydrogen and carbon cause environmental impacts like depleting the ozone, greenhouse effect and climate change, reduction of photosynthetic ability of plants, and certain diseases in humans. Seismic techniques involved in drilling and exploring make changes in the land and marine system. Oil spills comes during the time of transportation from well to refineries disturbs the respiratory mechanism of living beings in the marine environment and also causes fire and explosion. The large drilling area contributes to the loss of vegetation. The oil refineries omit dust particles and chemicals such as sulphur dioxide (SO2), nitrogen oxide (NO2),carbon dioxide, carbon monoxide, methane, hydrogen fluoride, chlorine, benzene, etc., and causes severe health damage.

Natural Gas and Other Unconventional Gases

Natural Gas is comparatively viable option rather than other hydrocarbon resources. However, it is a fossil fuel and emits carbon dioxide to the environment. The extraction activities require high amount of water in this case. In India, the natural gas production is 31.90 Billion Cubic Meters in 2016-17. It has 15,000 km of gas pipeline network to distribute the resource to various parts of the country. Around 67% of offshore natural gas contributes to the total natural gas capacity. Coal Bed Methane is produced from 10 States including Andhra Pradesh, Arunachal Pradesh, Assam, Gujarat, Rajasthan, Tamil Nadu, Tripura, Jharkhand, Madhya Pradesh and West Bengal. Shale Gas exploration has been undertaken in Cambay, Cauvery, Krishna-Godavari and Assam and Arakan Basins. Krishna Godavari and Mahanadi area, Cauvery and Kochi Coast are rich in gas hydrates. The technological and financial requirements are huge for every stage of production process in these types of big projects. As a developing nation, the projects need infrastructure facilities such as roads and pipelines. Transmission and distribution are two pivotal challenges in Natural Gas industry. The population density and the land acquisition issues are certain barriers to establish domestic pipeline network and other infrastructure facilities in a country like India. Even in Massachusetts, the USA, the over pressurization of natural gas pipelines led to the explosions and fires in residential areas. This was due to pumping of more natural gas into pipelines and thus causing leakage. Several homes were destroyed or damaged, one man killed and several people were evacuated due to this fire and explosion. Thousands of homes disconnected from power supply and many people were severely injured and approached hospital due to smoke inhalation and blast trauma etc. The maintenance of pipeline networks is a heavy responsibility for public safety and old pipes invite more risks against people and property. So safety checking, replacement and upgradation are the major tasks for distributers and the customers. Land acquisition and the compensation procedure are other problems to implement the projects.

The natural gas industry depends 45% on import and has long term contracts with Qatar, the US, Russia and Australia. The lack of LNG transferrable ships and import terminals are certain constrains and the major pipeline projects like Turkmenistan-Afghanistan-Pakistan-India (TAPI) pipeline and the Iran-Pakistan-India (IPI)pipeline are delayed due to political and security issues. The newly proposed Iran-Oman-India, Central Asia-India and Russia-India gas connectivity networks need much diplomatic initiatives and good will from the concerned countries as well as from the US (Mallya and Deshmukh 2015).

Shale gas, tight gas, coal bed methane and methane hydrates are some unconventional natural gas which is more complicated to utilize than other hydrocarbons (Singh and Khanna 2012). But the availability of technology and the possession enhance the extraction of these resources. Shale gas explorations needs large quantity of water and land area and contribute to air pollution and contamination of water. The horizontal drilling and hydraulic fracturing may affect seismic issues like earth quake (Sinha 2015). The drilling requires huge quantity of fluid with high pressure to extract the resources. It disturbs the earth patterns and the ground water get contaminated by several metals, chemicals as well as methane. The transportation is now highly advanced, but it is also difficult. Ohio, West Virginia, and Pennsylvania witnessed the gas leakage and the fire which caused burning of around ten acres of land and the vegetation loss. In 2010, an explosion on the Deepwater Horizon drilling rig in the Gulf of Mexico resulted in the death of 11 workers and discharge of 4 m barrels of oil into the sea. It reduced the biodiversity and marine ecology for a long period (Anthony 2018).

Several European countries banned hydraulic fracturing and the European Union has issued certain policy recommendations for member nations about the risks and safety measures about the hydraulic fracturing (*Down to Earth* 2018). The necessity of huge quantity water for drilling reduces the essential water availability of the nation. Almost all the drilling areas are located in water scarce areas and it depletes ground water level. Seismic problems such as weak earth quakes are the consequent factor of hydraulic drilling. In the US several incidents were reported (Zoback, Kitasei and Copithorne 2010) during the time of shale gas productions. Though India requires a huge quantity of energy, the nation should understand the challenges and constraints like population density, water scarcity, seismic issues and the environmental concerns.

Nuclear Energy

As an independent country India recognized the significance of nuclear energy since 1950s. But the country's nuclear sector has been isolated due to the tests conducted in 1974 and 1998. The reluctance to sign NPT created the situation more problematic. The 2008 NSG waiver and Indo US nuclear deal allowed India to import nuclear technologies and uranium from NSG member countries after the long term isolation. It has increased India's nuclear prospects and energy ambitions. The Department of Atomic Energy expects a 40GW nuclear power by 2020 (Ministry of Power 2008). It has been answered in the parliament that the present capacity 6780 MW will be elevated to 22,480MW by 2031 after the completion of under construction projects. India's nuclear expectations failed many times, because it was manipulated for attracting nuclear vendors. Ramana (2009, 127-52) explains that the failures were not by the lack of resources, but the projected growth of nuclear sector increases competition of nuclear suppliers and the government hopes for better price. India predicted 25,000 MW of nuclear power by 1987 and updated it to 43,000 MW by 2000, but actually the installation capacities were in 600 MW (1980), 950 MW (1987), 2720 MW (2000), 4120 MW (2009) etc., and it was only 2.8% of the country's total electricity generation capacity. In 2000, the Department of Atomic Energy argued for 20 GW by 2020 and 275 GW by 2052. However, it still produces only less than 7GW (The Telegraph 2018). Currently nuclear energy constitutes only 3.06 % of the total electricity generation (DAE 2018).

Nuclear power generation is not as cheap as claimed by the advocates of this energy resource. They argue it is more economical than a thermal power plant, but the nuclear power from the Kaiga reactors is about eight percent more expensive than thermal power from Raichur (Ramana 2007, 169-71). The actual cost includes construction of the reactor, operations and maintenance, storage, decommissioning, liability insurance against accidents, the costs of disposal of radioactive waste, initial heavy water inventory and of replacing the heavy water lost during routine operations and working capital (Seethi 2008, 135-37). The social and environmental cost is not included in this and it cannot be measured in an easy way.

India uses imported uranium with an accelerated manner after 2009. It imports from Russia, France, Kazakhstan and Canada (DAE n.d) and has done agreements with Uzbekistan, Namibia and Mongolia. India keeps strategic uranium reserves and increases the import for uninterrupted functioning of reactors. In Nuclear Fuel Complex, workers are suffering from high radiation as the process of transformation of uranium cake into powder and then pellets produces radioactive dust. It causes several hazardous health impacts. The safety standards are determined by the nuclear industry related experts and the inspections are also done by like minded people. The confidentiality and restriction surrounding nuclear power plants, enables the authorities to hide away adverse issues from public scrutiny (Abbott 2011).

There are Indian agreements with Bangladesh, Vietnam, Japan, Sri Lanka, Russia, Australia, Canada, France, the USA and the UK for peaceful cooperation of nuclear technology. The Indo-US and the resultant agreement could not fulfil the energy requirement of the nation or the projected nuclear expectation.

The Nuclear Industrial Complex (NIC) is the prime factor behind India's nuclear thirst. The trade of nuclear technology and material became a big busyness after the deal. For boosting the technology, several established environmentalists also supported the nuclear technology due to its claim of zero carbon emitting property (Seethi 2008, 134). They avoid all the impacts of radiation from the time of mining of uranium to waste disposal. The industrial giants such as France, Germany, Canada, Britain and the United States are benefitted from the dealings. The international commercial banks and several nuclear companies make profit, but the local residence and workers of the plant suffer from issues of the project. There are arguments that one then has to count the cost, consider the safety, the complexity, and the issues surrounding governance of nuclear power. Also if the technology cannot be fundamentally scaled further than 1 TW, one has to ask if the same investment would have been better spent on a truly scalable technology (Abbott 2011).

The Environmental Impact Assessment (EIA) supposed to regulate the reactors of India; it is done by the representatives from the The Department of Atomic Energy (DAE) and its allied organizations. The resistance from the part of the local people and the civil society are largely ignored even during the time of the public hearings (Ramana 2009, 1-34). In every stage of nuclear development such as mining, transportation and processing as well as from reactors, radioactive by-products are produced. India's significant Uranium mining is located in Jaduguda and other places in Jharkhand. Uranium is used for the purpose of weapons and nuclear power programmes. The imported one is mainly used in power sector and the domestically produced one is used for defence purpose. The Uranium mining started since 1967 and it has made much visible impacts on the environment, human health and socio economical spheres of Jaduguda region. The villagers of the region, who belong to the Santhal, Munda and Ho tribal communities got evacuated from their homeland without receiving any adequate rehabilitation facilities. The displacement due to the pollution from tailing spills is not even addressed because it happened several years after the establishment of the mine. There are pipelines which connects

Jadaguda mine to tailing ponds consisting of treated waste. The mines like Bhatin and Narwapahar are also sending mine water to Jaduguda effluent treatment plant (ETP). The pipes often break down and the tailing reach nearby homes. In 2006, the flood water combined with the tailing pond water contaminated the nearer farming areas and rivers. The large area of forest needed for the mines, other infrastructure facilities and related transportation lead to mass deforestation and biodiversity loss. The transportation of Uranium ore and other materials are in unsafe condition and the pipelines containing mine water often encounters leakages (Pallavi 2015). It is causing soil contamination, ground water pollution and serious health hazardous to the nearby areas. The small amount of Uranium which is obtained from the large quantity of ore needs abundant water (Jadaguda Uranium Mine 2009). After the extraction of Uranium the remaining waste contains thorium, radon and radium which are highly radioactive and this tailings cause skeletal distortions, tuberculosis, cancer, skin diseases and loss of fertility etc.

Nuclear reactors are not exempted from radiation, accidents and other social environmental impacts. Even though there is no catastrophic incidents occurred in Indian reactors, most of them witnessed several accidents due to human as well as mechanical error. Level 1 radiation affected in Kakrapar Atomic Power Station (KAPS) by heavy water leakage in 2016. It led to the temporary shutdown of the power station. It is the 220 Mega Watt Pressurized Heavy Water Reactor and experienced issues in 1992 and 1995. In Kalpakkam, the workers got radiation from high level radioactive waste due to the damage of waste management system. The Bhabha Atomic Research Centre admitted that it was a hazardous incident and kept the reactor shut down for six months (Subrahmanian 2003, 16-29).

Tritium leakages happened in 2012 accident in Rajasthan Atomic Power Station (RAPS) at Rawatbhata. The labourers of the plant have chances to contact with the radioactive elements, especially the contractual labourers and cleaning staff. In Narora in Uttar Pradesh, Level 3 nuclear accident was happened due to the fire at turbine blades. It led to a loss of Rs. 150 crore, which is a huge repairing cost comparing with other alternatives. Excessive vibrations in turbine bearings and oil leaks are common in Indian reactors.

Abundant water is required for the functioning of nuclear reactors, so all the plants such as Tarapur (Arabian Sea), RAPS (Rana Pratap Sager), Madras (Bay of Bengal), Kaiga (Kadra Dam Reservoir), Narora (River Ganga), Kudankulam (Indian Ocean) and Kakrapar (Tapi River) are situated near to the large water bodies. The 40% of water used in these plants is getting evaporated and the rest of the hot water flows to the original water body. This hot water disturbs the aquatic life and affect the livelihood of fisher folk. The impact of climate change creates threat to the nuclear reactors. The Fukushima disaster occurred as a result of the tsunami and the earthquake. Earthquakes, tsunami, hurricanes, flood and sea level rise are some examples of common natural disasters that may affect the nuclear establishments. The authorities always claim that the current nuclear reactors are safe from such natural calamities and precautions have been taken to overcome any such occurrence. They assert that there are mechanisms to manage loss of power, loss of communication, evacuation problems and mechanical error (DAE n.d).

In fact, nuclear power plants need huge area of land including exclusion zone which is 1.6 km from the periphery of the project. People around 30 km surrounding area need to evacuate at any time and they have chances of getting affected with radiation (AERB 2010). The threats like evacuation and radiation affect residents of nearby areas. Land acquisition is also a major problem and Gujarat Mithivirdi nuclear plant was shifted to Kovvada in Andhra Pradesh due to this problem.

Nuclear waste is another grave problem as it remains as radioactive for thousands of years. These waste are categorized as low level, intermediate level and high level waste. In India, nuclear waste are stored in the plant itself with high protection measures (DAE 2017). But radioactive garbage left for future generation is a heinous crime. The cost of maintaining the nuclear waste and the decommissioned reactors are considerably very huge. The reprocessing of nuclear wastes is also not economical and produces another waste (Ramana 2007, 169-71).

Renewable Energy

Until 17th century, the world solely depended on renewable energy such as the sun, muscles, water and wind etc. The fossil fuel ridden energy transition has helped the modern growth, but the heavy reliance leads to environmental calamities. India, with a growing energy demand, depends heavily on coal and oil for its energy aspirations. It has now become the fourth largest carbon emitter in the world, so the transformation towards sustainable energy or its commitment towards 40% of clean energy by 2030 will be a challenging factor for a country like India. There are several options regarding renewable energy like wind, solar, small hydro, bio power (biomass &gasification and cogeneration), waste to power, biogas plant, water mills, and micro hydel projects etc. Now India has 60.98 GW and the country has planned to achieve 175 GW by 2022, including 100GW of solar energy.

Solar Energy

Solar energy is one of the most feasible resources to fulfil India's energy ambitions. The capital cost, storage capacity, irregular availability of solar radiation, unawareness and the required land area are major hurdles for its popularity. Solar energy is not considered a popular source of electricity for domestic consumers, because the public electricity grid is economical and easily available option. Though the government provides 30% of subsidy for solar equipment and the initial capital cost, the long procedures and the involvement of multiple agencies such as Ministry of New and Renewable Energy, Ministry of Power, Central and State government agencies empanelled agencies or service providers, and DISCOMs (Distributing Companies) etc. Unnecessarily complicate the system (Phillip 2014). Most of the consumers are unaware about the necessity, benefits, quality, cost, grid connection, net metering, subsidy and contribution to the clean environment. Even though, the consumer wants to purchase solar power, the initial capital cost is a huge barrier to the large section of people of India. The present roof top mechanism is not effective in net metering, which means the surplus power can send back to the grid or DISCOMs by consumers. But, the grid instability due to multiple small plants connection with public grid, fear of revenue loss of DISCOMs and weak policies are limiting the growth of roof top solar deployment. However, the price increase of grid power and the declining cost of solar power are making it a popular source of electricity (Dutt and Kuldeep 2018).

The conventional energy is easily available from the market and the people are synchronized over time with them. The lack of efficient technicians and quality products prevent the acceptability of solar energy. The storage capability of solar power is another concern, because the weather conditions have significant influence on solar radiation (Bandyopadhyay 2013). So, better, economical and environmental friendly batteries are essential in the case of this resource. The strong political leadership with effective research programs can develop the better technologies and measures to adopt solar power and they can rectify the current mistakes or weaknesses (Ansari et al. 2013). The larger solar plants need huge area for infrastructure development and power production (Srivastava and Srivastava 2013). But the large scale and centralized solar power production has got momentum than the small scale decentralized projects in India. The captive solar plant can save electricity by avoiding transmission loss, because either the consumers and producers are the same or power is generated from nearby plants. Solar power plants are devoid of land loss and it can be built even in remote locations.

Wind Power

Wind power potential is located in limited settings. The efficient intra-state transmission system is necessary for the development of wind power generation. There are wind and solar hybrid systems with aero generator or small wind turbine and solar PV technologies. Such plants have energy production capacity during strong wind or shiny days. Gujarat, Tamil Nadu, Maharashtra, Karnataka and Andhra Pradesh are rich in wind and solar. The transmission grid system and the storage technologies are still a barrier to the newly coming sources of energy. In recent years there are developments in offshore wind farms, but it is expensive and difficult to build and maintain.

There is lack of updated data on wind energy potential in India which is needed for installing modern equipment in expected locations. Land availability is an issue in this sector also. Improved transport facilities are needed for wind farm installation in forest and hilly areas. The construction of roads leads to deforestation. For example, in Bhimashankar sanctuary, around 300000 trees were destroyed for the construction of a road for the wind farm. Also, constructing massive numbers of wind powered turbines have the potential to leave an impact on wildlife populations, especially the local and migratory birds. It has been reported that several birds in India, including the Great Indian Bustard which is a critically endangered species, are threatened by the installation of wind turbines. Worldwide, these turbines kill 2 lakh birds every year (Bindra 2017). The large scale wind and solar farms are often utilizing forest grassland and desert. Therefore, proper planning and location study is needed before windmill installation as it affects the habitat and ecosystem.

So, we need an eco-friendly policy to develop renewable clean energy for future generation. There is a need of strong political will, updated policies and research programs for the development of this field.

Geothermal Energy

At present, India is at nascent stage of exploration for geothermal resources. The Geological Survey of India found 340 hotspots with low surface temperature (Sharma and Trikha 2013). It can be used for direct and indirect applications and clean energy. But the hot spring locations are found in certain locations only. The difficulty in transportation leads to use of this resource only in the surrounding areas. Installation and research activities need huge cost for effective usage. Sometimes during drilling, steam run out from inside earth and the improper drilling may h lead to earthquake. However, attempts are being made to make use of the resources as it can provide a clean energy.

Hydroelectricity

Globally, hydroelectricity is the major source of renewable energy. However the construction of huge hydroelectric power projects damage and destroy forest, wildlife habitat, agricultural land, and settlement areas. It dries up the downstream rivers on its way to nearby sea and it affects the riverside ecosystem. It disturbs the habitat of birds and plants which are necessary for the particular locality. Loss of forest and downstream less river flow force to relocate human beings as well as animals from their territory. Tribal people are not paid adequate compensation for the loss of their livelihood. The rehabilitation process is not well equipped and thousands of people have lost their land and livelihood. Micro hydel projects are more effective than large scale dams. But the micro projects in ecological sensitive areas are also a threat to the society. The small hydroelectric power projects in the Himalayas and the Western Ghats are not feasible for long-term benefit.

Biomass Energy

Agricultural waste after harvesting season is the source of biomass in India. Yet, agricultural farms hardly practice such system for their own power generation. They simply burn down the residue and thus causes air pollution. The small scale farmers can not adopt the technology easily, so there is a need of government intervention in the form of awareness generation and investment in this sector. Biomass Gasification is one of the methods to utilize solid waste and avoid waste dumping problem. But wood smoke contains carbon monoxide and other polluting matters. The demand of wood for energy may lead to deforestation. In the case of waste to energy, it contributes to air pollution. But biogas plant and biodiesel in transportation sector are eco-friendly. Supporting measures to counter the technological weakness of biogas and bio-fuel methods is necessary for its utilization in urban, rural, agricultural and non-agricultural fields. Wood and agricultural residue are limited and seasonal, so the availability of sources should be ensured and coordinated for the development of biomass energy.

Hydrogen Energy

Hydrogen is an energy carrier; not an energy source. In India, it is only in the initial stage of development and is used in power and transportation sector on an experimental basis. Now it is an expensive option, because the separation and storage of hydrogen need more effort. It takes a long time to separate hydrogen from other elements and the conversion of gaseous form of hydrogen to liquid form for storage is very expensive. The transportation of fuel and its distribution and maintenance are the other difficulties which cause constrain to develop this fuel. It has efficiency to replace the fossil fuels in transport sector but the cost and the need of structural modification become barriers to the development of this area (Chenoy 2009). Development of high pressure cylinders, compact storage capacity and fuel cell efficiency etc., determine the future of Hydrogen fuel. So, financial support with better research and development programs are imperative for the replacement of fossil fuel.

Lack of effective research, political will, comprehensive policy measures, international, regional or intraregional cooperation, technological advancement, public awareness and financial incentives are barriers for the development of renewable energy sector in India.

Energy: End Use Sectors

The major energy consuming sectors of India are agriculture, industry, transport, building etc. Industry is the main driver of the energy demand and it constitutes nearly 50% of total energy consumption globally. Industrial nations are now focusing on energy efficiency and clean sources (EIA 2017). Among the different energy sectors, industry plays a significant role in the consumption pattern. The use of non - combustible fossil fuels is rising in the current scenario. The building sector which consists of cooling, lighting and appliances also contributes the growing energy demand. Developing nations, especially India, needs more industrial and economic development. So it is focusing to fulfil its basic energy requirements, instead of energy efficiency. In industrial sector, the nation requires more development and depends on many inefficient energy sources. In industrial sector, energy is needed for many activities like process and assembly, steam and cogeneration, lighting, air conditioning for buildings etc., and as chemical feed stocks. Natural gas feed stocks are used to produce agricultural chemicals. Natural gas liquids and petroleum products like naphtha is used in the manufacturing of organic chemicals and plastics etc. So energy efficiency and clean usage are the biggest issues to tackle for a better future.

Transport is another sector which consumes considerable part of energy and it is mostly dependent on oil. The major carbon emission is also coming from this sector. Both transport and industrial sector consumes more energy and they grow rapidly every year. Coal and oil are the major sources of energy. Oil is the main contributor in transport, coal in industries, and electricity from almost all sources are industrial, residential as well as agriculture.

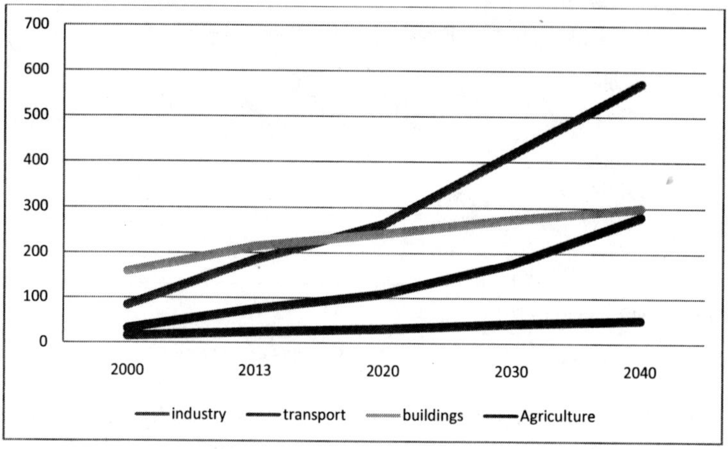

(EIA 2017)

Figure 4.2: Sector wise energy consumption Pattern (Mtoe)

India's energy consumption from sectors such as industry, transport, buildings and agriculture are together contributing 3.3% per year on average up to 2040 (EIA 2017). From figure 4.2, it can be discerned that the growth of industrial and transport sector is very high compared to other sectors. The growing economy is the main factor behind the industrial consumption and the rise of per capita income and lifestyle changes affect the transport sector. The poor quality of roads and old vehicles affect the fuel efficiency of this major sector. The mechanized and electrical power after 1960s contributes to the growing energy demand from agricultural sector. However, the major sources in Indian energy mix are fossil fuels. The oil dependency of transport sector and coal ridden thermal power plants and industries are major barriers for adopting new alternatives. The natural gas is the comparatively viable option which government put forward to overcome the GHG emission causing energy mix. Natural gas has considerable share in Indian fertilizer industry and in electricity generation. The import dependence, geopolitical barriers and the lack of infrastructural facilities, including pipelines and grids, are preventing the growth of natural gas industry in India.

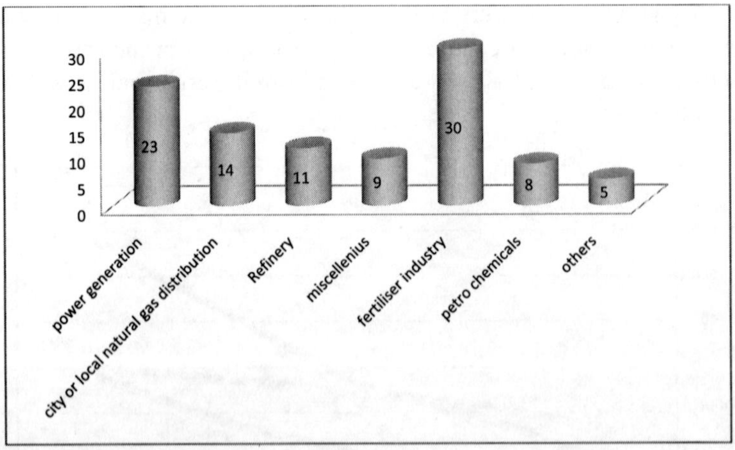

(Central Statistics Office 2018)

Figure 4.3: Sector wise natural gas consumption

India has around 62 GW of renewable installed capacity with 57244.23 MW grid interactive power. It has 33.39% of growth during 2016-17 period(Central Statistics Office 2018). The renewable energy sources are not prioritized through policy regulations and implementation level. However, now there is a visible increase of renewable power in Indian energy scenario. Large scale industries and Telecom companies are using the wind, solar and other hybrid options to fulfil the energy needs. In transportation sector also, the use of CNG, ethanol and biodiesel and electricity are increasingly used instead of oil.

Power Sector

In India, the electricity demand is indicating an increase from 1115BU to 3175 BU during the period of 2015 to 2030 and it is the third largest producer with 1160.10 BU after China with 6015 BU and the US with 4327 BU (Tripathi 2018). The compound annual growth rate is 8.42% in installed capacity from 2008 to 2017. Total installed capacity consists of 70.83% thermal power plants, 11.81% of Hydro, 1.80% of Nuclear and other renewable accounts 15.56%. Wind power is the major source among renewable installed capacity and comprises 56.39% which increased from 26866.66 MW to 32279.77 MW from 2016 to 2017. Biomass power constitutes 14.29% and increased 4831.33 MW to 8181 MW. The installed capacity of power from waste to energy and small hydro power are 114.08 MW and 4379.86 MW respectively. Solar power is the second largest contributor from renewable energy and which shows an increase of 6762.85 MW to 12288.83 MW (Central Statistics Office 2018). Even if renewable sources are contributing significantly to the development of energy sector growth, the fossil fuels and large-scale hydro electric projects encompasses the major share of electricity sector.

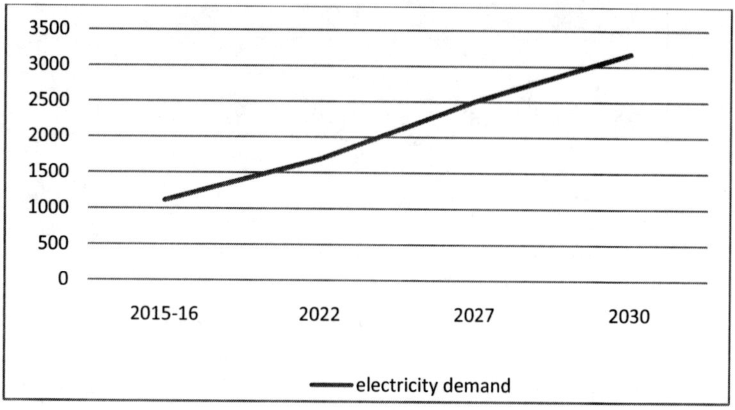

(TERI 2017)

Figure 4.4: India's electricity demand

Electricity consumption of industrial sector (40%) accounts the highest share in India and domestic (24%) as well as agricultural sector (18%) also have a significant role in the electricity sector. The total estimated electricity consumption stood at 10, 66,268 GW in the year 2016-17 which consists of 4, 26,665 GW (industrial sector), 2, 59,311 GW (domestic), 1, 95,473GW (agriculture), 98,333 GW (commercial usage), 17217 GW (railways and traction) and the remaining 69269 GW. The compound annual growth rate (CAGR) of total electricity consumption of 2016-17 over 2015-16 is 7. 82 and industry and domestic sector show the greatest increase (Central Statistics Office 2018). Indian electricity sector has to focus on access, efficiency, quality, affordability and clean electricity for a sustainable future.

India's total installed capacity of electricity is 3,44,689 MW and its 64.3% is from thermal power plants which is 2,21,803 MW. Hydro projects contribute 13%, that is 45,457 MW. Renewable energy sources like solar, wind, waste to power, biomass and small hydro projects have 20.5% share in the installed capacity of 70.649GW. The targeted 175 GW can provide around 50% of the current installed capacity. However, there is no policy

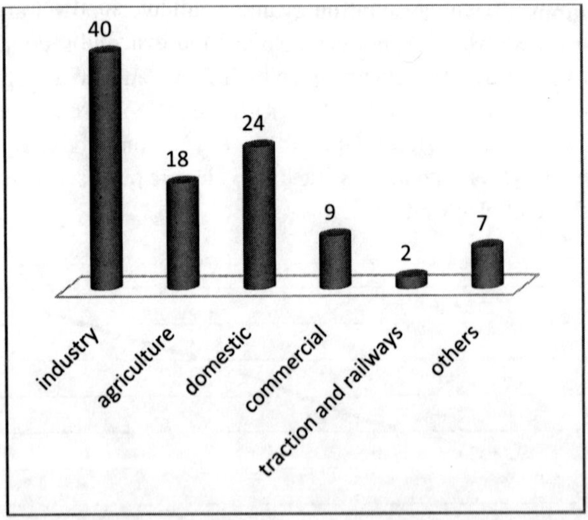

(Central Statistics Office 2018)

Figure 4.5: Sector wise Electricity consumption

to reduce the dependence on thermal power plants. In 2017-18, the overall generation of electricity shows 5.35% growth which includes 4.27% of thermal power plants, 3.07% hydro projects, 0.87% nuclear source, 13.55% of Bhutan import and 23.48% other renewables. That means, even though the generation from the above conventional sources remained at 1265 Billion Unit (BU), the generation from thermal power plants increased by 4.27% (Ministry of Power 2018).

Nonetheless, the per capita electricity consumption was 1075 units in 2015-16 (TERI 2017). The lifestyle changes of middle class population, the increasing use of electrical appliances in kitchen and for other purposes, the growing industrial and service sectors, the large electrification process etc., are the some of the reasons for the increase. The industrial, agricultural as well as residential usage of electricity is largely coming from northern India. There will be huge demand from transport sector in near future due to the reduction of fossil fuel usage in that sector. Production of electricity from renewable source is not effective for meeting the need.

In the transmission sector, India faces certain challenges. Lack of access in certain geographical locations is such a challenge. For example, the north eastern states experience the highest power deficit due to the geographical and insurgency issues. Inadequate transmission capacity is another major problem. The surplus power of certain regions cannot be utilized by other deficient regions. Power evacuation is not efficient, so it leads under utilization of certain plants. The transmission and distribution losses are also high compared to other developed nations due to lack of upgradation and poor maintenance. Weak billing and collection, frequent interruption flickers and electricity theft etc. also affect the power transmission system.

Transport Sector

Transport sector is one the fastest growing energy consuming sector with 4.4% growth per year as shown in the figure 4.6. Oil is the major fuel used in this sector and adopting alternate resources is very difficult. Transport sector is the major consumer of petrol and diesel. The sector consumes 70% of diesel and 99.6% of petrol from the total consumption.

Import dependence, CO2 emission, pollution and finite resource are some of the major problems in this area. Urban population is continuously growing in India from 1952 to 2011 (MHA 2011). The growing urbanization and the rise in per capita income contribute to the development of automobile industry. People buy vehicles for travelling, personal status and asset. The purchase enhances the automobile industry and its production, but the resulting oil consumption is a biggest challenge in this sector.

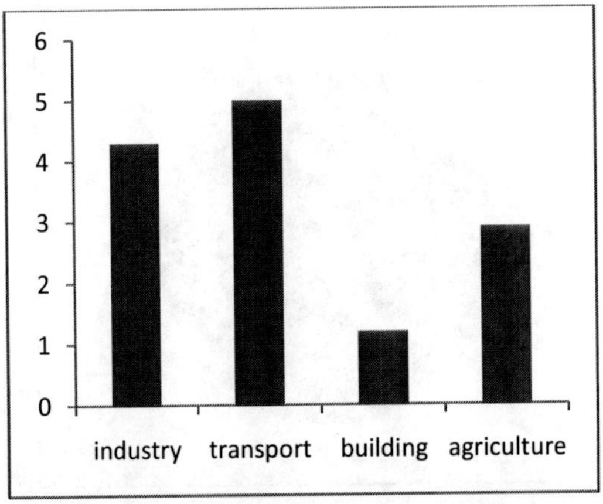

(Ministry of Petroleum & Natural Gas 2014)

Figure 4.6: Compound Average Annual Growth Rate of different sectors

The figure shows the greatest increase is coming from transport sector. India's 60% of goods are transported by using road network. The 90% of the passengers are also utilizing this opportunity. Rapid urbanization and improving connectivity increase the road transportation. The energy consumption of transport sector increases annually by 1.5% (EIA 2016) and most of the consumption growth is happening in non OECD nations.

Table 4.2: Consumption of Petrol and diesel in Transport sector

Diesel		*Petrol*	
cars, UVs, 3 wheeler	28.48%	Twowheeler	61.44%
Trucks	28.25%	Car	34.33%
Buses	9.5%	Three wheeler	2.34%
Railway	3.24%		

(Ministry of Petroleum and Natural Gas 2014)

Diesel is mostly used in transport sector. It accounts 70% of total diesel consumption, in which private cars and UVs (13.15%), commercial cars & UVs (8.94%), three wheelers (6.39%), trucks (28.25%), buses (9.5%) andtrains are included (3.24%). Petrol accounts 99.6% in transport sector in which two wheelrs consumes 61.42% and cars are using 34.33%. Cars, utility Vehicles and three wheelers together contribute to the major share in transport sector. In agricultural sector, tractors consume significant amount of enrgy for agricultural as well as transportation purpose (Ministry of Petroleum and Natural Gas 2014).

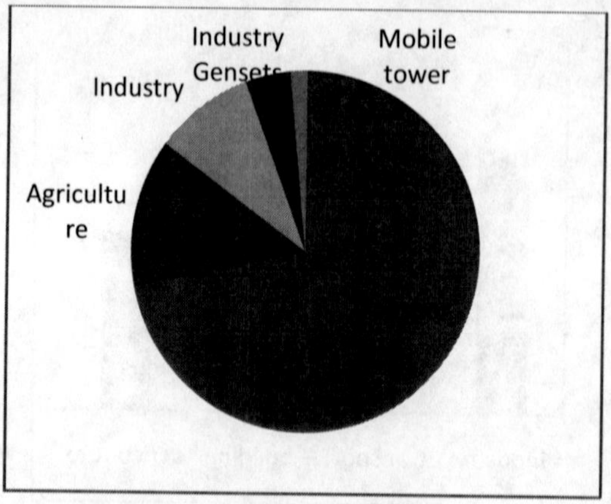

(Ministry of Petroleum and Natural Gas 2014)

Figure 4.7: Diesel consumption sector wise

Biofuel, electricity as well as natural gas are used in transport sector. But oil is more efficient and affordable fuel source in transportation. The availability and feasibility are the other factors which provide popularity to the petrol and diesel. Long term efforts are needed for better technologies.

Reduction of fuel consumption in transportation sector is difficult.The railway also consumes 3.24 % of diesel, as 37.5% of total routes are only electrified until 2017 by Indian railways (Ministry of Railways 2017). The inefficiency of vehicles such as lorry, buses,trucks etc., and terrible roads are also causing huge consumption fuel.

India has the second largest road network in the world, but in terms of efficiency and safety,it stands far below inglobal standards. Poor quality of roads,heavy trafic, toll stations, multiple check points and older vehicles are affecting the traffic and fuel usage. Personalised transportation due to increased urbaniztion and standard of living constitutes a major share of energy consumption in this sector. The inefficient public transport, goods and services are also reasons for the energy demand from the transportation sector. Certain legislations can reduce the oil consumption such as decrease the number of vehicles- personal as well as public, implement cycle friendly approaches, efficient and ecofrindly vehicles etc. But such legislations generally are considered as a threat to the private intests and choices.

Building Sector

Residential and service sectors such as public buildings, offices, shops, hotels etc., are included in the building sector. Urbanization and rising income have certain impact upon the people of every nation. The urban population rise by 24% which now encompasses 377 million and 200 million will be added to this by 2030 (MHA 2011). In India, the lifestyle changes affect the residential pattern, including cooking fuel, electrical appliances, thermal comfort and luxury items etc. In older days, kerosene was a common lighting fuel in all parts of India. Now also, it is used as fuel for lighting and cooking. Still, a huge population has been living without access to electricity and using firewood, coal and cow dung for cooking purpose.

The updating of appliance also contributes to the huge energy demand. Implementation of energy conservation building and alternative energy using measures are the need of the time. Because, as we consume more energy as electricity and the electricity is produced from thermal power plants, nuclear reactors as well as large scale hydro electric plants. Adoptions of new options for energy production are necessary to save the environment.

As far as cooking fuel is concerned, the majority of households in rural India used firewood, agriculture residue, cow dung, charcoal, kerosene etc. Of late, LPG, biogas and electricity are the main source behind cooking (Thampi 2017). Biomass produced health effects, especially on women and girl children are the major adversities in the rural cooking sector. Rising income, convenient appliances for kitchen and the various programmes for reduction of energy poverty increase the electricity consumption in households.

Cooling is another part of energy consumption for residential as well as service sector. The demand of fans, air cooler and air conditioners are in rising proportions. Implementation of energy efficient appliances are necessary because these equipment consume more energy in building sector. Affordability is the main factor behind lifestyle changes. Private ownership of vehicles with the consumption of oil and possession of modern appliances consume large quantity of electricity. The process of urbanization lead to big houses, new equipment, new life style and high energy requirement.

Agriculture

Agriculture is the most important sector of Indian economy and more than 70% of rural areas depend on this sector (FAO n.d). But, industrial and service sectors show greater growth percentage than this. In the case of livelihood, food security as well as employment, agriculture plays a vital role in the development of the nation. In agriculture sector, irrigation equipment and tractors consume more energy than others. Electricity is used more than diesel in irrigation purposes. Increasing shortage of water requires more efficient pump sets leading to more energy usage (India Energy Portal n.d). Tractors are more in use after 1960s. Traditionally, muscle power has been the only energy source during the time of harvesting, threshing, drying and warming. But after 1960s, the agricultural sector is more or less mechanized in all parts of India. That means the structural change of agriculture affects the energy landscape which includes animate power to mechanized power and electricity consumption for irrigation (Jha et al. 2012). In crop production, processing and transportation, huge mechanized and electrical energy are used through pump sets, tractors and others. India is an agricultural based country and it is the significant source of livelihood for 70% of the rural people.

Industry

Industrial sector is one of the highest energy consuming sectors in India. It includes fertilizers, cement, iron and steel industries and so forth. In addition, it needs buildings and transportation through rail, road and air. Coal is the main source of energy which drives the Indian industry. Abundant domestic reserves and the cheap availability are the main reasons behind the coal consumption. After independence, India took more effort on industrial development for the economic well-being of the society. But the industrialized nations used coal as their primary fuel in 18th and 19th centuries only. After that, they sought for alternative options to reduce the environmental damages. But the developing nations like India still depend on coal for their whole industrial purposes. The huge demand from industrial sector led to the growth of short term and large scale projects like nuclear energy, thermal power plants, LPG and natural gas. Energy demand from industrial sector influences the policy measures of the nation for immediate supply of huge amount of energy. The steel industry is the largest consumer of energy and India is the only country which uses coal for the production of direct reduced iron. Lack of energy efficiency measures and policy gaps are the major issues in this sector (IEA 2018).

Energy Poverty: The challenging Aspect of India's Energy Sector

Access to modern and affordable energy is a basic need for every human being which is a major factor behind every country's social, economic as well as human development. But in the case of India, per capita energy consumption is one of the lowest among world's average. And around 31 million people have no access to electricity and the majority people are still using the biomass such as firewood and cow dung and crop residue as cooking fuel. The inefficient use of cooking fuel is causing indoor air pollution which is mostly affecting health of the women and girl children of rural area (Saghir 2004; Barnes and Toman 2006). About 80% of rural population is using firewood, kerosene, cow dung, lignite, charcoal, coal and crop residues which are unhealthy for human being and ecology. They use it as their convenient and affordable fuel source for cooking, lighting, and heating. The resulting carbon emission and PM 2.5 impact cause severe harms to human health (NITI Aayog 2017). Tripura, Uttar Pradesh and West Bengal are depending more on biomass for cooking. Madhya Pradesh, West Bengal, Uttar Pradesh, Bihar and Rajasthan are the states which utilize cow dung as their fuel for cooking (PPAC 2016).

Access to energy is essential for people's well-being and their health. Electric lighting helps to extend the productive hours and modern cooking fuels enhance the health level of women and children. The necessary medical services require energy services for storage. The local unavailability of medical facilities deprives the poor people. Reliable, modern and clean fuel with affordability is the concern for every human being. The traditional unsustainable usage of cooking fuel leads to respiratory diseases, premature deaths and increases the gender inequities in a nation like India (Moss et al. 2011). Time consuming firewood collection reduces the working hours and study time of a large section of people in poor nations. The electricity access can reduce the unwanted labour of women in the household works through different equipment like washing machine, mixer grinder; pump sets etc. So, modern energy access can enhance the gender equality also. Still the affordability makes barrier to the usage of adequate energy. The high cost of energy stands against a good standard of living.

Even though the rural electrification process was almost completed in the year 2018, still 32 million homes, which is 15% of India's population, do not have access to continuous and good quality power. In rural electrification programme, if it is claimed that 10 % households and public places have power, it means that the government approves that the particular rural area is electrified, but in most of the cases, several households may possess only one bulb or like that. Lack of access to electricity deprives overall development of the society, including health, education and wealth. Bihar, Odisha, Jharkhand, Madhya Pradesh, Rajasthan and Uttar Pradesh are socially deprived and have no access to electricity for several households. The North eastern states suffer from energy poverty due to its geographical locations, insurgencies, poor financial and infrastructural development. The quality, reliability and affordability of energy are significantly critical for the states in these parts. Supply disruptions, transmission loss, voltage variation and hurdles for grid connectivity are main problem in the electricity sector. The distribution of oil and other energy resources are difficult in this region, because the insurgents may forcefully collect the tankers and sell it through black market (Kumar 2007). In a country like India, state intervention is needed for the access of adequate electricity and clean cooking fuel for people's daily lives.

India's per capita consumption of electricity is only 914 KWh which is very low compared to the global average of 3026 KWh. However, India's energy demand is one of the highest in the world and the consumption would grow by 4.2% per year which is greater than that of all the developed countries. The energy demand growth of all non OECD countries is 61% and it is lesser than the 165% of India (BP 2018). The huge demand from industrial sector, rising automobile supply, household electric equipment and large portion of people without accessing modern energy contribute to the growing energy needs of India.

So far, India has electrified 92% of the total 21, 49, 35,879 un-electrified households and 1, 72, 21,652 are remaining to be completed. The table shows that the less energy accessible states are the most backward states in the nation. More than 10% of households have to be electrified by states

Table 4.3: Electrification Status

State	*Electrification status (%)*	*To be electrified (No. of Households)*
Jammu & Kashmir	87	206995
Himachal Pradesh	99	11090
Punjab	100	0
Haryana	99.61	13345
Uttarakhand	89	248799
Uttar Pradesh	71	9849521
Rajasthan	93	829186
Gujarat	100	0
Madhya Pradesh	99	132770
Bihar	94	781247
Sikkim	93	4108
West Bengal	98	298705
Jharkhand	87	838823
Chhattisgarh	98	113202
Maharashtra	99	123813
Odisha	88	1151856
Telangana	95	328303
Andhra Pradesh	100	0
Goa	100	0
Karnataka	96	371928
Kerala	100	0
Tamil Nadu	100	0
Arunachal Pradesh	76	78010
Assam	78	1399400
Meghalaya	69	163549
Nagaland	78	94399
Manipur	83	71407
Tripura	88	94478
Mizoram	93	16718

(Saubhagya 2018)

like Jammu & Kashmir, Jharkhand, Uttarakhand, Odisha, Manipur and Tripura. States such as Nagaland, Assam, Arunachal Pradesh and Uttar Pradesh are needed to provide around 25% of electricity access to their own people. Meghalaya is far behind in the case of percentage of electrified households. Meanwhile, Uttar Pradesh has more than 98 lakh households to be electrified. Assam and Odisha also have to electrify about 11 lakhs of household in their states. So the data reveals that energy poverty is a major constraint for India and as a developing nation. As the state is obliged to provide energy access to meet the basic needs of the citizens, the nation's energy demand is increasing.

Insecurities of Indian Energy Scenario

Energy is considered as the strategic component of every nation and it is imperative for every society as well as human being. But industrialisation and the resulting changes affected the energy paradigm also. The fossil fuels played a key role in the development of the human society. Now these fuels challenge the survival of the humanity as well as our ecosystem. As a developing nation, India needs more industrial growth and economic development, so it needs continuous accessibility of modern fuels. India is the third largest energy importing country in the world due to the high energy demand and the unavailability of the domestic oil resources. Large scale coal usage in industry as well as in electric sector, crude oil dependent transport sector, traditional biomass ridden cooking sector and the nuclear developments are the major ingredients of India's energy sector. Even though there are certain visible developments are happening in clean energy area, there are no significant developments to reduce the usage of hydrocarbons like containing the hazardous coal mining, oil import dependency, domestic exploration of oil import dependency, domestic exploration of oil and liberal policies for large scale selling of traditional vehicles etc. This pattern of energy search is affecting the structure of environment and well-being of the society.

India's Energy Engagements: Import Dependence

India's energy sector is mainly depending upon import of crude oil, coal, uranium, natural gas etc. The dependence on import for energy sources is a challenging aspect due to several reasons. The higher level of import than the export affects the Indian economy and foreign exchange reserves of the country. The oil import is a major determinant of Indian economy and the fossil fuels contribute a huge share in the import sector. Recently, the huge demand and low supply of oil in international market has worsened the situation and raised the oil price. The import bill increased heavily in 2018 and it affects every sections of society in India. Price fluctuations affect the Indian rupee and it has its own repercussion on different spheres of society. The Rupee devalues and enlarged trade deficit as well as fiscal deficit have the power to disturb Indian economy. India imports around 80% of its oil needs and this import dependence drawdown the foreign reserves. India is the third largest energy consumer in the world and has not much crude oil reserves. So the energy demand will not fall in near future and that will increase the import dependence.

Sanction on Iran, decreasing oil production of Venezuela and Libya, conflicts in Iraq, Yemen, Libya and Syria, tensions between Saudi Arabia and Iraq and above all the output cut down by OPEC countries are the main problems behind price hike in 2018 which touched $85 per barrel. The price hike in import goods raises the inflation and interest rate here. Global oil price influences domestic price and leads to the increase of price in petrol and diesel and decrease in GDP growth rate. Common man experiences the problems of price hike such as inflation in every field and rise of interest rate. So diversification of the energy sources is necessity for India to strengthen its economy. India depends 80% of oil from foreign countries. Again, the nature of the import dependence of India is an issue because half of its oil requirement is depended on a few countries. The price rise of oil affects all people from bottom to top. The resulting inflation also harm the well being of the common people. Rapid industrialization since the independence developed the energy sector and now India is one of the highest energy consumption countries. Energy became a prominent part of India's foreign policy and the quest for energy security influence the nation's foreign policy.

India depended around half of the oil requirement from the Persian Gulf region. Saudi Arabia, Iraq, and Iran are contributing the major part. Qatar is the highest natural gas importer for India. Even though there is a strategic partnership between the countries of Persian Gulf and India, the energy decisions and policies of these countries influence the economy of our nation. The US sanctions on Iran played a critical role in India Iran relationship. The influence of the US in India's energy sector is significant from 1960s. The nuclear cooperation sanctions, as well as NSG waiver are certain recent developments in India's energy relation with the US. Nevertheless, the question of feasibility of nuclear power plants poses questions regarding the relationship.

Now the sanction on Iran also affects the oil import of the country. The involvement in war on terror in Afghanistan is also backed by the India's energy interest on central Asia. India followed neo-colonial policies on certain resource rich African states. India and China are energy hungry nations and they follow the completion to acquire energy sources. India allows private companies to explore oil resource to tackle the energy challenge from China. And both countries agued for common but differentiated responsibilities' in the United Nations for their developmental needs as well as for maximum energy utilization (Muller-Kraner 2008).

India's energy engagements with other nations also follow the traditional state centric energy security framework. It imposes certain insecurities to the people of other nations also. The price fluctuations affect even the ordinary man. The large scale energy projects influenced by developed nations such as nuclear power plants work against the rights of the society, their livelihood and safety.

Domestic constraints in Energy Sector

India's energy demand includes aspiration to curb the energy poverty and the reality that a major chunk of the population from the rural areas suffer from energy poverty. At the time of India's independence, only 1500 villages were electrified. The basic energy concerns of vast population and the growing sophisticated energy needs of the middle class population constituted the energy demand of India. The increasing per capita income enabled the urbanized section to attain modern energy appliances. They avoided biomass ridden cooking fuel and favoured LPG or other electric appliances. The weather change increases the use of heating or cooling equipment such as fans and air conditioners. The energy demand is increasing and the rich can attain through their purchasing capacity. But the sources of this energy are not clean in most of the cases. LPG is coming from petroleum products and electricity is coming from thermal power plants, large scale hydro projects and nuclear power plants. In India, the transport sector is growing at the higher rate compared to OECD nations. Agriculture sector also mechanized after 1960s and most of these contributed to the fossil fuel dependence of the developing nations. The developed countries consumed hydrocarbon resources and achieved their development in 19th century. Now they changed their perspective on energy usage and focus on green or clean technologies. Most of the countries in the European Union do not allow the drilling or exploration or inefficient usage of hazardous energy resources.

Energy security of India, largely considered uninterrupted supplies to support economic and commercial activities is necessary for sustained growth of economy (Singh 2010). Most of the literature shows energy independence or dominance are the indicators of economic strength of the particular nation. Availability of energy at affordable price is considered as a developmental concern for a state like India. So, for energy security India uses its domestic resources as well as foreign resources. International cooperation and overseas assets help to access adequate resources from abroad. Lack of energy or supply disruption affects the economy as well as national power. So, India maintains the continuous availability of energy largely unsustainable, with affordable price. Energy supply comes mostly from coal, oil and natural gas. Even if the contribution of nuclear power plants are very less, but it is significant in the energy sector, because large scale trade is happening in this sector. Even in renewable sector the government adopts large scale projects and causes threats to the environment and the people.

So, the concern for the energy security of a nation sometimes threatens people's security. The mining of coal, its production process and transformation lead to displaced people, deprivation of livelihood and health hazards, deforestation, water contamination and other pollution. Dependence on oil and the subsequent GHG emission and the resultant extreme weather conditions force to search for other options. Nuclear energy production is comparatively a new technology and it is carbon free, but the environmental threats of the power plants, hazards of uranium mining and threats from nuclear wastes are terrific. Needles to say, large scale renewable technologies also generate harms to the populace and environment.

A large chunk of the literature on energy consider it as a strategic and security factor of state. Adequate availability is the mainstream concern about energy. Environmental and legal norms are avoided for the sake of ensuring availability and economic development. However, the energy threats are borderless and the impact of sustainable energy of certain states will be a cause of disaster for other regions in the world. Climate change and extreme weather situations are the result of anthropogenic greenhouse gas emission and 60% of carbon emission from the world energy usage. Sea level rise, loss of biodiversity, desertification, water and food insecurities etc., are from the GHG emission and high level global temperature. These impacts are having much effect on ecologically fragile areas and the people residing in those areas are mostly poor. They cannot afford remedies for environmental causalities and it increases the depth of climate calamities. So, in most of the cases, the energy consumers are not directly affected with the issues.

The environmental problems are boarder less. Nonetheless, like in the case of mining, the nearby areas are directly affected with severe consequences. The pollution of transport sector directly affect the poor in urban areas and the rich has several facilities including efficient building, vehicles and hospital access for the protection from the environmental threats. Mining of coal and uranium are mostly done in forest areas, so the health impacts and genetic disorders mainly occur among the nearby tribal people and the deforestation affects the global environment and weather conditions. The livelihood issues and the health problems faced by marginalized sections near to the project areas are not considered as a grave social issue by the mainstream society. The changing weather conditions like strong wind, rain, flood, drought, extreme hot or cold temperature etc., make huge calamities to the marginalized societies.

So, the current energy security landscape shows a quest for acquiring maximum energy while even avoiding the security of the society and environment. This is mostly associated with the traditional state centric security approach which upholds that security is inextricably linked with national power and deals with external threats. After the cold war, the security concept was re-conceptualized and questions like security for whom and how and securitized by whom and on what issues etc., were posed (Buzan et al. 1998, 25-34). Industry and the transport sector consume more energy than other sectors, that means, the interests of the elites are protected in national energy security approaches. And it sacrifices the interests of the vulnerable section for the sake of the security of certain privileged section of the society. Waever (1995, 46-86) argues that security problems are the consequence of elite efforts to shape the world. The fact that India which is one of the highest energy consumer nations in the world, acquires its energy from insecure options reflects the national perspective towards the concept of security. For short term requirement and for the satisfaction of mainstream society, the entire focus is narrowed down towards the availability and affordability of energy, discarding the larger issues.

The short term energy goals satisfy the energy requirements of the mainstream society, but it creates insecurities to the environment and large section of people. In security discourses, the primary referent object is changed to human centric after the cold war (Booth 1991, 313-326). It addresses the economic, food, health, environment, personal, community as well as political security (UNDP 1994). Kaldor (2008) argued for the inclusion of individual human rights and their basic needs to the current security discourse. Freedom from fear and freedom from want are constitutionally recognized human security needs by several governments like Canada and Japan (Gasper 2005).

Many large scale energy projects displace a certain sections of people, often most of them are tribal population, who depend on agriculture, fishing or forest products. The developmental projects affect the livelihood opportunities and the compensation or rehabilitation facilities are not addressing their societal security. So they become marginalized and deprived. The residents near to the locations like coal and uranium mines, thermal and nuclear power plants, industrial firms, as well as near to the transport routes are affected by the pollution and radiation. Water bodies nearer to the projects also get contaminated and it affects the aquatic life which in turn changes the life of fishing community there. In coal mines, so many children are working for their daily bread. The low level workers including women and children of these mines, plants etc. are facing risks of high level pollution, radiation and accidents. They are deprived of protective measures or health measures due to unaffordability.

The security of energy resources and the dependency on fossil fuels make damages to the environment. The resource capture[4] (Homer-Dixon 1999) is being done by the elites and in the process, the vulnerable section of people are getting marginalised. Current consumption pattern of energy causes ecological destruction and the environment is not under the control of human beings (Dalby 2002, 95-108). Inevitably, structural changes are needed for a sustainable future. It requires a comprehensive policy for environmental as well as human security. Unsustainable human activities in the energy sector disturb the air, water, soil and the living things. For exploration and the production of energy sources, the forest and other ecosystems are destructed and the resulting environmental insecurities itself threatens the human security. The fossil fuel explorations methods like drilling and mining disturb geographical structure. The pollution from energy sources from its exploration stage to consumption as well as waste management affects the environment. Fossil fuel consumption and its carbon emission affect the weather condition. The resulting catastrophes like flood, earth quake, tsunami, hurricanes, extreme hot or cold climate condition etc. also leads to societal damages especially on 'eco-system people'[5] (Gadgil and Guha 1995) as well as urban poor. The weather patterns affect their livelihood practices and act as threat to their life itself.

Lack of access to sufficient energy, especially clean energy, and the environmental and human security threats from the unsustainable usage of energy are the main challenges for India. Short term and large scale energy projects for the economic development of the country lead to environmental and societal calamities. Expanding accessibility is the priority policy concern for India. The access of clean energy is still a faraway concept. Affordability is the major constrain for rural and poor populations to access energy. So the cheap and continues availability of coal, oil and gas remain to be the viable option. The involvement of giant energy companies, coal mafias, automobile industries, political leaderships and corruption are crucial factors involved in the implementations of energy policy in a country like India.

Innovative policies and technologies are the only solution for a sustainable future. But the nation focuses on the affordable availability of the resource and it leads to environmental destruction and human insecurities. The developed nations acquire this position through unsustainable energy usage. But geographical and social features are different in developing nations and cause huge environmental damages and human security issues. Future generations also have to right to inherit a healthy planet (Annan 2000). The needs of the mainstream society act as a threat to the powerless marginalized section. The structural violence in the developmental activities affects security of the people and provides insecurity in health, food, water, livelihood and environment (Cilliers 2004). The fulfilment of sustainable developmental goal is a responsibility of India, which argues for access to affordable, reliable, sustainable and modern energy for all (UNDP 2016). Greater awareness, strong political will and technological advancement are needed for a greener future of the planet.

Reference

Abbott, Derek. 2011. "Is Nuclear Power Globally Scalable?." In the *Proceedings of the IEEE (Institute of Electrical and Electronics Engineers)* University of Adelaide, October, 1611-1617.99(10):1611-1617. Adelaide, Australia: IEEE.

Aduloju, Ayodeji, and Omowunmi O. Pratt. 2014. "Human Security and Developmental Crisis in the Contemporary West Africa."*Journal of Human Security* 10 (1): 46-58.

AERB (Atomic Energy Regulatory Board). 2010. "Convention on Nuclear Safety." AERB, Government of India. Accessed February 10, 2018.https://aerb.gov.in/index.php/ english/convention-on-nuclear-safety.

Annan, Kofi A. 2000.*We the Peoples: The Role of the United Nations in the 21st Century.* New York, USA: United Nations Department of Public Information.

Ansari, Md. Fahim, Ravinder Kumar Kharb, Sunil Luthra, S.L. Shimmi, and S.Chatterji. 2013. "Analysis of barriers to implement solar power installations in India using interpretive structural modelling technique." *Renewable and Sustainable Energy Reviews* 27 (November): 163-74.

Anthony, Augusta, Ray Sanchez, and Nicole Chavez. 2018. "Pressure increase reported in Massachusetts gas pipeline, NTSB says." CNN, September 16, 2018. https://edition.cnn.com/2018/09/15/us/massachusetts-explosions-fires-gas-pipeline/index.html.

Bandyopadhyay, Bibek. 2013. *Prospects and challenges of Solar Power in India.* Under Industry Institution Interaction Programme of TEQIP Phase II, Jadavpur University. October 28.http://teqip.jdvu.ac.in/for website/ Program%2028.10.2013/ Presentation Dr.%20Bibek%20Bandyopadhyay.pdf.

Barnes, Douglas. F and Michael A. Toman. 2006. "Energy, Equity and Economic Development." In *Economic Development and Environmental Sustainability: New Policy Options*, edited by Ramon Lopez, and Michael A. Toman. Oxford: Oxford University Press.

Barton, Barry, Catherine Redgwell, Anita Ronne, and Donald N Zillman. 2004. *Energy Security: Managing Risk in a Dynamic Legal and Regulatory Environment.* New York: Oxford University Press.

Bindra, Prerna. 2017. "The Bustard and the Windmill." *The Hindu,* September 2, 2017. https://www.thehindu.com/sci-tech/energy-and-environment/the-bustard-and-the-windmill/article19608564.ece.

Booth, Ken. 1991. "Security and Emancipation." *Review of International Studies* 17(4): 313-326.

BP (British Petroleum). 2017. *B P Statistical Review of World Energy 2017*. https://www.bp.com/content/dam/bp-country/de_ch/PDF/bp-statistical-review-of-world-energy-2017-full-report.pdf.

BP (British Petroleum). 2018. B P *Statistical Review of World Energy 2018.*https://www.bp.com/en/global/corporate/energy-economics/statistical-review-of-world-energy.html.

BP (British Petroleum). 2018. *BP Energy Outlook Country and Regional Insights – India.* https://www.bp.com/content/dam/bp/en/corporate/pdf/energy-economics/energy-outlook /bp-energy-outlook-2018-country-insight-india.pdf.

BP (British Petroleum). 2018. *Energy Demand by sector.* Accessed January 12, 2019. https://www.bp.com/en/global/corporate/energy-economics/energy-outlook.html.

Business Line. 2018. "Coal production 2018, Coal production up 15% this fiscal." June 11, 2018. https://www.thehindubusinessline.com/economy/coal-production-up-15-this-fiscal-piyush-goyal/article24135551.ece.

Business Standard. 2018. "Emission standards for thermal power plants: SC asks govt to file detailed affidavit." April 25, 2018. https://www.business-standard.com/article/pti-stories/emission-standards-for-thermal-power-plants-sc-asks-govt-to-file-detailed-affidavit-118042501253_1.html

Buzan, Barry, Ole Waever, and Jaap de Wilde. 1998. *Security: A New Framework for Analysis*. US: Lynne Rienner Publishers.

Central Statistics Office. 2018. *Energy statistics.* New Delhi: Ministry of Statistics and Programme Implementation, Government of India. http://mospi.nic.in/sites/default/files/publication_reports/Energy_Statistics_2018.pdf.

Chenoy, Dilip. 2009. "Overview of Indian Hydrogen Programme&Key Safety Issues on Hydrogen Fuel." In *Workshop on Compressed Natural Gas and Hydrogen Fuels Lessons Learned for the Safe Deployment of Vehicles.* December 10-11.Washington D C: US Department of Transportation and US Department of Energy.

CIL (Coal India Limited). 2018. *Coal Vision 2030*. https://www.coalindia.in/DesktopModules/DocumentList/documents/Coal Vision 2030 document for Coal Sector Stakeholders Consultation 27012018.pdf.

Cilliers, Jakkie. 2004. *Human Security in Africa: A Conceptual Framework for Review*. Nairobi, Kenya: African Human Security Initiative.

Cilliers, Jakkie. 2015. *Future (im)perfect? Mapping conflict, violence and extremism in Africa.* Pretoria, South Africa: Institute for Security Studies.

DAE (Department of Atomic Energy). n.d. "Important Agreements"DAE, Government of India.Accessed November 2, 2018. http://www.dae.nic.in/?q=node/75.

DAE (Department of Atomic Energy). n.d. "Myths and Facts." DAE, Government of India. Accessed February 16, 2019.http://www.dae.nic.in/?q=node/926.

Dalby, Simon. 2002. "Security and Ecology in the Age of Globalization." *Environmental Change and Security Project Report* 8 (Summer): 95-108. Washington DC: Woodrow Wilson Center of Scholars.

Dalby, Simon. 2002. *Environmental Security.* Minneapolis: University of Minnesota Press.

*Down to Earth.*2015."Narora fire." July 4, 2015. https://www.downtoearth.org.in/ news /narora-fire-30932.

Down to Earth. 2018. "Ireland becomes the fourth EU country to ban fracking." July 11, 2018.

Dutt, Arjun, and NeerajKuldeep. 2018. "Discoms Rooftop Moment," *Business Line,* April 10, 2018. https://www.thehindubusinessline.com/opinion/columns/ discoms-rooftop-moment/article23495195.ece.

EIA (US Energy Information Administration). 2016. *International Energy Outlook 2016 with Projections to 2040*. Washington DC: Office of Energy Analysis, U.S. Department of Energy. https://www.eia.gov/outlooks/ieo/pdf/0484(2016).pdf

FAO (Food and Agricultural Organization).n.d. "India at a Glance."FAO, United Nations.http://www.fao.org/india/fao-in-india/india-at-a-glance/en/.

Gadgil, Madhav, and RamachandraGuha. 1995. *Ecology and Equity: The Use and Abuse of Nature in Contemporary India*. New York: Routledge.

Gasper, Des. 2005. "Securing Humanity: Situating 'Human Security' as Concept and Discourse." *Journal of Human Development* 6 (2): 221–245.

Glaser, Alexander, and M.V Ramana. 2007. "Weapon-Grade Plutonium Production Potential in the Indian Prototype Fast Breeder Reactor." *Science and Global Security* 15(2): 85-105. Routledge.

Guha, Debasis. 2014. "A case study on the effects of coal mining in the environment particularly in relation to Soil, Water and Air causing a Socio-economic Hazard in Asansol-Raniganj Area, India."*International Research Journal of Social Science* 3(8): 39-42.

Homer-Dixon, Thomas. F. 1999. *Environment, Scarcity and Violence.* Princeton: Princeton University Press.

IBEF (India Brand Equity Foundation). 2018. "Oil & Gas Industry in India." IBEF.Accessed November 12, 2018.https://www.ibef.org/industry/oil-gas-india.aspx.

IBEF (India Brand Equity Foundation). 2018. "Road Infrastructure in India." IBEF.Accessed January 2, 2017. https://www.ibef.org/industry/roads-india.aspx.

IEA (International Energy Agency). 2006. "Energy for Cooking in Developing Countries." IEA.Accessed June 5, 2018.https://www.iea.org/ publications/ free publications/publication/cooking.pdf.

IEA (International Energy Agency). 2015. "India Energy Outlook: World Energy Outlook Special Report." Accessed July 1, 2018. https://www.iea.org/ publications/ freepublications/publication/IndiaEnergyOutlook_WEO2015.pdf.

IEA (International Energy Agency). 2017. *World Energy Outlook 2017.* https:// www.iea.org/weo2017/.

India Energy Portal.n.d. "Agriculture, Energy Sectors." Government of India, Accessed December 13, 2018. http://www.indiaenergyportal.org/subthemes_link.php? text=agriculture&themeid=15.

Jadugoda Uranium Mine – 1. 2009. Jharkhand Forum, April 22.https://www.youtube.com/ watch?v=-2z8EsV748I.

Jha, Girish Kumar, Suresh Pal, and Alka Singh. 2012. "Changing Energy-use Pattern and the Demand Projection for Indian Agriculture."*Agricultural Economics Research Review* 25(1) January-June: 61-68.

Kaldor, Mary. 2004. "A Force for Intervention: A Human Security Doctrine for Europe and Beyond." *The New York Times.* September 30, 2004.

Kumar, B.B, ed. 2007. *Problems of Ethnicity in North East India*. Delhi: Concept Publishing Company.

Lahiri-Dutt, Kuntala. 2007. "Illegal coal mining in Eastern India: Rethinking legitimacy and limits of justice." *Economic and Political Weekly* December: 57-66.

Lok Sabha. 2018. "Share of Atomic Energy."Lok Sabha Unstarred Question No.2064 to be Answered on 07.03.2018. Department of Atomic Energy, Government of India. http://dae.nic.in/writereaddata/parl/budget2018/lsus2064.pdf.

Mallya, Sameer and Shreyas D Deshmukh. 2015. *Viability of India's Gas Pipeline Options: A Geo-political Perspective: (Pakistan as a spoiler in TAPI and IPI venture)*. New Delhi: The Centre for Land Warfare Studies.

MHA (Ministry of Home Affairs). 2011. *Census of India 2011: Rural Urban Distribution of Population, Provisional Population Totals*. New Delhi: MHA, Government of India. http://censusindia.gov.in/2011-prov-results/paper2/ data_files/ india/ Rural Urban 2011.pdf.

Ministry of Petroleum & Natural Gas. 2014. "70% of Diesel, 99.6 % of Petrol consumed by Transport Sector: M/s Nielsen submits All India Study Report to PPAC on sale of Diesel and Petrol." Press Information Bureau, Government of India. January 28. http://pib.nic.in/newsite/PrintRelease.aspx?relid=102799.

Ministry of Petroleum and Natural gas. 2017. *Indian Petroleum & Natural Gas Statistics 2015-16*. New Delhi: Economic and Statistics Division, Government of India. http://petroleum.nic.in/more/indian-png-statistics.

Ministry of Power. 2008."Power Generation, Overview." Government of India. Accessed August 19, 2018.https://powermin.nic.in/en/content/overview.

Ministry of Power. n.d. "Power Sector at a Glance All India". Accessed June15, 2018. https://powermin.nic.in/en/content/power-sector-glance-all-india 2018.

Ministry of Railways. 2017. *Facts & Figures 2016-17*. Government of India http://www.indianrailways.gov.in/railwayboard/uploads/directorate/stat econ/IRSP 2016-17/Facts Figure/Fact Figures%20English%202016-17.pdf.

Ministry of Statistics and Programme Implementation. 2011. *Statistical Year Book 2011*. Central Statistical Office, Government of India. http://www.mospi.gov.in.

Mishra, Niharranjan. 2015. *Coal Mining, Displacement and Rural Livelihoods: A Study in Mahanadi Coalfield Odisha*. Rourkela, Odisha: Department of Humanities and Social Sciences National Institute of Technology.

MNRE (Ministry of New and Renewable Energy). 2017.*Year End Review 2017*. New Delhi: Press Information Bureau, MNRE, Government of India.

Monga, Ritu, RichaBajpai, and Purnima Swarup Khare. 2006. "Energy Consumption, Sectoral Activity, and Structural Change in the Indian Economy." *Journal of Environmental Research and Development* 1(1): 68-71.

Moss, Jeremy, Michael McMann, Jessica Rae, Andrea Zipprich, Darryl R.J. Macer, Aori R. Nyambati, Diana Ngo, MingMing Cheng, N Manohar and Gregor Wolbring. 2011. *Energy Equity and Environmental Security.* Bangkok: The United Nations Educational, Scientific and Cultural Organization (UNESCO).

Müller-Kraenner, Sascha. 2008. *China's and India's Emerging Energy Foreign Policy.* Bonn: German Development Institute.

Nakano, Jane, David Pumphrey, Robert Price and Molly A. Walton. 2012. *Prospects for Shale Gas Development in Asia: Examining potentials and Challenges in China and India*. Washington D.C: Center for Strategic and International Studies.

National Portal of India.n.d. "Power & Energy."Government of India.Accessed June 2, 2018. https://www.india.gov.in/topics/power-energy.

NDTV. 2017. "India in talks with countries like Uzbekistan to create Uranium Reserve." September 24, 2017. https://www.ndtv.com/india-news/india-in-talks-with-countries-like-uzbekistan-to-create-uranium-reserve-1754479.

Neslen, Arthur. 2016. "The rise and fall of fracking in Europe."*The Guardian*, September 29, 2016. https://www.theguardian.com/sustainable-business/2016/sep/29/ fracking-shale-gas-europe-opposition-ban.

NITI Aayog. 2017. *Draft National Energy Policy*. Government of India. June 27. https://niti.gov.in/writereaddata/files/new_initiatives/NEP-ID 27.06.2017.pdf.

Pallavi, Aparna. 2015. "Uranium Mine Waste Imperils Villages in Jaduguda." *Down to Earth.* July 4, 2015.

Perera, Pradeep.2018.*Challenges of Integrating 175 GW of Renewable Energy in India and Policy Options.* Philippines: Asian Development Bank.

Philip, Annie. 2014. "Filling the Gaps: Rooftop Solar Projects in India." *Economic and Political Weekly* 49(10).https://www.epw.in/journal/2014/10/web-exclusives/filling-gaps- rooftop-solar-projects-india.html.

Pinna, B, Dalla Chiara, and K. Pant. 2014. "Energy used by transport systems in India: the role of the urban population, sources, alternative modes and quantitative analyses." *WIT Transactions on Ecology and the Environment* 190: 661-675. WIT Press.

PPAC (Petroleum Planning & Analysis Cell). 2018. *Ready Reckoner Snapshot of India's Oil & Gas data.*Ministry of Petroleum & Natural Gas. https://www.ppac.gov.in/ WriteReadData/Reports/20190 12205 54381340 355 Snap shot of India % E2%80%99s Oil & Gasdata, December 2018.pdf.

PPAC (Petroleum Planning and Analysis Cell). 2016. *Assessment report: Primary survey on household cooking fuel usage and willingness to convert to LPG*. Ministry of Petroleum and Natural Gas.Government of India. http://www.ppac.org.in/ WriteReadData/Reports/2017103 104493 42512219 Primary Survey Report PPAC. pdf.

Rajya Sabha. 2016. "Per Capita Consumption of Power. "Rajya Sabha Unstarred Question No.2392.Ministry of Power, Government of India. http://www. india environmentportal.org.in/files/file/Per % 20 capita % 20 consumption % 20 of % 20 power. pdf.

Rajya Sabha. 2017. "Disposal of Radioactive Waste Materials." Rajya Sabha Unstarred Question No.2086. Department of Atomic Energy, Government of India. http://dae.nic.in/writereaddata/parl/monsoon 2017/rsus2086.pdf.

Rajya Sabha. 2017. "Production and Import of Uranium."Rajya Sabha Starred Question No.368. Department of Atomic Energy, Government of India.

Ramana M.V. 2009.*The Indian Nuclear Industry: Status and Prospects, Nuclear Energy Futures*. The Centre for International Governance Innovation Nuclear energy Futures Papers, The Nuclear Energy Futures Project: 1-34, https://www.cigionline.org/sites/default/files/nuclear energy wp9.pdf.

Ramana, M V, and Ashwin Kumar. 2010. "Safety First? Kaiga and Other Nuclear Stories."*Economic & Political Weekly*xlv (7). February 13.

Ramana, M.V. 2007."Economics of Nuclear Power."*Economics and Political Weekly*. January 13: 169-71.

Ramana, M.V.2009. "Nuclear Power: Economic, Safety, Health, and Environmental Issues of Near-Term Technologies."*Annual Review of Environment and Resources* 34(1): 127-52.

Redgwell, Catherine. 2004. "International Energy Security." In *Energy Security: Managing Risk in a Dynamic Legal and Regulatory Environment,* edited by Barry Barton, Catherine Redgwell, Anita Rønne, and Donald N. Zillman. Oxford: Oxford University Press.

Remme, Uwe, Nathalie Trudeau, Dagmar Graczyk and Peter Taylor, 2011.*Technology Development Prospects for the Indian Power Sector.* IEA Energy Papers 2011/4: OECD Publishing.

Saghir, Jamal. 2004. *Energy and poverty: myths, links, and policy issues*. Energy and Mining Sector Board.World Bank. http://siteresources.worldbank.org/INTENERGY/Resources/EnergyWorking Notes 4.pdf.

Sahel and West Africa Club/OECD. 2006. "Workshop on Human Security in West Africa: Challenges, Synergies and Action for Regional Agenda." Lome,Togo, March 26–28. Governance, Conflicts Dynamics, Peace and Security Unit, Sahel and West Africa Club/OECD. https://www.oecd.org/swac/events/38522284.pdf.

Saubhagya. 2018. "House Electrification Status." Pradhan Mantri Sahaj Bijli Har Ghar Yojana, Saubhagya Dashboard, Ministry of Power, Government of India. https://powermin.nic.in/en/content/saubhagya.

Seethi, K.M. 2008."Perils of Nuclear Renaissance and the Indo US Civil Nuclear Deal."*Indian Journal of Politics and International Relations* 1(1): 129-40.

Sethi, Girish. 2017. "Industrial Energy Efficiency." In *Workshop on SDG7: Affordable and Clean Energy,* New Delhi, February 23: TERI and NITI Aayog.

Sharma, Oum Prakash and Poonam Trikha. 2013. Geothermal Energy and its Potential in India.*Renewable Energy, AkshayaUrja:* Ministry of New and Renewable Energy. https://mnre.gov.in/file-manager/akshay-urja/july-august-2013/EN/14-18.pdf.

Singh, Bhupendra Kumar. 2010. *India's Energy Security: Changing Dynamics.* New Delhi: Pentagon Press.

Singh, Hemant K. and Aman R Khanna. 2012. *India's Energy Options: the Road Ahead: an Analysis of the Prospects of Shale Gas in India's Energy Future.* New Delhi: Indian Council for Research on International Economic Relations.

Sinha, Bibhulal. 2015. "*Shale gas in India challenges and opportunities*" Master's thesis. Ljubljana University.

Srivastava, Swami Prakash, and Surat Prakash Srivastava."Solar Energy and its Future Role."*International Journal of Environmental Science: Development and Monitoring* 4(3): 81-88.

Subramanian, T.S. 2003. "Nuclear Safety, The Kalpakkam 'incident'." *Frontline* 20(17): August 16 – 29, 2003.

Sudarshan, Anant and Ligia Noronha. 2009. "Contextualizing India's Energy Security." In *India's Energy Security,* edited by Ligia Noronha, and Anant Sudarshan, 3-8. Abinton, Oxon: Routledge.

TERI (*The Energy and Resources Institute)*. 2017. *Transitions in Indian Electricity Sector 2017–2030.*New Delhi: TERI. http://www.teriin.org/files/transition-report/files/downloads/Transitions-in-Indian-Electricity-Sector_Report.pdf.

Thampi, Simi. 2017. *Access to Clean Cooking for Rural Women: Food for Thought*. NITI Aayog, Government of India. http://niti.gov.in/content/access-clean-cooking-rural-women-food-thought.

The Economic Times. 2018. "India needs 600 MMT refinery capacity by 2040." January 13, 2018.https://economictimes.indiatimes.com/industry/energy/oil-gas/india-needs-600-mmt-refinery-capacity-by-2040-dharmendra-pradhan/articleshow/62487735.cms.

The Telegraph. 2018. "Nuclear capacity to triple by 2031". August 10, 2018. https://www.telegraphindia.com/india/nuclear-capacity-to-triple-by-2031/cid/1216719.

The Times of India. 2018. "India discusses 'Oil Buyers Club' with China; seeks US crude to counter OPEC." June 13, 2018. https://timesofindia.indiatimes.com/business/india-business/india-discusses-oil-buyers-club-with-china-seeks-us-crude-to-counter-opec/articleshow/64575528.cms.

Tiwary R.K, and B.B Dhar.1994. "Effect of coal mining and coal based industrial activities on water quality of the river Damodar with specific reference to heavy metals." *International Journal of Surface Mining, Reclamation and Environment* 8(3): 111-115.

Tripathi, Bhasker. 2018. "Now, India is the third largest electricity producer ahead of Russia, Japan." *Business Standard.* March 26, 2018.

UNDP (United Nations Development Program). (1994). *Human Development report: New Dimensions of Human Security.* Oxford: Oxford University Press.

Waever, Ole.1995. "*Securitization and Desecuritization.* "In *On Security,* edited by Ronnie D. *Lipschutz.46-86. New York: Columbia University Press.*

Wheeler, Deborah. 2011. "Freedom from Want, and Freedom from Fear: A Human Security Approach to a New Middle East?. " *Journal of Human Security* 7(1): 37-52.

Zoback, Mark, Saya Kitasei and Brad Copithorne. 2010. *Addressing the Environmental Risks from Shale Gas Development.* World Watch Institute, Natural Gas and Sustainable Energy Initiative.

Notes

1. This type of mining is prevalent in Northeastern states of India, especially in Meghalaya. Very small tunnels with 3-4 feet diameter and having two types like vertical and horizontal and leading to another pit upto 5-100 m^2. It is a very hazardous method of mining and children are the main workers in these mines.

2. It is largely a surface mining method and the area it is open for the lifetime of the mine.
3. Population growth encourages the resource distribution to the favour of powerful groups in the society. It results in the scarcity of resources for poor people.
4. Land acts as the centre of identity for rural poor and other indigenous communities. Due to its dependence on ecosystem, Gadgil and Guha (1995) called them as ecosystem people.

Chapter - V

India's Sustainable Future: Lessons From Abroad and Prospects of Green Energy Transition

Introduction

Global energy scenario is witnessing a transition from hydrocarbon ridden energy landscape. The climate change impacts and quality of air are the prime reasons to rethink about the present energy order. It does not provide security to the people, environment as well as society. The Paris agreement, 2015 wanted to limit the global temperature rise well below 2^0 C. The carbon emission is the major cause behind the global warning and the major share is coming from the dependency on fossil fuels in the energy mix (Stec and Baraj 2009). The global commons are the main victims of the vulnerabilities of unsustainable energy usage. The environmental concerns and threats are addressed globally in recent decades. The large scale development of renewable energy and technological advancement are the major ways for a sustainable society and environment. Most of the countries are in the pathway of renewable energy transition.

Green Initiatives: Lessons from Abroad

The energy transition is not only the installation of renewable energy systems, but it consists of energy efficiency measures, sustainable urban planning, research and development on renewable energy sources and their business models, technological advancement in storage sector and integration of end use sectors for efficient usage of clean energy. Solar and wind energy systems are standing in the frontline due to its rapid decline of capital cost. But the focus of energy transition in developing countries especially India is still onto the power sector. The end use sectors are crucial in the energy landscape of every nation. Some nations consider these sectors efficiently and help to reduce the emission (Beatley 2012 107-90). Countries like Denmark and Germany provide attention on each sector, including the installation of clean energy technologies.

In the European Union, several countries are adopting clean energy option for their adequate energy supply, low carbon emission and for the sustainable development. In the global level, the EU stands at the forefront of the green energy development. Electricity sector and heating/cooling domestic purposes have the highest percentage of renewables and the EU adopts several measures to green the transport sector as well. Biofuel usage and electric vehicles are growing among the EU countries. Even though, during the industrialization period they were the highest carbon emitters, now they are trying to reduce all kinds of pollution which hamper the nature as well as human being. The developed economic sector as well as technological advancement have been helping them for adopting these clean energy measures, which is a model for all of the countries worldwide. They are using their own energy resources, mostly domestically available, for their energy needs and purposes.

Sufficient research, financial support and the availability of various resources and the initiative from the part of government and the EU are the motivating force behind the development of renewable energy in the European Union. Along with the oil crisis of 1973, geopolitical dimensions and environmental factors together contribute to the rethinking of European nations to begin a sustainable energy approach. The experiences of these nations are influencing the green transition of countries of different parts of the world.

The green transition of energy sector is not a difficult goal for any country and it is the need of the time. Every state undergoes certain changes but some goes beyond that. An overview of the energy transition process in other countries will be useful to assess and evaluate the potential and prospects of the energy landscape of India in a better perspective.

Germany

Germany is one of the major renewable energy countries in the world. *Energiewende*,[6] the policy of transition to low carbon and nuclear free nation, transformed it as a clean energy friendly country. As a nation, it accepted the problems of climate change and the dangers of nuclear energy. Wind and solar are the major green energy sources for the country. The Fukushima disaster in 2011 led to a quick decision to shut down the country's 17 nuclear reactors by 2022. Out of the 17 reactors, 10 have already been closed. Now they discourage new power plants in this sector (World Nuclear Association 2018).

Germany's electricity sector is changing towards a greener future and its share of clean energy is increasing every year. It constitutes 33.3% in 2017 which indicates a growth from 6% in 2000. The renewable energy mix contains wind, hydro, biomass, photovoltaic solar,[1] geo thermal and municipal waste (BMWi 2017). Energy transition is the policy of the country towards a more environmental friendly future. The coalition government with Alliance 90/ The Greens[2] came into power in 1998. The influence of the Greens led to the decision of nuclear phase out of Germany before 2020. However in 2009, the new government cancelled the decision. The civil resistance in 2011 after the Fukushima incident compelled the government reintroduced the Act.

The joint action by the European Union and Germany started in 1997 for a renewable energy scenario. The European Union's Renewable Energy Directive[3] proposed the 12% target by 2010 and Germany achieved it in 2007. The Renewable Energy Sources Act, key policy in the establishment of a well-developed and renewable energy sector of Germany, came into force in 2000. The Renewable Energies Heat Act instructs builders to generate a minimum percentage of their heating needs from their own sources. The Act provides assistance for the existing buildings to establish a heat generating system. In the transport sector, 5.3% of renewable energy is used. Bio Ethanol, biodiesel and biogas are the major bio fuels used in this sector (BMWi 2017) Germany's 90% of domestic consumption of energy comes from heating. So, the government is implementing energy efficiency by supporting the people with CO_2 Building Rehabilitation Programme.[4]

The German *Energiewende* is a guiding line to the world. Economically viable, stable and clean energy is the motive behind this programme. The research and innovation in the field of renewable energy are promoted by the programme. The renewable base electricity generation increased from 36.2 billion kWh of year 2000 to 216.3 billion kWh in 2017 (BMWi 2017). The country has a target of 60% in 2050 for total consumption and 80% for electricity sector. There are also policies to reduce energy consumption through energy efficiency and to promote efficient technologies, industries, buildings etc. Financial support for all these efforts is a major feature for the *Energiewende* programme. Storage is the other factor in energy issues of Germany. The excess energy from wind and solar is being used to split water and the resultant hydrogen is used to produce electricity. Efficient storage options and intelligent power grids are also a part of the German 'energy transition' programme. Around 180 universities and 120 research institutions are contributing for the cause of the country's clean energy scenario (BMBF 2017).

Iceland

Every nation has its own potentials and limitations. Iceland is a geologically and volcanically active country as well as suffered from poverty and colonial rule for a long period. However, the country recognized its potential as geothermal and hydel energy sources for their sustainable development. Renewable sources are contributing to 80% of Iceland's energy needs. Fossil fuels are used in transportation and for industrial purposes. Iceland is a small country with around 3.4 lakhs people, but its 100% electricity comes from renewable sources. Since 1940s it started its geothermal energy usage in a structured manner. The district heating purpose is also completely done by renewable sources. Seasonal meltdowns of glaciers of the country provides hydro sources and active volcanic zones contribute the geothermal power. The increasing oil prices and unstable supply influenced the local farmers to use domestic energy sources. The municipalities, districts and government began to support these initiatives gradually and made effort to build a long term energy infrastructure. They succeeded in their effort and now only the transport sector depends on non-renewable sources (ORKUSTOFNUN[5] 2017). The country hosts the geothermal department of the United Nations for the research of new developments in renewable energy and assists other countries with their practical experiences (MFA Iceland 2018).

The Iceland government provides low interest loans to communities for geothermal development such as for drilling to obtain hot water from underground and there is an option for cost recovery also. The community based hydro projects are also common in Iceland. Large scale development of renewable energy helps to increase the international cooperation and trade. Now the energy intensive industries have been translocating to Iceland for sustainable growth. Hydrogen development is also a major initiative from the part of Iceland. Hydrogen research and experiments are conducted here and a hydrogen fuelling station has also been established here.

Earlier, Iceland was a poor country in Europe depended upon on imported coal and peat for energy requirement. Now it is the only country with 100% electricity consumption from renewable sources. Public willingness, cooperation and support among state government as well as local authorities, and the mutual assistance between people helped to develop community based energy projects. So, the local empowerment and the public participation are key factors in the development of Iceland's energy initiative. Long term perspectives for a better energy alternative of the government from the beginning of the transition period contributed a lot to its energy sector. The government's policies, actions and legal frameworks supported the achievement. Every country has its own resources, but the matter is how it can be utilized by them. Iceland used its opportunity and developed a green energy nation becoming a role model for other countries.

Sweden

Sweden is a leading European Union country in terms of renewable energy usage. Oil crisis was the primary factor behind Sweden's search for alternative energy sources. The country's electricity generation depends on renewable sources by 57% and nuclear sources by 41% (IEA 2017). It implemented energy tax[6] on electricity and fuels and CO_2 taxation[7] since 1991. It has been working for the target of 50% renewable energy by 2020 in the total energy usage and at least 10% achievement in transport sector also. It has comparatively low emission than the higher per capita energy usage countries. The high dependence on nuclear power is a major criticism against Sweden's energy sector. But now they raised the nuclear energy tax, stopped all new nuclear power plants and plans to close the existing plants.

Energy efficiency is another matter of significant for industries and buildings. Even for privately owned buildings, houses or flats, the individual can approach energy advisors and build the home according to expert advice. The growing investment in renewable sector is a vital feature in Sweden's energy landscape. It achieved its 50% renewable energy target in 2012 itself. In almost all the sectors including, electricity, transport and heating the nation maintains a significant proportion of green energy. The transport sector is the only area which is dominated by fossil fuel. However, in 2017 Sweden achieved a 20.8% biofuel used in transport sector. The country used HVO biodiesel which is hydro treated vegetable oil produced from different bio raw materials. As the catalyst hydrogen is used for HVO production instead by methanol, it is cleaner and environment friendly. Green electricity certification[8] is another feature Sweden's energy consumption and it was started since 2003. Research and development in wind energy and ethanol are rapidly growing nowadays. Fossil free transportation by 2030 and heating by 2020 are the main energy policy targets of Sweden. The Green electricity and biofuels have been helping them to achieve its longer term goal of 100% renewable for its total energy usage. The usage of HVO biofuel, tax exemption for biofuel dependent transportation, tax regulation mechanisms and energy efficiency initiatives are the most meritorious achievement for Sweden.

The United Kingdom

Achieving a sustainable future and reducing the carbon emission are significant policy concerns of the United Kingdom like other the EU countries. The dependence on fossil fuel produces disastrous consequence to the nature and increasing foreign dependence. So, the UK is also trying to explore all of its renewable energy resources. The country is using wind, wave, marine, hydro, biomass and solar sources for its clean future and it contributes 20% of its electricity production. In its share of renewable energy (31%), bioenergy (35%), onshore wind (22%), offshore wind (20%), solar PV (19%) and hydro (3.6%) are included (United Kingdom National Statistics 2017). Bioenergy is obtained from different living sources like biodegradable waste, food waste and animal manure and it is used as a source for electricity generation and heat production. Feed in Tariff (FIT)[9] is a good attempt to encourage production of small scale renewable energy in which government pays for every unit of electricity produced and it is transferred back to the public grid. Community energy sector with small scale solar, hydro, wind and biomass technology installations are prevalent in England. However, relatively low financial incentives reduced the growth of this sector. The capacity of this project infrastructure is 121 MW with a production capacity of 265 GWh which is equal to the energy demand of 85, 500 houses (CEE 2017). It enables the groups to invest in other social economic and environmental development programmes of their locality and helps in reducing the environmental degradation.

Micro generation of England's energy sector is a model for every nation. Instead of large scale projects, the energy sector entails small scale, cost effective, low carbon and affordable energy supply. Government provides financial support to the small scale renewable energy production that generates electricity as well as heat for domestic purposes. It is a major initiative in the decentralized energy systems and has solar photovoltaic panels, micro-scale wind turbines, combined heat power[10] (CHP) systems. England achieved the "greenest year ever" in 2017. It announced the clean energy strategy in 2017 with 50 energy efficiency improving measures boosting clean energy steps. It establishes cross sectoral policies for improving the energy efficiency and emission reduction. England is committed to shut down all coal power stations and has a target 1.5 GW by 2025, comparing to the 13.8 GW in 2016. The nation has abundant renewable sources such as wind, wave and tidal and is a major power in the wind energy.

Finland

Finland has the second largest share of renewable energy in the European Union. The country is using bioenergy, more than that of oil, and it is produced from wood, side streams of agriculture, forest, industry, biodegradable waste and municipal waste. Its 80% of electricity is emission less. Finland has achieved its 2020 target of 38% in 2014 itself. Bioenergy contributes 25% of its energy share and the oil contributes only 24%. The country has the plans to increase its share of renewable energy as 50%, complete phase out of coal and reduction of oil by half in 2020. Long cold winter season due to the country's location at the northern part contributes to the large requirement of energy for electricity and heating. Solar thermal systems and small wind turbines are common in households and it sells excess energy to the grid. In 2011, feed in tariff was implemented and small scale renewable energy production was promoted. Energy efficient buildings and support to investments in green initiatives in industries are also major features of energy policy of Finland. The leftover and black liquor are used in heating and electricity purposes. Agricultural residues, field biomass animal manure etc., are utilized in biogas plants. Efficient wood burning practices with clean dry wood is a major factor behind the low emission district and local level heating. Biofuels usage in transport sector is from wastes, wood and agricultural residues and is available in liquid and gaseous forms.

Latvia

Hydroelectric capacity has helped the country to become the highest clean energy producing nation in the world. It has 12400 rivers and 4000 lakes. There is water cooperation with neighbouring countries. Energy efficiency and the promotion of clean energy services are the prime policy features of Latvia. The forest resources contribute a large share of biomass for the energy sector. Investment subsidies, tax credits low interest bank loans etc., are the major measures which support the sector's development. National support schemes for the development of renewable energy programmes are the main cause for this achievement.

Austria

Austria accounts 33.5% renewable energy share in the total primary energy usage and 71.7% in electricity generation. Hydro electric power plants with small scale hydropower stations are the major factor behind the renewable energy development in the country. It is estimated that 36.4% of energy is coming from hydro power. Wood fuels, black liquor, biofuels and biogas together contribute another large share and it is increasing in recent years. Green Energy funding is the main reason behind the Austrian clean energy nature.

Denmark

Denmark achieved 43% of power from wind in 2016 and announced its target which is a 50% usage of renewable energy of total energy needs by 2030. Denmark plans to phase out coal producing electricity before 2030. Government supports all clean energy initiatives with research and finance. The country is trying to reduce coal powered plants and now the energy scenario is driven by bioenergy and wind. Electric powered vehicles with efficiency in all dimensions of transport sectors are important in Denmark. Wind is the major energy source and there are certain wind farms which are owned by several local entrepreneurs to meet their agricultural needs. Stakeholders can get less interest loans and financial support from the part of the government which enables the wide acceptance of the renewable sector. In Denmark, the supply of bioenergy through waste management mechanism is ensured. From agriculture, forest, livestock, households and industry, they collect the raw materials for biomass production.

Norway

Norway possesses the largest number of per capita electric cars with plug in facility. The electricity comes from hydel power. Clean transport sector is a nearby goal for Norway. It is an inspirational initiative from the government side and the buyers are exempted from import tax and VAT for the electric vehicles. The reduction of road tax and low price of electricity are influencing factors for buyers. Government provides a lot of facilities for electric car owners. About 98% of the electricity of Norway comes from renewable sources and hydropower dominates the energy sector.

Table 5.1: Experience in green transition of different countries

Countries	*Green transition experiences*
Germany	Energiewende, comprehensive energy policy Reduction of nuclear energy Wind, Hydro, Biomass, Photovoltaic Solar, geo thermal and municipal waste Green Political Party Building codes to produce heat by renewable and provided with financial assistance (CBRP) Biodiesel from waste, residue and rape seeds Bioethanol

(Contd...)

Iceland	Using of local resources Hydel and geothermal sources Low interest loans are available District heating from renewable Hydrogen research and development Community based energy projects Cooperation among public, government and influence of local level authorities
Sweden	Carbon tax since 1991 Closure of nuclear plants Energy advisors are available for residential and commercial building construction Monitoring and maintaining the green contents in every sectors Green Electricity Certification 20% of transportation depends on Biofuel especially HVO
United Kingdom	wind, wave, marine, hydro, biomass and solar sources Feed in Tariff Community Energy sector Micro generation Decentralised energy system Combined Heat Power Industrial standards, removal of fossil fuel heating, recycling of heat efficiency in buildings, support for homes Green house gas removal technologies charging station development
Finland	Policy to phase out coal and limit by half the usage of oil Significant role of bioenergy, clean burning technologies, use of agriculture residue, animal manure and waste for energy
Latvia	Hydel Efficient biomass usage Investment subsidies, tax credits low interest bank loans
Austria	Green Energy funding
Denmark	Importance of research and finance Effective transport sector, less congestion, efficiency in public transport and rail system, electric and hybrid vehicles, fuel efficiency, green measures in freight sector
Norway	• More electric vehicles, biofuel and hydrogen also used in vehicles • Electric initiatives in aviation sector • LNG in ships • Tax exemption for electric vehicles

India and Energy Transition

India's energy landscape relies heavily on hydrocarbon resources. In the primary energy consumption, renewable constitutes only 6%, that is 4% from hydro projects and 2% from other renewable except nuclear energy (BP 2018). As a developing country, with huge energy demands and complex peculiarities of social and political compulsions, the sustainable transition of India's energy sector, is a difficult option. But to adapt green energy measures is the need of the timc duc to the climate change casualties which are more visible in every part of the world. Sea level rise, melting of the ice, earthquake, strong winds, flood, drought etc., are affecting a lot of people as well as the ecosystem. The natural disasters are directly or indirectly linked to the wrong usage of energy. To reduce the warming 1.5 degree Celsius became imperative for the nations to reduce these calamities. In 2016, India's carbon emission increased by 4.7% than 2015. It is much higher than other heavy emitting countries like the US and China, which was declined by 2% and 0.3% respectively in this year. India has submitted the target to the United Nations Framework Convention (UNFCCC) on Climate Change, to cut down its emission intensity of its GDP by 33 to 35% by 2030 below 2005 level. For this India committed 175 GW of installed renewable capacity by 2022.

In the total energy mix as we understand only 2% is the contribution from renewable other than hydro and nuclear resources. Since 2014 in power sector, the renewables provide 27.07 GW of installed capacity which comprises 12.87 GW from solar power, 11.70 GW from wind 0.59 GW from small hydro and 0.79 from bio power (MNRE 2017). The reduction in tariffs of solar and wind facilitates the growth of the two resources in the energy system. At the same time, the energy demand of the country is also increasing due to its population, urbanization and industrialization. So, in order to curb this energy aspirations, the country need comprehensive energy policy framework.

The renewable energy policies are mainly addressing the power sector which is comparatively easier than others. Nearly 70% of diesel and 99.9% of petroleum are used as fuel for transportation. The transformation of this sector is very difficult and it contributes a heavy part to the energy demand of the country. The high energy consumption sectors are transport and industries. The industrial sector constitutes 45% of energy consumption and the major energy sources used for this purpose are coal, oil and natural gas. Automobile industry has introduced certain electric vehicles, but they are not commercially available. The vehicle manufacturing industry prefers Hybrid Vehicles (HV) than 'plug in Hybrid Electric Vehicles' (PHEV). These vehicles help to increase the energy efficiency but not completely avoiding the fossil fuel consumption. There are no effective policies to change the usage of electricity from thermal power plants in the industrial sector. In residential usage, there is certain policy prescription to reduce or remove traditional biomass ridden cooking fuel to LPG, but that is again leads to fossil fuel dependency. In the residential as well as commercial building sector, the demand of electricity is increasing due to the extreme weather conditions and the growth of electrical appliances.

We need to address the huge energy demand and universal clean energy access with the inclusion of marginalized sections and socio environmental benefits through our energy system. Rapid energy transition is crucial for global as well as national level to cut down the carbon emission and global warming. The planet can no longer tolerate the mistakes committed by the industrialized nations to be repeated again by the developing nations. There are certain innovative policies by the government for energy transition. Yet, the carbon free consumption is a faraway concept for the nation. Installation of renewable energy is not the only aim of energy transition. Emission reduction as well as secure usage of energy sources are also steps to green energy future.

End Use Sectors: Need of Green Reforms

In India, energy transition debates are more or less focused on power sector only. The growth of installed renewable capacity is not only the solution for an energy secure country. Addressing the end use sectors and its problems are the basic necessity for achieving a green future. Adoption of more renewable sources and energy efficiency are the key factors to reduce the environmental impact of current energy usages. Now we have a lot of opportunities to reduce the problems of the current end use sectors of energy in India. There are barriers like financial weakness, less awareness and lack of strong policies. In spite of it, rectification of the mistake which we have committed earlier is a necessary obligation towards the future generation.

The sustainable planning will help to improve the transport, agriculture, industrial and building sectors to implement the environmental friendly options. Government should take steps to provide effective and reliable supply of raw material for the production of energy through effective planning. Burning of agriculture residue is a problem affecting air quality and human health. Nevertheless, industries can use this residue for energy production and they can avoid all fossil fuel usages. Another significant hydrocarbon dependent is transport sector. The urban planning and usage of public transportation will improve the energy efficiency. So, the sector wise clean energy initiatives and the integration of the policies are the ways for energy security of the nation.

Building Sector

The building sector includes residential as well as commercial constructions which consumes significant share of energy. It was 41% in 2013 and used 214 Mtoe of 527 Mtoe of total energy consumption (EIA 2015). In this sector, only a few of them are energy efficient or using renewable energy for the various requirements. The growing urban population, rising income and lifestyle changes, increase the energy needs in urban areas. The environmental damages necessitates to rethink about the energy efficiency measures and green effort to improve buildings of commercial sector. Here, the consumption of electricity shares by lighting (59%) air conditioning (31%) and others (10%). In residential sector, fans (34%) and air conditioning (7%) together contribute largest share and lighting (28%), refrigeration (13%) others (18%) etc., constitutes the remaining (BEE 2017). Energy Conservation Building Codes (ECBC)[11] has stablished standards for building, lighting, ventilation, air condition, solar water heating and other electrical equipment. Energy efficient buildings can reduce the unwanted consumption of energy through the usage of daylight, controlled ventilation, shading and renewable energy usage. Daylight consumption is an effective method for residential as well as commercial buildings.

Thermal comfort is affecting daily productivity of every human being. But a large section of people has no access for this opportunity. The energy intensity of individual air conditioning is very heavy and causes carbon emission. Energy efficient buildings with usage of clean energy can maintain the thermal comfort. In cooling, water can be the major resource of energy. The Infosys building at Pocharam, Hyderabad provides an example regarding this and it reduces 56% of energy consumption (GRIHA 2012). The sustainable site planning and high performance building with solar passive principle[12] help to save energy. It uses maximum daylight for the work from 8 am to 5 pm. The smart building system ensures the indoor air quality. The windows are designed by efficient glazing and shading to reduce heat and avoid glare of delight. The building is divided into two halves, the traditional air conditioning is used in one half and the other is utilized radiant cooling[13] method. The chilled water flows through pipes installed in walls, roofs and floors. It cools the entire building and reduces the energy consumption by 50% compared to 2007-08 level. The capital cost also lower than the convention systems (Sastry 2012).

District heating[14] and cooling options are also available across different parts of the world. The capital intensive cooling and heating technologies can be implemented through centralized system. Urban areas and its commercial as well as residential sectors can be managed through district heating and cooling methods. India's climatic conditions do not require huge heating mechanisms. But the district or local level energy systems or heat pumps[15] can provide adequate energy according to the local atmosphere. Municipal solid waste (MSW)and other combustible waste, electricity and geothermal energy can be used in heating of this sector. Copenhagen and

Rotterdam adopted the recycle mechanism of waste management to replace oil consumption. Biogas plant, bagasse co-generation,[16] solid biomass boilers and solar heat pumps can be used in building's thermal comfort purposes.

As a hot country India needs efficient cooling mechanisms in most of the days in a year. Electric chillers are used in Doha and Paris, cold water from water bodies and industrial waste water can be used in district cooling mechanism. Lake Ontario provides Toronto's cooling system and deep sea water is used in Port Louis's commercial buildings. Absorption chillers are used in London's new Olympic Park. Sweden, Finland, Latvia, Estonia, Lithuania and Denmark are using biomass for its heating requirement. Iceland uses geothermal energy and meets 92% of residential heat demand. Biomass and municipal solid waste treatment plants help the heating requirement of industries and buildings in Sweden (REN 21 2017). Demand of heat for industries, hot water and space cooling is increasing in India. The sugar residues of India can provide fuel for this and satisfy the industrial heat requirement. Solar water heater can provide hot water to the industries, commercial buildings and residents.

Water pumping is another energy consuming services in the building sector. Hydro-pneumatic pumping system[17] or gravity based water distribution system[18] and clean energy usage are helpful for this area. LED bulbs and daylight consumption are workable for lighting part. Occupancy sensors can reduce the energy consumption in huge buildings. Energy options are available for lift mechanism also. Inefficient fuels are common in cooking sector, especially in rural area. Firewood, wood chips, cow dung, coal and kerosene are in use because of its cheap availability. Large scale cooking also uses traditional biomass and LPG. House hold usage creates indoor air pollution and the LPG has problems from the time of extraction to the period of consumption. In household sector, most of the traditional fuel usage has changed to LPG, but they still use unsustainable energy sources as their primary or secondary fuel for cooking. Though LPG and natural gas contribute less carbon emission, we cannot ignore their environmental impacts. In urban areas LPG, electricity and natural gas are common in kitchen. The usages of electrical appliances are more convenient, easy to use and time saving.

But the cost of appliances and the electricity are not affordable for the large section of people. So, the traditional biomass cantered cooking is common in urban and local area. The awareness about indoor air pollution and carbon emission are very weak among rural people. They opt LPG due to the unavailability and inconveniences of old fuel sources. But the cost of

LPG and electricity is a cause of concern for them. The improved biomass cook stoves and local biogas plants are better options to overcome these issues (Tyner 2012). The localized energy plants with wind, solar and biomass is the only remedy for that. These plants can use locally and ecologically feasible energy sources. Only 1% of the rural households adopt improved cook stores since 2000 and the free gas connection also faces affordability issues and usage practices (Niti Aayog 2011). So, a strategic and long term perspective is necessary for the clean cooking sector.

The residential sector dramatically changed in recent decades. The kerosene usage for lighting purpose in rural areas has almost changed to electric bulbs. Due to the climatic conditions, the use of cooling equipment increased recently. There is visible growth in electric appliances in residential as well as commercial buildings. So the planning in construction sector is imperative for the sustainable well being of the society. District, municipal as well as local level renewable energy plants can provide clean energy for the particular locality. District level heating and cooling options are good for urban development.

Table 5.2: Renewable Options for Building

End use	*Methods*	*Resources*	*Implemented places*	*Options for India*
Thermal Comfort	District heating	Biomass	Rotterdam, Finland	District heating and cooling for major cities
		Municipal solid waste	Sweden Copenhagen	
		Geothermal	Iceland	
		Excess heat from industries, commercial buildings CHP[1]		Radiant cooling for commercial buildings
	District cooling	Electric chillers	Doha	Biogas plant bagasse co-generation solid biomass boilers heat pumps (electric, solar, geothermal) Solar water heater
	heating individual buildings	Biogas plant, bagasse co-generation solid biomass boilers and solar heat pumps Solar water heater	common	
	Radiant cooling	Chilled water	Infosys building, Hyderabad	
Energy efficiency	Building efficiency codes Efficient appliances	Policy Measures	EU member countries	Improve the present efficiency measures Implement without delay

(*Contd...*)

Electric purposes	Renewable electricity	Stand alone Micro Grid Mini Grid Public grid	
Water pumping	Renewable electricity Technologies	Hydro-pneumatic pumping system gravity based storage system clean energy usage	
Lighting	Renewable electricity Efficiency measures	LED Daylight consumption Occupancy sensers	
cooking	Technologies	Improved cook stoves Solar cooker Biogas (individual or community based) Renewable electricity (stand alone, mini, micro or public grid	

Transport Sector

Transport is a major energy consuming sector in India. Effective planning and implementation with strong political will can change this fast growing end use sector to a sustainable one. It is the second largest energy consumer and produce environmental pollution mainly through carbon emission. The sector needs comprehensive policy instruments for the sustainable development. Efficiency of vehicles, introduction of EVS, charging facilities, clean electricity production, research and development of clean fuels, improved public transport system and urban planning are necessary for the green future of transport sector. The roads, rails, air and waterways in the Indian transport sector depend on fossil fuels. In global level also, only 3.1% uses renewable energy in this sector. The main challenge of India's energy sector is import dependence and which mainly comes from petroleum products. The transport sector consumes its major share and the transition of this sector towards green will reduce the import dependency of the country and would enhance the economy.

However, the implementation of this green energy transition in transport sector is more difficult than others. Nevertheless, it can change slowly by certain initiative from the part of government as well as society. The UK and France introduced purchase incentives[19] for electric vehicles. The United States offers tax credits to certain vehicles. Germany provides incentives for EVs and allocates a fixed amount in the budget. Norway gives subsidies and Estonia provides fast charging facilities to the citizens (Shakti Sustainable Energy Foundation 2017). In India, the electric and biofuel vehicles are less and the fossil fuel based automobile industry is growing rapidly. Most of the electric cars would be HEV or PHEV due to the preference by the automobile industry. The availability of charging facilities, components and the cost are not favourable for electric vehicles currently. So, there is a significant need for centralized policy decisions.

Urban and rural level planning is an important step for energy efficiency in transport sector. There must be space for pedestrians as well as bicycles. Efficient and sophisticated public transport systems are suitable for poorer sections, students as well as various sections of the society. Efficient taxi system can reduce the use of private vehicles. There is a need to connect all the roads with sophisticated transport mechanism. Traffic congestion and huge number of vehicles are another problem in the efficiency measures of transport system. In the 1970s, Singapore faced this situation and now it manages efficiently the public transportation system. The cost of ownership of vehicles is high in Singapore and the state encourages the use of public transport, walking and cycling (MOT Singapore 2018). The country improves the rail network and bus service more people centred. It improves the balance of quality, affordability and profitability of transportation.

Reduced vehicle transport, enough parking facility, effective traffic management etc., are essential factors in the urban planning. The poor freight management and the inefficient or old vehicles create another problem. Indonesia has accomplished a good model for this (UNCTAD 2015). They strengthened their rail road and marine transport system. Traffic information system is also transparent and easily available in certain countries. The old vehicles with no environmental certificates are prohibited in some cities of the EU and Tokyo. China also introduced Green Freight initiative which shows the energy efficiency measures have huge power to reduce the carbon emission. They coordinated it with national and sub national governments. They adopted various cleaner technologies and provide loan facilities to change the vehicle as energy efficient (Reja 2016). The transportation of goods and service delivery are the backbone of the economy. But the reduction of associated environmental impacts is the necessary step to improve human health. So, effective freight management with efficient carriers, mode of transport and operational strategy will help to advance this sector (US Environmental Protection Agency 2004). The US government connected environmental protection agency with freight industry including trucks, trains, flights and ships. The government has ensured the availability of fuel efficient technologies in the market and the collaboration of national as well as international organizations to the project.

Transformation of railway from diesel to electricity is easier than other transportation sectors. India has made the plan to electrify the railway sector by 2022. In the Netherlands, all electric train consume clean energy from wind mills. In Australia, fully solar powered trains proved its efficiency. India also introduced solar powered train coaches, which can provide power to air conditioners, fans, lights etc. Guwahati provides a successful story for solar equipped railway stations. Sophisticated railway mechanism can reduce road transport as well.

Renewable energy adoption in transport sector is based on the willingness of political leadership and effective policies. There are several examples worldwide to show how successfully green energy can be used even in aviation and shipping sector. The third largest ferry service in the world runs on a blended biodiesel fuel which is Washington Department of Energy Efficiency 2013). In aviation field, 1700 commercial flights are using sustainable aviation fuels and are willing to reduce the emissions. The technologies are at the beginning stage in global level also. But the aviation sector is ready to adopt easily the green technology than road transport. Nowadays the airports are tearing towards clean energy. Cochin International Airport functions with 100% renewable energy. It is the fourth largest in India and it meets its whole power requirement through solar. The cost of construction can maintain by 5 years and it has 25 years of life expectancy. The 20 year period is the savings to the airport authority and the environment. Urban and local level planning, research on clean energy technologies and batteries, and maintaining the energy efficiency are the main factors for this sector. The changes in the energy mix, the consumer behaviour and policy developments are also influencing the green transport. Solar powered electricity can change the sector to a clean future.

Table 5.3: Sustainable options for transport sector

<table>
<tr><th>Mode of transport</th><th colspan="2">Options</th></tr>
<tr><td rowspan="2">Road</td><td>Efficiency</td><td>Fuel efficiency
Vehicle efficiency</td></tr>
<tr><td>Efficient transport system</td><td>Urban Planning
Foot path
Cycle Path
Mass transit system
Reduce traffic congestion
Public transportation system</td></tr>
<tr><td></td><td>Fuel</td><td>Biofuel
Blended biofuel
Ethanol
Hydrogen
electricity</td></tr>
<tr><td>Rail</td><td colspan="2">Renewable electricity</td></tr>
<tr><td>Ship and Aviation</td><td colspan="2">Biofuels, electricity (developing stage)</td></tr>
</table>

Industrial Sector

The industrial sector consumes 40% of oil. But biomass, solar, geothermal and heat energy will be good options for future clean energy scenario in the industrial sector. The heat generation demand of this sector can be mainly addressed by biomass. However, the availability is still very low. Steam is largely produced from coal but biomass like wood waste, rice husk, wood chips, coconut shell etc. can be used in steam production. Biomass can be used with charcoal and coal consumption can be reduced. In medium and low applications, solar thermal can provide results. Heat pumps make heat from various sources and geothermal energy is used for low temperature purposes. The huge electricity demand from industrial sector should be addressed by renewable (IRENA 2014).

The efficient and continuous functioning of industries is necessary for the development of every nation. The industrial sector of India constitutes steel (29%) brick (19%), chemicals (14%), sugar (5%), cement (6%), aluminium (2%), textile (4%), paper (1%) and others (29%). The steel, bricks and cement industries itself shares 45% of the sector and mostly run by coal. Natural gas, oil and biomass are used in chemical, cement, aluminium and steel industries. They are large scale industries and energy efficiency policies are implemented here. But the small scale industries are still out of the policy purview. Being energy efficiency measures are at the beginning stage in India, the clean energy usage needs a great effort from the government and the society. Large scale industries adopted the Energy Conservation Act 2012 in their operation.

Biomass is a viable option for industrial sector if we can ensure the availability. Netherlands and Finland are already using the technologies for their renewable progress (Vesterinenet et al. 2010). Sectors like fertilizer, cement, aluminium can utilize the facilities of biomass. The methods of combustion and gasification of biomass can be used in this sector.

Heat pumps are other source of energy which is operating with the help of electricity, solar or geothermal. Solar energy devices also can enhance the energy efficiency of the industrial sector. The pressurized hot water steam or hot air is the main requirement for the industrial sector. The solar water heating has successful background in India from Godavari Fertilizer and Chemical Ltd and Textile factory of Gorgon. Normal water heating mechanism can raise water temperature from 25^0C to 85^0C. Solar air heating with plate collectors is used in food, leather, textile, chemicals, rubber, paper and pharmaceutical industries. Solar concentrated technologies are available in two types. The one provides low temperature steam comparing with the other in between 120^0 C -200^0 C and the other gives up to 300^0 C which is the maximum requirement of industries. Shirdi Community Kitchen in Maharashtra is fully operationalised by solar cooking system. Food and cleaning industry can adopt solar technology (MNRE 2017). The initial capital cost and high payback period are the main barriers. But the government's policies and the subsidized loan can promote the renewable technologies for the industrial sector.

Agriculture

India's 10% people depend on agricultural income. The increased mechanization of the sector contributes to the food security, but affects the energy requirement of nation. The good quality power supply is necessary for the satisfaction of the food security of increasing population. Tractor and power tillers (49.29%), diesel engines (16.76%) and electric motors together contribute to the energy consumption of this sector in 2013. Agriculture sector used 15% of total diesel and 18% of total electricity for pumps and tractors which consumed 237 GWh energy in 2012. Meanwhile, it is estimated that 728 TWh is needed in 2040 (Niti Aayog 2017). The subsidized rates of electricity and less energy efficiency are the other problems (EIA 2015). So, localized planning and green energy implementation will be helpful for solving the problems.

Even though agricultural sector consumes a considerable share of energy, it can contribute to bioenergy for various purposes. Ethanol and soya bean oil are also produced by agricultural sector which are useful as energy resources. Agriculture residue has the potential of producing biodiesel, bagasse, ethanol etc. India's sugar industry is the second largest after Brazil and it can produce ethanol and bagasse cogeneration. Ethanol is a by-product of sugar industry. Some crops are used for biomass production such as corn, sugarcane, Napier grass, sorghums etc. Some others like agricultural residue of rice, wheat maize, cotton, pulses, oilseeds sugarcane are burnt in the field itself. Energy crops needs low investment and maintenance and hence it will be profitable for farmers also.

The availability of biomass throughout the year is the basic problem regarding this sector. In India the bioenergy is totally depended on sugarcane industry only. The large number of small scale farmers is a barrier for the biomass supply to the power plant. The collection and transportation costs are the biggest challenges in India for the development of the sector. For the reliable supply, we can adopt decentralised collection centres for two or three villages and grow energy crops like bamboo or Napier grass.

As a result of the recent climatic conditions, more field irrigation is required. Therefore, it consumes huge electricity as well as diesel. Solar pumps are an ideal substitute for the irrigation needs of the farmers. Option for selling to the public grid can reduce the wastage of electricity. But the initial cost is the only hindrance to implement the technology widely. Now government provides subsidies to solar pump sets. Solar powered bore wells are also available in market. Solar solutions can manage the entire purpose of agriculture. We can use it in a combined way also. Solar, wind and biomass are locally available for agriculture farms according to the climatic conditions. So, it can be utilized through decentralised power plant.

Power Sector

The new green approach increases the demand of electricity. Public consumption of electricity is increased due to modern equipment. Now the country is solving the issue of accessibility problem. Certain sectors are shifting to electrification from direct hydrocarbon usage, like railways. Now there is a task to change our hydrocarbon dependent power plants to cleaner fuel. Energy efficiency is the first and foremost need of this sector. Energy loss and theft etc., are common in Indian electricity grid. Transmission and distribution loss consist around 21% in every year. In 2007-08, the loss was 1,87,513 GWh of total 6,77,095 GWh which is around 27%. In 2016 - 17 the loss increased up to 2,48,834 GWh which is 21.30% of the total generated electricity of 11,51,971 GWh (Energy Statistics 2018). So there is a need of planned investment in transmission and distribution sectors. Updating and rectification of damaged parts are necessary for the energy efficiency. Reliability of power supply is another problem and even in the time of peak demand, it cannot provide adequate supply to the consumers.

In remote areas, we need mini grid as well as off grid development. It can satisfy through renewable energy. For the public grid and mini grid, a transparent as well as efficient auctioning is necessary. Introduction of regulatory mechanism can avoid power theft and non-payment. It can update and repair the infrastructure individually or through social enterprises or private investors by taking up the local power plants through auction. So the development of renewable power in huge quantity is significant for the country. We have solar, wind, biomass, geothermal, tidal and oceanic energy sources. However, the renewable energy constitutes only around 20% of total installed capacity. Therefore, the sector wise green energy initiatives are need of the hour.

Brazil is the third largest nation in renewable energy development and its 64.7% of installed capacity depends on hydropower due to abundant water resources. But it focuses on biomass, wind and solar due to the risks associated with hydropower. The sugarcane industry and the solid waste contribute to the significant development of biomass power. It has more than 350 GW wind power installed capacity also. So the renewable energy depends on the local circumstances. The better business models with locally available resources and capital cost can change present energy condition of India. The effective policies with carbon tax, subsidised loans and other incentives can build the sustainable future. It can implement through national as well as local level. Japan increased their renewable power through several community level projects.

Standalone energy systems can also satisfy the electricity needs of several sectors. India adopted certain policies for the development of clean energy and achieved around 80 GW (MNRE 2018). West Bengal Renewable Energy Development Agency (WBREDA) made community based renewable solutions in the Sundarbans region. It consists of 23 mini grids and now they are using wind, solar and biomass sources. Chhattisgarh implemented mini grid with cluster approach. Each cluster contains more than 10 villages with technicians and operators for maintenance (Halff et al. 2014). Mini grids are the most cost effective and adaptable for the local area by available resources. Namibia (Solar and Biomass), Zimbabwe (Solar and Hydro), Brazil (Solar and Hydro) and China (wind and solar) have already installed mini grids successfully for the electrification of not reachable areas (REN 21 2014).

Table 5.4: Sustainable options for Industrial, Power and Agricultural Sector

Purposes	*Options*
Industrial Sector	
Biomass, solar and geothermal technologies for heating reqluirement	Blending coal with biofuel Solar thermal Heat pumps solar and geothermal Solar water heating Solar air heating Solar heating technologies for Up to 300 C heating requirements
Renewable electricity for electric purposes	Solar Biomass Wind farms Hybrid Individual and Cooperative ownership of micro or mini renewable power plants Public grid
Efficiency	Energy Efficiency Policies
Agriculture	
Pumping	Solar pumps

(*Contd...*)

Irrigation	Solar powered bore well
Renewable electricity	Install wind mills, solar plants in farmland Plant energy crops in barren land Use agricultural residue and animal manure for biomass Individual, private or cooperative management of single or hybrid renewable farms

The green initiatives of all sectors together contribute the growth of electricity sector. The electrically powered vehicles including buses, trucks, cars, two wheelers, rail, flights etc., need more electricity. As far as building sector is concerned, lightening, heating, cooling, cleaning and cooking increase the electricity demand. Industrial and agricultural technologies also enhance the electricity consumption. Sector coupling[20] is a viable option to reduce the electricity needs for the entire energy structure.

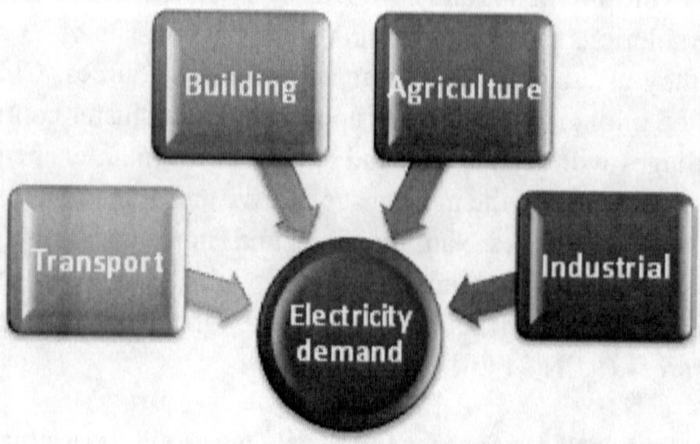

Renewable energy is not only the option for emission free future, but also it ensures energy access and enhances the standard of living of all sections of the society and leads to a sustainable future. The most suitable energy resource is solar for India due its availability of abundant sunny days. Now there are a lot of technologies to adopt profitably. In the case of wind energy, the state of Tamil Nadu produces more wind energy than Denmark and Sweden. Abundant agriculture residue, solid biomass waste and energy crops can play a major role in biomass power. Enormous hydro power, untapped geothermal power, and tidal and hydrogen energy sources are there for the clean power production. Financial support and extensive research are needed for the development of this sector.

India: Green Energy Initiatives

India has an estimated potential of around 1000 GW of renewable power from commercially exploitable sources including solar (649 GW), bioenergy

(25 GW), wind (302 GW), small hydro (21 GW) and others (Energy Statistics, 2018). Solar is the largest source of energy which contributes 65%, followed by wind (30%), small hydro (2%) and others contributes 3%. The other 3% consists of biomass power, cogeneration bagasse and waste to energy. The states of Rajasthan, Gujarat, Maharashtra and Jammu and Kashmir have more potential renewable than other states. But in the installed capacity, Tamil Nadu (10,625 MW), Maharashtra (7648 MW), Karnataka (7458 MW), Gujarat (6672 MW), Rajasthan (6238 MW) and Andhra Pradesh (6,164 MW) are the leading states (Niti Aayog 2017). The cumulative renewable energy capacity increased from 35500 MW to 70000 MW in 2017. India is a growing country as far as of installed renewable power is concerned, with a status of 4th in wind power, 6th in solar power and 5th in total renewable power.

India is the third largest GHG emitter and energy consumer in the world. The usage of energy is the significant part of GHG emission. So it is high time to green the energy usage of India. Renewable energy and sustainable energy usage in every end use sectors and energy efficiency are the only way to reduce the emission as well as pollution to the environment. So, India is aiming to achieve 175 GW installed renewable capacity by 2022. It constitutes 100 GW solar, 60 GW wind and 15 GW biogas.

Solar Energy

The solar energy is the most growing renewable energy sector of India. The installed capacity is increased from 2630 MW to 22000 MW in between 2013 to 2017. The reduction of tariff and transparent bidding reduced the per unit cost of solar power from Rs. 6.17 to Rs. 2.44 and wind power from Rs. 4.2 to Rs. 2.4. The country has installed 40 solar parks and produces around 30 GW power. Kurnool Solar Park, situated in Andhra Pradesh, is the largest solar park in the world. Lack of awareness is the major barrier to the solar deployment. Under KUSUM scheme government planned to provide 27 lakhs solar pumps and small scale power plants. The shared infrastructure for solar project provides loans to the states for installing solar parks.

Schemes under rural electrification programme (2006) promoted different solar projects. The scheme provided solar lanterns and solar pumps. It promoted the home lighting, street lighting and solar home systems. As part of National Action plan on climate change, government introduced the Jawaharlal Nehru National Solar Mission Scheme in 2010. Earlier the target was 20GW by 2022, but the Narendra Modi Government increased its target to 100GW by 2022. It includes large scale, medium and connected projects and rooftop schemes (Rachit & Vinod 2016). The solar rooftop scheme can use vacant rooftops on commercial as well as residential buildings. It can avoid energy loss in terms of transmission, distribution as well as technical flaws (MNRE 2017). SRISTI scheme gives opportunity to access subsidies for installing rooftop solar plants.

Solar energy is the most potential resource for India. However, the usage of this resource is very limited till now. In India, almost the total consumption of electricity comes from public grid. Lack of awareness and burden of huge capital cost are the barriers for transformation.

Wind Energy

Though, India has a potential of 302 GW wind source above 100 m from ground level and now we have only 32 GW installed capacity. MNRE has 794 wind monitoring stations all over India. And now it plans to install 1000 MW in the coast of Gujarat. Tamil Nadu, Andhra Pradesh, Karnataka, Kerala, Madhya Pradesh and Maharashtra have significant potential of renewable energy. Some states are producing more electricity than Denmark and Sweden. India plans to install 60 GW of wind power by 2022 The Electricity Act 2003 announced 'Renewable Purchase Obligation.'[21] The tariff also reduced in last decade, but the wind potential states are less integrated with the interstate transmission lines and it needs policy formulations. The Ministry of Power waived the Interstate Transmission System (ISTS) charge in 2016. Green Energy Corridor Project with the cooperation of Germany provides funds for synchronizing solar and wind power with public grid. The resources are available in limited places and the voltage fluctuation at the time of integration needs a comprehensive investment scheme.

Biomass

There are 288 biomass and cogeneration projects and 158 bagasse cogeneration projects in India. Several financial incentives are available for biomass projects including accelerated depreciation[22] and tax holidays for certain period. For starting biomass projects, government provides loans to the beneficiaries (MNRE 2016). Maharashtra, Uttar Pradesh and Karnataka have grid connected biomass installed power. But still it lacks continuous supply and modern equipment (Seth et al. 2015). The present industrial and domestic waste can be utilized as energy source. In 2016-17, India had 115 MW installed capacity from this sector. Andhra Pradesh, Maharashtra, Delhi and Punjab are the major contributors.

In the case of ocean energy, biofuels and geothermal energy, India has enormous potential and research programmes are under progress. Similarly, research, development and demonstration projects are undertaken to explore the possibilities of hydrogen as the fuel of the future.

End Use Sectors and Energy Transition

The smart city mission of government supports urban planning and sustainable environment. It promotes renewable sources of energy and green buildings. Atal Mission for Rejuvenation and Urban Transformation supports pedestrians, bicycles, public transports and parking facility. HRIDAY (Heritage City Development and Augmentation) plan also plans to improve the urban life. Swachh Bharat Mission is linked with waste management.

In automobile sector, the Draft National Automotive Policy 2018 proposes clear emission standards for future vehicles. India has adopted National Electric Mobility Mission Plan (NEMMP) 2020 to promote hybrid and electric vehicles. GUTS 2017 (Green Urban Transport Scheme) promotes the shift to usages of hybrid/electric and non-fossil fuels for public transport by setting up public bike sharing, bus rapid transit programme, intelligent transport system, urban freight management etc., (NITI Aayog and BCG 2018). UJALA Scheme replaces the old lighting infrastructure with new LED bulbs and the Ministry of Power implemented a star rating labelling system for electrical appliances, including air conditioners, refrigerators etc. The energy conservation Building Codes 2017 encourages the energy saving measures and integration of clean energy sources for buildings. However, the energy efficiency measures as well as new sustainable developments are only at the beginning stage in India

The sustainable solutions for India's energy landscape are not a far away concept. There are effective solutions in all walks of life to transform a better green future. There is a huge potential for clean sources of energy like solar, wind and biomass in India. We can also learn and apply lessons from the green initiatives of other countries.

Reference

Arora, Rajat. 2017. "India to be first in world to run all government ports on green energy." *Economic Times,* May 31, 2017. https://economictimes.indiatimes.com/industry/transportation/shipping-/-transport/india-to-be-first-in-world-to-run-all-government-ports-on-green-energy/articleshow/58917369.cms.

Beatley, Timothy. 2012. *Green Urbanism: Learning from European Cities*. Washington D.C. Island Press.

BEE (Bureau of Energy Efficiency). (2017). *Energy Conservation Building Code*.Ministry of Power, Government of India. http://www.aeee.in/wp-content/uploads/2017/05/ECBC-presentation-by-BEE.pdf.

BEE (Bureau of Energy Efficiency).2018. *Energy Conservation Building Code Rules 2019*.Ministry of Power, Government of India. https://beeindia.gov.in/news-events/energy-conservation-building-code-rules-2018.

BMBF (Federal Ministry of Education and Research). 2017. "German Energy Transition." Accessed May 18, 2018. https://www.bmbf.de/en/german-energy-transition-2319.html

BMWi (Federal Ministry for Economic Affairs and Energy). 2017. "The Renewable Energy." Accessed April 13, 2018. https://www.bmwi.de/ Redaktion/EN/Dossier/renewable-energy. html.

CEE (Community Energy in England). 2017. *Community Energy State of The Sector: A study of community energy in England, Wales and Northern Ireland*. https://communityenergyengland.org/files/document/51/1499 247266 Community Energy-State of the Sector Report. pdf.

EUEI PDF (European Union Energy Initiative Partnership Dialogue Facility). 2014. *Mini Grid Policy Toolkit: Policy and Business Framework for Successful Mini Grid Roll outs*.http://www.ren21.net/Portals/ 0/documents/Resources/MGT/MinigridPolicyToolkit Sep 2014 EN.pdf.

Gils, Hans Christian, Sonja Simon, and Rafael Soria. 2017. "100% Renewable Energy Supply for Brazil—the Role of Sector Coupling and Regional Development." *Energies* 10 (11): 1859.

GRIHA (Green Rating for Integrated Habitat Assessment) n.d "Infosys Green Building: GRIHA." Accessed March 15, 2018. http://www.grihaindia.org/images/casestudies/pdf/Infosys-hyderabad.pdf.

Halff, Antoine, Benjamin K Sovacool, and Jon Rozhon. 2014. Energy Poverty*: Global Challenges and Local Solutions.*Oxford: Oxford University Press.

IEA (International Energy Agency). 2015. "*India Energy Outlook: World Energy Outlook Special Report.*" Accessed July 1, 2018. https://www.iea.org/publications/freepublications/publication/IndiaEnergyOutlook WEO2015.pdf.

IEA (International Energy Agency). 2017. *World Energy Outlook 2017*. https://www.iea.org/weo2017/.

Infosys. n.d. "Commercial radiant cooled building: A first in India."Accessed April 24, 2018.https://www.infosys.com/ newsroom/features/ Pages/commercial-radiant-cooling-building.aspx.

IRENA (International Renewable Energy Agency). 2015. *Off-Grid Renewable Energy Solutions, Global and Regional Status and Trends*. https://www.irena.org/-/media/Files/IRENA/Agency/Publication/2018/ Jul/IRENA Off-grid RE Solutions 2018. pdf.

Mehndiratta, Shomik, Zhi Liu, and Ke Fang. 2012. "Motorized Vehicles: Demand Management and Technology." In *Sustainable Low-Carbon City Development in China,* edited by Axel Baeumler, Ede Ijjasz-Vasquez, and Shomik Mehndiratta, 299-322. Washington DC: World Bank.

MFA (Ministry of Foreign Affairs Iceland 2018).*Icelandic Foreign Affairs 2018.*https://www.government.is/library/01-Ministries/Ministry-for-Foreign-Affairs/PDF-skjol/MFA%20-%20Icelandic%20Foreign%20 Affairs%202018.pdf.

MNRE (Ministry of New and Renewable Energy). 2017. *Year End Review 2017.* New Delhi: Press Information Bureau, MNRE, Government of India.

MOT (Ministry of Motor Transport Singapore).n.d. "Infographics."Accessed April 9, 2018.https://www.mot.gov.sg/transport-matters/motoring/ infographics.

NITI Aayog and BCG (NITI Aayog and the Boston Consulting Group). 2018. *Transforming India's Mobility: A perspective.* http://niti.gov.in/ writereaddata/ files/ document_publication/BCG.pdf.

NRDC (National Resource Defense Council). 2017. *The Road from Paris: India's Progress toward its Climate Pledge.* https://www.nrdc.org/ sites/default/files/ paris-climate-conference-India-IB.pdf.

ORKUSTOFNUN. 2017. *Energy Statistics in Iceland 2017.* https://orkustofnun.is/ gogn/os-onnur-rit/Orkutolur-2017-enska-A4.pdf.

Philibert, Cédric. 2017. *Renewable Energy for Industry From green energy to green materials and fuels.* International Energy Agency. https://www.iea.org/ publications/insights/insightpublications/Renewable_Energy_for_Industry.pdf.

*Pinna,*Ivano, Bruno *dalla Chiara*, and K. Pant. 2014. "Energy used by transport systems in India: the role of the urban population, sources, alternative modes and quantitative analyses." *Energy Production and Management in the 21st Century.*1: 661-675.WIT Press.

Reja, Binyam. 2016.*China's Green Freight Initiative.*Conference Report, Busan: South Korea..The World Bank Group.http://cleanairasia.org/wp-content/uploads/2016/ 09/03 Binyam-Reja World-Bank1.pdf.

REN 21(Renewable Energy Policy Network for the 21st Century). 2018. *Renewables 2018 Global Status Report.* http://www.ren21.net/wp-content/uploads/2018/06/ 17-8652 GSR2018 Full Report web final.pdf.

REN 21(Renewable Energy Policy Network for the 21st Century). 2018. *Distributed Renewables for Energy Access.* http://www.ren21.net/gsr-2018/chapters/chapter 04/chapter 04/.

Sagebiel, Julian, Christian Kimmich, Malte Muller, Markus Hanisch and Vivek Gilani, ed. 2016."Background of the Agricultural Power Supply Situation in India and Andhra Pradesh."*In Enhancing Energy Efficiency in Irrigation A Socio-Technical Approach in South India,* edited by Sagebiel Julian, Christian Kimmich, Malte Muller, Markus Hanisch and Vivek Gilani 7-17. Washington DC: Springer.

Sastry, Guruprakash. Integrated Design Approach Question all assumptions 2011."Accessed April 23, 2018.http://www.grihaindia.org/images/ casestudies/ pdf/Infosys-hyderabad.pdf.

Sastry, Guruprakash. n. d. "First Radiant Cooled Commercial Building in India – Critical Analysis of Energy, Comfort and Cost. Green Initiatives Infosys Limited." Bangalore, India. Accessed April 23, 2018. http://portal.aeecenter.org/files/ newsletters/ESMS/Sastry.pdf.

Seth, Rahul, Rohit Seth and ShrishBajpai.2015. "Need of Biomass Energy in India." *Progress in Science and Engineering Research Journal* 3(2) March-April:013-17.

Shakthi Sustainable Energy Foundation. 2017. *Thermal comfort for all. Sustainable and Smart Space cooling.*https://shaktifoundation.in/wp-content/uploads/2017/09/Brochure-Thermal-Comfort-For-All.pdf.

Stec, Stephen and Besnik Baraj, ed. 2009.*Energy and Environmental Challenges to Security NATO Science for Peace and Security Series C: Environmental Security.* Berlin: Springer Science & Business Media.

The Danish Wind Turbine Owners' Association, n.d. "Cooperatives - a local and democratic ownership to wind turbines." Accessed April 5, 2018.http://dkvind.dk/html/eng/cooperatives.html

Tyner, Wallace Edward. 2012. *Energy Resources and Economic Development in India.* New York: Springer.

UNCTAD (United Nations Conference on Trade and Development). 2015. *Sustainable Freight Transport systems: Opportunities for Developing Countries.* https://unctad.org/meetings/en/SessionalDocuments/ cimem7d11_en.pdf

UNEP (United Nations Environmental Programme). 2015. *District Energy in Cities, Unlocking the Potential of Energy Efficiency and Renewable Energy*. https://wedocs.unep.org/bitstream/handle/20.500.11822/9317/-District energy in cities unlocking the potential of energy efficiency and renewable ene.pdf?sequence=2&.

United States Environmental Protection Agency. 2016. "Learn about Smart Way. " In the *17th World Clean Air Congress and 9 th Better Air Quality (BAQ) Conference.* Busan, South Korea. https://www.epa.gov/smartway/learn-about-smartway.

Vesterinen, Pirkko, Eija Alakangas, Kati Veijonen, and VTT Martin Junginger. 2010. *Prospects of bioenergy in new industrial sectors – D2.3.* Utrecht University. https://ec.europa.eu/energy/intelligent/projects/sites/iee-projects/files/projects/documents/eubionet iii prospects of bioenergy in new industrial sectors en.pdf.

World Nuclear Association.(n.d). "Nuclear Power in Germany." Accessed June 16, 2018. http://www.world-nuclear.org/information-library/country-profiles/countries-g-n/germany.aspx.

Notes

1. Roof top solar panels produce electricity directly from sun.
2. Green Political Party in Germany.
3. European Union directed its nations together to achieve 20% of energy production from renewable by 2020 and provides a target for each members.
4. It provides financial grant and low interest loans to the building owners to make them energy efficient especially to reduce the heating requirements.
5. ORKUSTOFNUN is the government agency of Iceland deals with production, maintenance of energy resources and supply of electricity and other energy issues.
6. It began from 1930s onwards for and petrol and diesel, and now it include coal, coke and natural gas also. The tax rate depends on energy content and its usage. The tax applicable for all end use sectors and it varies according to the intensity.
7. It was one of the first countries to introduce a carbon tax (1991) and helps to reduce CO2 emissions. It affected on Co2 emissions from electricity and other fuel usage. It The tax provides incentives to energy efficiency also.

8. Norway and Sweden aims to increase the renewable energy production through electricity certificate system and the producers get certificates for each MW and purchasers with quota obligation can buy these certificates for their needs.
9. Tariff for individual installations of renewable energy per unit of electricity which goes back to the public grid.
10. It can produce heat and electricity at the same time. Heat is the by-product during power generation.
11. It aims to build energy efficient buildings for energy conservation and low carbongrowth which is institutionalized by Ministry of Power and Bureau of Energy Efficiency since 2017.
12. Solar radiation is used in building design as heating, cooling and other purposes. The natural energy can be used by efficient building design.
13. It cools a floor or ceiling by absorbing the heat from other objects of the room.
14. Central production of heat and transmitted through underground pipes.
15. It extracts heat from one place to another that is warmer to cooler or cooler to warmer. It used for cooling and heating.
16. Generation of electricity and thermal energy through biomass combustion is known as bagasse cogeneration.
17. It ensures continuous water supply solution with equal pressure for high-rise buildings and commercial complexes. It is energy efficient also.
18. The energy efficient and low cost system can be used for rural water distribution especially in hilly areas.
19. Combined Heat and Power Plant produces heat and electricity from the same plant.
20. Provides financial incentives for buying low carbon emission electric vehicles.
21. Different energy sectors are needed to be interacted such as buildings, transport, agriculture and industry - with the power producing sector.
22. The obligation compels consumers to by renewable electricity or renewable energy certificates.
23. Renewable energy promoting tax incentive.

Chapter - VI

Conclusion

Energy is an indispensable part of every one's life as well as the society since the very existence of human being. Along with solar energy, muscle power, simple tools, animals and fire contributed towards the primitive energy landscape. The biomass, wind and water were also instrumental in enhancing the quality of human lives. But with the arrival of hydrocarbon resource in the energy sphere has accelerated the growth of modernization, industrialization, mechanization and in all sectors of social life. Invention of oil added to the progress of human development in a rapid pace. The new energy applications reduced the labor and increased the productivity. The industrial efficiency and transportation facilities boosted the energy consumption causing the possession of certain energy sources in determining the power of the nations. Sometimes it did lead to conflict or even war. Even though the fossil fuel energy sources played an essential role in the development of human society, it also provides a lot of environmental threats to the very existence of planet Earth and the living things. Nuclear energy came at this juncture. Nevertheless, the large scale accidents and the radiation problem limited the scope of this source. Now the world recognizes the impact of our energy choices, its economic, political, social and environmental consequences as well as significance of energy transition and efficiency.In this study an attempt has been made to analyze India's pattern of energy landscape and the prospects towards a sustainable future.

India is the third largest consumer of energy in the world and it is one of the major contributors to the growth of global energy demand. It is mainly because of the fact that India is a major economy and wants to satisfy the energy aspirations of more than 1.3 billion and it needs to solve the energy poverty of the large section of the people who has limited access to electricity and clean cooking fuels. For this, currently the country depends more on hydrocarbon resources. It consumes Coal (56%) Oil (29%), Gas (6%),

Nuclear (1%) Hydro (4%) and Renewables (3%) and it is predicted thatcoal and oil would continue to dominate India's energy scenario for the next 20 years. In power sector,around 63% comes from thermal power plants. The cheap and abundant availability of the resource is a major attraction for the energy intensive sectors. The transport sector is the significant contributor to the greenhouse gas emissions and 99% of it depends on the fossil fuel. The 80% of India's oil requirement depends on import, while also importing coal, natural gas and uranium from other countries.India is an emerging economy in the world and its development aspirations require continuous availability of energy. So, the present energy engagements try to ensure the rich commercial energy supply.

India's energy policy asserts four key objectives such as access at affordable prices, improved security and independence, greater sustainability and economic growth. For sustainability, India agreed to reduce oil imports by 10% and produce 175 GW renewable energy capacities by 2022. But accessibility, affordability and reliability are the mainstream concerns about the energy security. India produced 676.48 million tonnes of coal in 2017-18 which is as much higher than the 70 million tonnes of 1970's. And over the years, the coal production shows a significant increase from the previous year. Now the commercial coal mining has been opened for private sector and it can boost the production capacity of the sector. The import policy of coal also helps the consumers which ensures the easy import for their needs. India's energy policies are determined by differentministries of energy and they themselves work for better productivity for each sector. The high import dependence forcedthe Ministry of Petroleum and Natural Gas to explore and produce more hydrocarbon resources from domestic land. The Ministry actively engage in exploring oil, natural gas, CBM, gas hydrate and shale gas in India's offshore and onshore land. It undertakes to increase the refining and distribution capacity for the resource. To diversify the source nations, India maintains its energy relation with several nationsand has already established its presence in 26 countries. Around 80% of crude oil and 40% natural gas import keep up the energy security of the nation and needs the momentum for future also. Nuclear sources also play a significant role in India's energy policy. Department of Atomic Energy agrees to produce 20GW of nuclear power by 2020 but now it produces only 6 GW which is 2% of total electricity production. Even though, they produce more environmental and social problems than energy security, Government continuous to follow building up of new reactors.

India's energy search is led by the huge energy demand of the country. It is a significant challenge for a developing nation to ensure the basic energy requirements of its people. For the development of the economy, it needs continuous availability of energy. So, it depends on other resource rich nations and it affects the foreign exchange reserves of the country. The fluctuating oil price has severe impact upon value of Indian Rupee and even the poorer sections of the society.

Oil consumption especially in the transport sector is the major contributor in the Green House Gas emission. Coal is the major energy resource in India's primary energy mix. Deforestation, displacement, livelihood problems for indigenous people, child labor, death of workers, harmful working condition, pollution and health hazards are the major problems of coal mining and its usages. The new alternatives for traditional fuels are Natural Gas, LPG, CBM, Shale Gas, Gas Hydrate and others are also hydrocarbon resources and the stages of exploration, drilling, production and the consumption of itaffects environment as well as human society. In fact, Carbon free nuclear energy is also not free from threats to the ecosystem.

Fossil fuels are the imperative part of human civilization. Industrialized nations achieved its development through the abundant use of hydrocarbons. But it deteriorated the environment and made uncomfortable for future generations. It became a cause for climate catastrophes and vulnerabilities on global commons. The greenhouse gas emissions and the resulting climate change have been affecting the humanity and ecology through heavy rain falls, changes in wind pattern, loss of agriculture, shift in seasons, floods, storms, epidemics, spread tropical cyclones, sea level rise, extinction of species, loss of fishery etc. The developed nations can take necessary actions to rebuild their life, but in developing countries extreme weather events affect their livelihood, shelter, education, etc. The unsustainable energy use affects air and water quality. Sulphur dioxide particulate matter nitrous oxide and other chemicals which spread in the air and it create respiratory heart and other health risks. It deteriorates the water quality and reduce underground water level. Large consumption of fresh water in the hydrocarbons and nuclear power plants change the temperature level of water source which led to the loss of life of marine and riverine creatures. Toxic waste disposal has degraded the forest and barren land. Large areas required for power plants and most of them are destroyed in huge parts of forest area.The disposal of radioactive waste or the storage of the same needs high financial cost and increases the risk of environment, including human beings. The policy makers of India preferred the nuclear energy for the energy security of the nation without any carbon emission. However, the carbon free energy source produces more environmental and social consequences. The actual cost of nuclear power includes the cost of maintenance of externalities, waste storage and disposal. The impact of fossil fuels and nuclear energy usage will be affecting for generations. In Russia, a huge town was destroyed by the Chernobyl accident.Now there are no single creatures in this area and people can not live there, due to the high radiation level in the atmosphere. At the time of accident, millions of people could not even take their own basic amenities. They started a new life after the accident with a lot of disease including genetical disorders. Hence, the cost of externalities is inconceivable for human being. The accidents and problems from the energy infrastructure, climate catastrophes environmental and health hazards are affected by poorer sections of the society and mostly they are not the beneficiaries of the projects. Often, they have not even any capacity to resist or for tackling the risks.The unsustainable energy consuming pattern produces the externalities which extend to local, national, regional as well as global level. The energy poverty is another problem for a country like Indiaand is not only lack of electricity access but also the usage of traditional fuels. In the cooking sector the major section of India still uses biomass, wood, cow dung, kerosene, coal etc. The indoor air pollution largely affects women and the children.

The clean energy sources and its sustainable usage are the requirement of humanity as well as the existence of the healthy ecosystem. The energy security goals through the traditional pathway are a threat to the environmental and human security. Global energy landscape is in a transitional period.The Paris Agreement is a milestone in the global energy transition towards a green future. India is also a part of it and commits to reduce 33 to 35 percent emission intensity by 2030 from 2005 level and agreed to produce 40% of electricity from non-fossil fuels. For Intended Nationality Determined Contribution by 2030, it announced its renewable target 175GW by 2022.The new green energy goals are becoming significant in the country's energy policy. But without the coordination of institutional mechanism of different sectors, it will not be fulfilled. Eradication of energy poverty is a challenging aspect in the case of India.Through *Soubhagya*, *Ujala* and other programmes energy access has reached many remote areas in recent years. But the quality and problems during the maintenance period reveal that the initial accessibility cannot ensure the energy security of the poor. Cheap availability of traditional fuel, replacement cost of modern fuel, maintenance cost, cultural preferences, less consideration to the cooking sector in the household and less negotiating power of women in the rural poor family are some of the factors affecting the use of modern energy equipment in the poor sections of the society. LPG and natural gas are the initial energy transition method for cooking in India. They are not environmental friendly or less cost resource for a green future. The energy needs are minimum in poor rural area, so the availability or unaffordability of modern fuels leads to search traditional sources after the implementation of certain welfare projects.

So there is a need of a comprehensive energy framework to ensure the benefit to all sections of the society. The usage of green energy sources, energy efficiency measures for every end use sectors and above all a pro green approach should be there in every aspect of governance. The renewable sources like solar, wind and biomass etc. have no emission relative pollution, no threats to human health, sustainable for ecology and there is no need of import dependence, price fluctuations, and geopolitical risk as in the case of fossil fuels. Utilization of local resources and the small power plants can reduce the risk on energy infrastructure through war, terrorist attacks and other natural calamities like flood, tsunami and earth quake etc.The locally available renewable sources can empower the poor sections of the society. It can empower the rural population as well as women.It assures the minimum standard of living to all sections of the society and can solve the issues of energy access and poverty which are the main problems for India in energy security discourses.

Several EU countries adopted certain measures for green energy transition. Most of them are in the process closing the nuclear power plants. They use the locally available clean resources for their requirements. Waste management and energy production are go hand in hand for these countries. Most of them provide low interest loans, subsidyor financial assistance to clean energy usage. Decentralized and community owned energy projects prevail and the sustainable usage of energy can ensured by the maintenance of different end use sectors in a coordinated way. US government's renewable portfolio standards compel the electric utilities to produce a certain percentage of clean electricity and each state determines the suitable resource with less environmental impact. Even hydropower also banned in certain areas due to ecological risks and they provide incentives in the form of rebates which is a cash back offer for energy efficient appliances and also in the form of tax credit. They enjoyed the financial benefit from net metering,feed in tariff, performance premiums and solar renewable energy credit. Lowinterest loan with long term repayment facility and fixed feed in tariff are the major reasons for the development of Germany's solar energy sector. Bio energy is a widely available source for India in three forms as solid,liquid and gas. It can produce electricity, used as fuel for cooking, thermal comfort for buildings and also for industrial purposes.

The biomass can be collected as agricultural residue, waste from residential as well as commercial sector, energy crops and forest produces. The cogeneration plants can provide heat and electricity. The advanced biomass plants can enhance the waste management mechanism and satisfy the energy needs of the locality. Brazil, India and the US use bioenergy for industrial heat production. The EU utilizes it for space heating and biofuels are used in transport sector. *Renovo Bio* program of Brazil encourages the biofuel productionlike biodiesel, ethanol and bio methanefrom the agricultural residues. In India biomass utilization is very rare except in the bagasse cogeneration plants and some biogas plants. However, it is a potential resource for generation of electricity, heat and fuel for transportation sector. As an agricultural based country with a huge pollution affected by burning of agricultural residue has the power to transform this resource to energy. In India, there is no effective mechanism to manage the wastes like food waste, sewage, animal manures and industrial waste. The bio energy from the waste is a remedy for the energy needs as well as alternative to landfills.China has biomass energy policy which ensures low interest loans funding and subsidies for feedstock and house hold biogas plant.It has implemented the fixed feed in tariff for biomass energy production. Japan has also FIT (feed in tariff)since 2012 for biomass power.Japan uses solid biomass like wood chips and pellet are used in space heating and boilers. Liquid biofuels are used in boilers of industry and transportation process. Bio gas is used in power sector and transportation field.Denmark offers waste to an energy plant in Copenhagen town to recycle the waste to produce electricity and solves the district heating requirements. The Netherlands also uses waste to heat methods for space heating.Croatia energy action plan targeted to achieve 10 % of transport sector will be biofuel source.The country provides subsidy for eligible producers of biomass and established certain quota for blending of biofuel and diesel. Supply of feed stock is the basic problem of production in bioenergy. So the continuous availability and infrastructure facilities for processing transportation of raw materials such as forest produces, agricultural residue and solid waste are necessary in this sector.Financial incentives subsidies, quota mechanism, feedin tariff are other needs for the development of various form of bioenergy.

Though the geographical location is a matter of fact for the availability, wind power is also an adaptable resource for several regions of India. Several states successfully manage wind farms and in Odanthurai, a Panchayat in Tamil Nadu state owns windmillwith 350kw capacity which is located near Udumalpet in Coimbatore. This is the first of its kind a panchayat which acts like a private enterprise to own wind farms. And, they repaid the bank loan within seven years from the revenue earned from the wind farm itself. Because the project generates 7.5 lakhs unit of electricity and the panchayat needs only 4.5 lakhs. They earned through selling remaining energy to the Tamil Nadu electricity board. So, the availability is not a matter for the development of the sector. Here panchayat owns a windmill and satisfies their needs through clean energy, then private companies, NGOs and other cooperate groups can buy and use windmills. Several countries follows the same path, the farmers together buy wind farms for their working. The potential of renewable energy is vast and available from biomass, wind, solar, geothermal, small hydro-ocean and hydrogen etc.

Solar energy is the most feasible source for India and now a visible growth is happening in recent years. Many parts of the country have access to effective radiation around 300 days in a year and it can build every part of India. Now the falling price enables the resource as cost effective and an alternative than others. India ensured a transparent auction process and certain financial incentives like viability gap funding accelerated depreciation,subsidies and concession in debt financing for the development of solar sector.Renewable purchase obligation and mandatory rooftop solar installation for certain buildings help to the growth of this resource. The large buildings, institutions and government buildings are not even take up the solar power. Even though the residential buildings are willing to install solar power for their energy needs, the initial cost, and maintenance difficulties are the major barriers to adopt this mechanism

Now a days, fossil fuels, unhealthy biomass and energy consuming electrical appliances are fulfilling the needs of thermal comfort of building, fuel for purpose of industry and cooking. Solar thermal and heat pumps, biomass boilers are available technologies for industries improved cook stores like solar or biomass, renewable based electric appliances, and biogas plants can minimize the unsustainable cooking practices. District heating systems are common in European Countries andseveral cities of China. In India, for more energy efficiency,can adopt district heating and cooling system for commercial buildings in major cities. Radiant cooling is an available and sustainable technology for cooling the buildings. Rain water harvesting can ensure the availability of water for anywhere in India.Building sector is one of the most electricity consuming sector. Stand alone, micro, mini or public grid can provide renewable power to building sector. Decentralized minor energy projects with solar, wind or biomass can ensure the electricity demand. Energy efficiency construction can tackle the thermal comfort and lighting purposes.

Transport is the most difficult energy intensive sector because 99% of it is runby fossil fuels in India. The increasing motorization, low fuel efficiency and inefficient freight transport are some to the unsustainable growth of the sector. Road transport can maintain through urban planning which includes better roads with foot path and cycle path, reduce traffic congestion, improve public transport system, promote the electric or hybrid vehicles, adopt mass transit system and avoid personal vehicle sector. Biofuels and blended fuels can be a way for the reduction of heavy usage of fossil fuels. Railways are more adaptive to renewable because it can use electricity in an easy manner. But shipping and aviation are the difficult sectors but technological advances will help them to change easily. Biofuels, solar power aircraft and hydrogen are the emerging developments in aviation sector. Individual or cooperative ownership renewable energy can satisfy the agricultural energy needs. Germany and Sweden provides examples regarding this. The Government can implement certain standards to reduce the energy intensity and usage of renewable energy resources. Several clean measures are available to satisfy the needs and they can own their own renewable energy power plants.

The centralized energy institutionalized mechanism has many limitations in providing energy access to the remote areas. Decentralization of energy structure can solve these issues effectively. Local, municipal, panchayat, block, urban and district level policies can implement energy solutions in a sustainable way. It can utilize the solar, wind and biomass resources locally and form micro or mini grids to transmit to all sections of the society. Mini grids can reduce transmission loss and cost of maintenance. Integration of various energy sources into public grid can contribute a significant development. Feed in Tariff and net metering policy can ensure the popularity for the mini grid programme. Decentralized policies can conduct awareness and training programmes for the people. Specific local resources can be utilized in this way. Local transmission grids can perform complimentary with central public grids. Local energy system can provide not only electricity but also fuel for cooking, lighting, heating, cooling, charging stations for transport sector and mechanism for waste management.

The current quest for India's energy security itself contributes insecurities to the environment, society and human being. There is an urgent need to address the issues of threats from energy searches. The people and the environment, nearby the resource rich area, are not only the victims who experience the sufferings, but also it has far reaching global level externalities. Some of the possible interventions are depicted here to assure a better and clean future. Effective energy efficiency measures, wider application of renewable energy and proper addressing of the energy poverty of the country are the ways for attaining a sustainable energy future for India.

- First of all, there is a need to implement the fossil fuel reduction policies in an effective way. Reduction policies to fossil fuel based vehicles and implement the electric vehicle policies with charging stations and other promotion factors. Implement the CO_2 emission standards, fuel efficiency standards and carbon tax for all vehicles. Efforts are needed to avoid ecologically fragile regions from the energy needs. Reduce the coal consumption and ban the hazardous mining. Promote the research development measures for alternative energy resources.
- Secondly, integrated energy efficiency measures should be adapted on all end use sectors such as buildings, transport, agriculture and all appliances. The effective implementation of energy performance building codes for new buildings for future energy savings is the basic requirement in this sector. The environmental clearance and sector coupling measures like usage of solar passive principle including daylight consumption, feasible measures for heating, cooling, lighting, pumping of water, efficient appliance and suitable renewable energy self-sufficiency are needed to include the building codes. Builders, architects, investors and consultants are the backbone of the building sector. So there is a need of training in energy efficiency for them. And ensure the availability of affordable energy consultants for the poorer sections of the society. Clear directives, renovation plan and financial incentive schemes are needed for the present building sector. Use the potential of domestic, commercial and agro waste for energy production and avoid the pollution. Implementation of effective urban planning for the reduction of carbon footprint is necessary. There is need to implement environmental regulations and establish targets of renewable consumption for industrial sectors and to implement renewable cogeneration plants to produce heat and power for this sector. Energy efficiency measures should cover electricity generation, transition, distribution and consumption.
- Thirdly, for renewable energy, identify the sources on the basis of availability and feasibility for the particular area. The current development in the solar and wind energy should be appreciable. Initiate the policies to secure the energy self sufficiency of every household, society and the state with a long term green perspective.

Instead of international bargaining, we can implement the energy policies in decentralized system. Decentralized efficiency measures can be implemented through state, district, regional and panchayat level. Solar installations and equipment can provide 100% rural electrification in India. Panchayat level waste management system can produce cooking gas for local level. Decentralized energy system can assure the needs of every locality with available resource. Government should provide the supply facility for abundant raw materials to the power plants in the case of biomass production. Enhance the growth of micro, mini and standalone grid.

- Besides, organise awareness program for mass behavioural change from school level itself. Ensure energy efficiency in work places, educational and religious institutions, then the people can easily adopt the mechanism at their home. The training and capacity building programmes by skilled persons in clean energy, technologies, storage facilities, problems of fossil fuel resources, financial sources etc, are imperative for the progress of green energy future.
- In addition, integration of different energy ministries and departments will enhance the sustainable development of the country. Ensure the financial sources for the adoption of green sources with subsidy, financial incentives and low interest loans. Transparent auctions, feed in tariff, net metering etc. should enhance the green energy sector.

The country's energy sector is a complex one to analyse and transform. But the local, national, regional and global level externalities have made a rethinking about global as well as national level energy aspirations. Now the concept of energy security is satisfying a certain sections of the people and provides insecurities to a large section in the global level. Fossil fuel and nuclear energy dependence produces environmental damages and human health problems. So a green transformation to the energy sector is a need of the time for a future generation. A cross sectoral policy framework is need for the complex character of energy spectrum. Abundant opportunities are available in the scenario. Better utilization of local resources with small scale projects and effective policy measures can alter whole energy system. But effective national level policies can only implement the green energy transition of India. It is to be underlined that green energy transition is essential for the large section of energy poor people in the country. The clean energy solutions provide environmental, human and societal security with sustainable future.

Reference

Books

Annan, Kofi A. 2000.*We the Peoples: The Role of the United Nations in the 21st Century.* New York, USA: United Nations Department of Public Information.

Awasthi, Shambhu Ratan. 2018. *Wind Power: Practical Aspects*. New Delhi: The Energy Resources Institute.

Barnes, Douglas. F and Michael A. Toman. 2006. "Energy, Equity and Economic Development." In *Economic Development and Environmental Sustainability: New Policy Options*, edited by Ramon Lopez, and Michael A. Toman. Oxford: Oxford University Press.

Barnett, Jon. 200. *The Meaning of Environmental Security: Ecological Politics and Policy in the New Security Era.* London: Zed Books.

Barton, Barry, Catherine Redgwell, Anita Ronne, and Donald N Zillman. 2004. *Energy Security: Managing Risk in a Dynamic Legal and Regulatory Environment.* New York: Oxford University Press.

Beatley, Timothy. 2012. *Green Urbanism: Learning from European Cities*. Washington D.C. Island Press.

Bithas,Kostas, and Panos Kalimeris.2015. "A Brief History of Energy Use." In *Revisiting the Energy- Development Link: Evidence from the 20th Century for Knowledge-based and Developing Economies,* edited by Kostas Bithas and Panos Kalimeris. 5-10. UK: Springer Briefs in Economics.

Brown, Marilyn A, and Benjamin K. Sovacool. 2011. *Climate Change and Global Energy Security: Technology and Policy Options.* Massachusetts: Cambridge.

Buzan, Barry, Ole Waever, and Jaap de Wilde. 1998. *Security: A New Framework for Analysis*. US: Lynne Rienner Publishers.

Chari, P.R. 2009. *Indo-US Nuclear Deal: Seeking Synergy in Bilateralism.* New Delhi: Routledge.

Chaturvedi, A.K. 2013. *Role of Pakistan in India's Energy Security: An Issue Brief.* New Delhi: Vij Books India Pvt Ltd.

Chauhan, D.S. 2006. *Non-Conventional Energy Resources.* Ernakulam: New Age International.

Dalby, Simon. 1997. "Contesting an Essential Concept: Reading the Dilemmas in Contemporary Security Discourse." In *Critical Security Studies: Concepts and Cases,* edited by Keith Krause, & Michael. C. Williams. Minneapolis: University of Minnesota Press.

Dalby, Simon. 2002. *Environmental Security.* Minneapolis: University of Minnesota Press.

Dalby, Simon. 2009. *Security and Environmental Change.* Cambridge, UK: Polity Press.

Dalby, Simon. 2010. "Critical Geopolitics and Security." In *Handbook of New Security Studies*, edited by J. Peter Burgess, London: Routledge.

Dannreuther, R. 2017. *Energy Security*. Cambridge: Polity Press.

Doyle, Michael W, and G.John Ikenberry, ed.1997. *New Thinking in International Relations Theory,* Colorado: Westview Press.

Ebinger, Charles. K. 2012. *Energy and Security in South Asia: Cooperation or Conflict.* Washington DC: The Brookings Institution.

Fouquet, Roger. 2009. "A Brief History of Energy." In *International Handbook on the Economics of Energy,* edited by Joanne Evans, and Lester C. Hunt. 1-19. Cheltenham, UK: Edward Elgar Publishing.

Gadgil, Madhav, and Ramachandra Guha. 1995. *Ecology and Equity: The Use and Abuse of Nature in Contemporary India.* New York: Routledge.

Gupta, Mitali Das. 2009. "Life Styles and Energy Consumption." In *India's Energy Security,* edited by Ligia Noronha and Anant Sudarshan. Abingdon, Oxon: Routledge.

Halff, Antoine, Benjamin K Sovacool, and Jon Rozhon. 2014. *Energy Poverty: Global Challenges and Local Solutions.* Oxford: Oxford University Press.

Homer-Dixon, Thomas. F. 1999. *Environment, Scarcity and Violence.* Princeton: Princeton University Press.

Jafar, Majid. 2004. "Kazakhstan: Oil, Politics and the New 'Great Game." In *The Caspian: Politics, Energy and Security*, edited by Shirin Akiner. London: Routledge.

Klare, Michael. T. 2004. *Blood and Oil: The Dangers and Consequences of America's Growing Dependency on Imported Petroleum.* New York: Metropolitan Books.

Klare, Michael. T. 2008. *Rising Powers, Shrinking Planet: The New Geopolitics of Energy.* New York: Henry Holt and Company.

Krausmann, Fridolin. 2011. *The Socio-Metabolic Transition. Long Term Historical Trends and Patterns in Global Material and Energy Use.Institute of Social Ecology.* Vienna: Institute of Social Ecology.

Kumar, B.B, ed. 2007. *Problems of Ethnicity in North East India*. Delhi: Concept Publishing Company.

Malik, Priyanjali. 2016. *India's Nuclear Debate: Exceptionalism and the Bomb.* New Delhi: Routledge.

Mehndiratta, Shomik, Zhi Liu, and Ke Fang. 2012. "Motorized Vehicles: Demand Management and Technology." In *Sustainable Low-Carbon City Development in China,* edited by Axel Baeumler, Ede Ijjasz-Vasquez, and Shomik Mehndiratta, 299-322. Washington DC: World Bank.

Noronha, Ligia and Anant, Sudarshan. 2009. *India's Energy Security*. Abington, Oxon: Routledge.

Pant, Girijesh. 2008. *India: The Emerging Energy Player,* Delhi: Dorling Kindersley.

Pant, Girijesh. 2015. *India's Emerging Energy Relation: Issues and Challenges,* New Delhi: Springer.

Pascual, Carlos and Elkind, Jonathan. 2010. *Energy Security: Economics, Politics, Strategies and Implications*. Washington DC: Brookings.

Pascual, Carlos. and Zambetakis, E. 2009. *The Geopolitics of Energy: From Security to Survival.* Washington DC: Brookings.

Prasad, Anubhuti Ranjan. 1986. *Coal Industry of India.* New Delhi: Ashish Publishing House.

Redgwell, Catherine. 2004. "International Energy Security." In *Energy Security: Managing Risk in a Dynamic Legal and Regulatory Environment,* edited by Barry Barton, Catherine Redgwell, Anita Rønne, and Donald N. Zillman. Oxford: Oxford University Press.

Sachdeva, Gulshan. (2015). Indian Energy Security and the Role of Renewables: Possibility of Cooperation with the EU. In *India's Emerging Energy Relatons: Issues and Challenges,* edited by Girijesh Pant (47-64). New Delhi: Springer.

Sagebiel, Julian, Christian Kimmich, Malte Muller, Markus Hanisch and Vivek Gilani, ed. 2016."Background of the Agricultural Power Supply Situation in India and Andhra Pradesh."*In Enhancing Energy Efficiency in Irrigation A Socio-Technical Approach in South India,* edited by Sagebiel Julian, Christian Kimmich, Malte Muller, Markus Hanisch and Vivek Gilani 7-17. Washington DC: Springer.

Sarolkar, P.B and K. Shivkumar. 2007. *Energy Scenario in 2020.* Nagpur: Gondwana Geological Society.

Sethi, Surya. 2009. "India's Energy Challenges and Choices" In *India's Energy Security*, edited by Ligia Noronha and Anant Sudarshan. 19-28. Abington,Oxon: Routledge.

Simpson, A. 2013. "Challenging Inequality and Injustice: A Critical Approach to Energy Security." In *Environmental security: Approaches and Issues,* edited by Rita Floyd, and Richard Mathew, London: Routledge.

Singh, Bhupendra Kumar. 2010. "Energy Security Options." In *India's Energy Security: The Changing Dynamics,* edited by Bhupendra Kumar. 52-100. New Delhi: Pentagon Energy Press.

Sinha, Bibhulal. 2015. "*Shale gas in India challenges and opportunities*" Master's thesis. Ljubljana University.

Sovacool, Bennjamin. K. 2011."Introduction: Defining, Measuring, and Exploring Energy Security." In *The Routledge Handbook of Energy Security*, edited by Benjamin. K. Sovacool, 1-42. London: Routledge.

Stec, Stephen and Besnik Baraj, ed. 2009.*Energy and Environmental Challenges to Security NATO Science for Peace and Security Series C: Environmental Security.* Berlin: Springer Science & Business Media.

Sudarshan, Anand, and Ligia Noronha. 2009. "Contextualizing India's Energy Security." In *India's Energy Security,* edited by Ligia Noronha and Anand Sudarshan, 3-19, Abington, Oxon: Routledge.

Trombetta, Maria Julia. 2010. "Rethinking the Securitization of Environment: Old Beliefs, New Insights." In *Securitization Theory: How Security Problems Emerge and Dissolve,* edited by Thierry Balzacq. New York: Routledge.

Tyner, Wallace Edward. 2012. *Energy Resources and Economic Development in India.* New York: Springer.

Vanderheiden, Steve. 2014. *The Politics of Energy: Challenges for a Sustainable Future*. New York: Routledge.

Vasudevachary, A. K.1996. *Problems and Prospects of Coal Industry in India: A Case Study.* New Delhi: Mittal Publications.

Vivado, Vlado. 2008. *The Return of the Obsolescing Bargain and the Decline of Big Oil: A Study of Bargaining in the Contemporary Oil Industry.* Saarbrücken: VDM Verlag.

Waever, Ole.1995. "*Securitization and Desecuritization.*"In *On Security,* edited by Ronnie D. *Lipschutz.46-86. New York*: *Columbia University Press.*

Willrich, Mason. 1975. *Energy and World Politics,* New York: Free Press.

Yergin, Daniel. 1991. *The Prize: The Epic Quest for Oil, Money, and Power.* New York: Free Press.

Yergin, Daniel. 2011. *The Quest; Energy, Security, and the Remaking of the Modern World.* New York: Penguin Books.

Articles

Aduloju, Ayodeji, and Omowunmi O. Pratt. 2014. "Human Security and Developmental Crisis in the Contemporary West Africa."*Journal of Human Security* 10(1): 46-58.

Ansari, Md. Fahim, Ravinder Kumar Kharb, Sunil Luthra, S.L. Shimmi, and S. Chatterji. 2013. "Analysis of barriers to implement solar power installations in India using interpretive structural modeling technique." *Renewable and Sustainable Energy Reviews* 27 (November): 163-174.

Anthony, Augusta, Ray Sanchez, and Nicole Chavez. 2018. "Pressure increase reported in Massachusetts gas pipeline, NTSB says." *CNN,* September 16, 2018. https://edition.cnn.com/2018/09/15/us/massachusetts-explosions-fires-gas-pipeline/index.html.

Arora, Rajat. 2017. "India to be first in world to run all government ports on green energy." *Economic Times,* May 31, 2017. https://economictimes. indiatimes.com/industry/transportation/shipping-/-transport/india-to-be-first-in-world-to-run-all-government-ports-on-green-energy/articleshow/58917369.cms.

Bansal, Alok. 2014. "US Iran Relations and their Impact on India." *Scholar Warrior.*8-14.http://www.claws.in/images/journals doc/78081265_AlokBansal.pdf.

Bhushan, Chandra. 2015. "Growth of Renewable Energy in India." *Down to Earth,* https://www.downtoearth.org.in/news/growth-of-renewable-energy-in-india-43605.

Bielecki, J. 2002. "Energy Security: Is the Wolf at the Door?." *The Quarterly Review of Economics and Finance* 42(2): 235-50.

Bindra, Prerna. 2017. "The Bustard and the Windmill."*The Hindu,* September 2, 2017. https://www.thehindu.com/sci-tech/energy-and-environment/the-bustard-and-the-windmill/article19608564.ece.

Blank, Stephen. 1995. "Energy, Economics and Security in Central Asia: Russia and its Rival." *Central Asian Survey* 14(3): 373-406.

Blinik, Adam. 2008. "Pipeline Diplomacy." *The New Atlantis 21(Summer): 122-127.*

Booth, Ken. 1991. "Security and Emancipation." *Review of International Studies* 17(4): 313-326.

Business Line. 2017. "Essar to announce Rosneft deal closer today." August 20, 2017.

Business Line. 2017. "OVL gets extension till 2049 for Azeri-Chirag-Deepwater project." September 18, 2017.

Business Line. 2018. "Coal production 2018, Coal production up 15% this fiscal." June 11, 2018. https://www.thehindubusinessline.com/economy/coal-production-up-15-this-fiscal-piyush-goyal/article24135551.ece.

Business Standard. 2018. "Emission standards for thermal power plants: SC asks govt to file detailed affidavit." April 25, 2018. https://www.business-standard.com/article/pti-stories/emission-standards-for-thermal-power-plants-sc-asks-govt-to-file-detailed-affidavit-118042501253_1.html.

Cesnakas, Giedrius. 2010. "Energy Resources in Foreign Policy: A Theoretical Approach." *Baltic Journal of Law and Politics* 3(1): 30-52.

Cherian, John. 2017. "From Non-alignment to Strategic Partnership". *Foreign Policy*, September 1, 2017.

Colgan, Jeff and Thijs Van de Graaf. 2013. "Mechanisms of informal governance: Evidence from the IEA." *Journal of International Relations and Development*. http://thijsvandegraaf.be/wp-content/uploads/2012/04/Colgan-Graaf-JIRD-July-8. pdf.

Dalby, Simon. 2002. "Security and Ecology in the Age of Globalization." *Environmental Change and Security Project Report* 8 (Summer): 95-108. Washington DC: Woodrow Wilson Center of Scholars.

Desai, Ronak. D. 2015. "A New Era for India Latin America Relations." *Forbes,* June 25, 2015.https://www.forbes.com/sites/ronakdesai/2015/06/25/a-new-era-for-india-latin-america-relations/.

Deudney, Daniel. 2000. "Geopolitics as Theory: Historical Security Materialism." *European Journal of International Relations* 6 (1):77-107.

*Down to Earth.*2015. "Narora fire." July 4, 2015. https://www.downtoearth.org.in/news/narora-fire-30932.

Down to Earth. 2018. "Ireland becomes the fourth EU country to ban fracking." July 11, 2018.

Dutt, Arjun, and Neeraj Kuldeep. 2018. "Discoms Rooftop Moment," *Business Line,* April 10, 2018. https://www.thehindubusinessline.com/opinion/columns/discoms-rooftop-moment/article23495195.ece.

Gasper, Des. 2005. "Securing Humanity: Situating 'Human Security' as Concept and Discourse." *Journal of Human Development* 6 (2): 221–245.

Gils, Hans Christian. Sonja Simon, and Rafael Soria. 2017. "100% Renewable Energy Supply for Brazil—the Role of Sector Coupling and Regional Development." *Energies* 10 (11): 1859.

Glaser Alexander, and M.V Ramana. 2007. "Weapon-Grade Plutonium Production Potential in the Indian Prototype Fast Breeder Reactor." *Science and Global Security* 15(2): 85-105. Routledge.

Goldthau, Andreas, and Jan Martin Witte. 2009. "Back to the Future or Forward to the Past? Strengthening Markets and Rules for Effective Global Energy Governance."*International Affairs* 85(2) March: 373-90.

Gopalakrishnan, A. (2002). "Evolution of Indian Nuclear Power Programme."*Annual Review of Energy and the Environment* 27 (November): 369-95.

Guha, Debasis. 2014. "A case study on the effects of coal mining in the environment particularly in relation to Soil, Water and Air causing a Socio-economic Hazard in Asansol-Raniganj Area, India." *International Research Journal of Social Science* 3(8): 39-42.

Hober, Kaj. 2010. "Investment Arbitration and the Energy Charter Treaty."*Journal of International Dispute Settlement 1(1):153-90.*

Ikenberry, G John. 1999. "Why Export Democracy? The 'Hidden Grand Strategy' of American Foreign Policy." *The Wilson Quarterly* 23(2): 56-65.

Indo-US Science & Technology Forum. (2014). "Here comes the Sun." *Connect* 6 (1): 4-9. Solar Energy Research Institute for India and US.

Jangir, Sunil Kumar. 2012. "Indo Us Nuclear Deal and 123 Agreement." *International Journal of Scientific and Research Publications 2* (10): 1-6.

Jha, Girish Kumar, Suresh Pal, and Alka Singh. 2012. "Changing Energy-use Pattern and the Demand Projection for Indian Agriculture."*Agricultural Economics Research Review* 25(1) January-June: 61-68.

Kaldor, Mary. 2004. "A Force for Intervention: A Human Security Doctrine for Europe and Beyond." *The New York Times.* September 30, 2004.

Kapoor, Karan, Pandey K. Krishan, A.K Jain, and Ashish Nandan, 2014. "Evolution of Solar Energy in India: A review." *Renewable and Sustainable Energy Reviews* 40.475–487.

Karasac, Hasene. 2002. "Actors of the New 'Great Game' Caspian Oil Politics." *Journal of Southern Europe and the Balkans* 4(1): 15-27.

Klare, Michael. T. 2002. "Global Petro-Politics: The Foreign Policy Implications of the Bush Administration's Energy Plan." *Current History* 101(653) March: 99-104.

Klare, Michael. T. 2003. "For Oil and Empire?Rethinking War with Iraq." *Current History* 102(662) March: 129-35.

Klare, Michael. T. 2008. "The New Geopolitics of Energy." *The Nation*, May 19, 2008.

Krausmann, Fridolin, Simone Gingrich, and Reza NourbakhchSabet. 2011. "The Metabolic Transition in JapanA Material Flow Account for the Period From 1878 to 2005", *Journal of Industrial Ecology* 15(6): 877-92. Yale University.

Kruyt, Bert.,*D.P. van Vuuren*, *H.J.M. de Vries*, and *H. Groenenberg.* 2009. "Indicators for Energy Security." *Energy Policy, Elsevier* 37(6) June: 2166 -2181.

Lahiri-Dutt, Kuntala. 2007. "Illegal coal mining in Eastern India: Rethinking legitimacy and limits of justice." *Economic and Political Weekly* December: 57-66.

Leal-Arcas, Rafael, and Andrew Filis. 2013. "The Fragmented Governance of the Global Energy Economy: A Legal-Institutional Analysis." *Journal of World Energy Law & Business* 167/2014: 1-59.Queen Mary School of Law Legal Studies.

Mamadouh, V. D. 1988. "Geopolitics in the Nineties: One Flag, Many Meanings." *Geo Journal.* 46(March): 237-253.

Mauawad, Jad. 2006. "Western Firms Feel a Pinch from Oil Nationalism." *The New York Times.* May 7.

Miles, Tom. 2017. "U.S. takes India back to WTO in solar power dispute." *Reuters,* December 20, 2017.

Mitavachan, H, and J. Srinivasan. 2012. "Is Land Really a Constraint for the Utilization of Solar Energy in India." *Current Science* 103(2), 163-68.

Monga, Ritu, Richa Bajpai, and Purnima Swarup Khare. 2006. "Energy Consumption, Sectoral Activity, and Structural Change in the Indian Economy." *Journal of Environmental Research and Development* 1(1): 68-71.

Mulligan, Shane. 2010. "Energy, Environment, and Security: Critical Links in a Post-Peak World." *Global Environmental Politics.* 10(4), November: 79-100.

Mulligan, Shane. 2011. "Energy and Human Ecology: A Critical Security Approach." *Journal of Environmental Politics* 20(5) September: 633-649.

Myers, Henry R. 1975. "Federal Decision Making and the Trans-Alaska Pipeline." *Ecology Law Quarterly* 4(4): 915-61.

NDTV. 2017. "India in talks with countries like Uzbekistan to create Uranium Reserve." September 24, 2017. https://www.ndtv.com/india-news/india-in-talks-with-countries-like-uzbekistan-to-create-uranium-reserve-1754479.

Neslen, Arthur. 2016. "The rise and fall of fracking in Europe."*The Guardian*, September 29, 2016. https://www.theguardian.com/sustainable-business/2016/sep/29/ fracking-shale-gas-europe-opposition-ban.

Pallavi, Aparna. 2015. "Uranium Mine Waste Imperils Villages in Jaduguda." *Down to Earth.* July 4, 2015.

Philip, Annie. 2014. "Filling the Gaps: Rooftop Solar Projects in India." *Economic and Political Weekly* 49(10).https://www.epw.in/journal/2014/10/web-exclusives/filling-gaps-rooftop-solar-projects-india.html.

Pinna, B, Dalla Chiara, and K. Pant. 2014. "Energy used by transport systems in India: the role of the urban population, sources, alternative modes and quantitative analyses." *WIT Transactions on Ecology and the Environment* 190: 661-675. WIT Press.

Raghavan, Sharad T.C.A. 2018. "What is International Solar Alliance." *The Hindu,* March 12, 2018.

Ramana, M V, and Ashwin Kumar. 2010. "Safety First? Kaiga and Other Nuclear Stories."*Economic & Political Weekly* xlv (7). February 13.

Ramana, M.V. 2007."Economics of Nuclear Power."*Economics and Political Weekly*. January 13: 169-71.

Ramana, M.V.2009. "Nuclear Power: Economic, Safety, Health, and Environmental Issues of Near-Term Technologies."*Annual Review of Environment and Resources* 34(1): 127-52.

Rasizade, Alec. 2002. "The Specter of a New 'Great Game' in Central Asia." *Foreign Service Journal* 79(11) November: 48-52.

Saini,Sunita. 2018. "Evolution of Indian Power Sector at a Glance." *National Journal of Multidisciplinary Research and Development* 3(1): 275-278.

Seethi, K.M. 2008."Perils of Nuclear Renaissance and the Indo US Civil Nuclear Deal."*Indian Journal of Politics and International Relations.* 1(1):129-40.

Sekhri, Sofiane. 2009. "Dependency approach: Chances of survival in the 21st century." *African Journal of Political Science and International Relations.* 3(5): 242-52.

Seth, Rahul, Rohit Seth and Shrish Bajpai.2015. "Need of Biomass Energy in India." *Progress in Science and Engineering Research Journal* 3(2) March-April: 013-17.

Sharma , Yogima. 2018. "Niti Aayog's new methanol push could be bad news for Modi's electric vehicles mission." *The Economic Times,* January 1, 2018. https://economictimes.indiatimes.com/niti-aayogs-new-methanol-push-could-be-bad-news-for-modis-electric-vehicles-mission/articleshow/62323639.cms.

Simpson, A. 2007. "The Environment: Energy Security Nexus: Critical Analysis of an Energy 'Love Triangle' in Southeast Asia." *Third World Quarterly.* 28(3) April: 539 – 54.

Smil, Vaclav. 2004. "War and Energy." *Encyclopedia of Energy* 6: 549-561. Elsevier.

Srivastava, Leena. and Neha Misra. 2007. "Promoting Regional Energy Co-operation in South Asia." *Energy Policy* 35(6) February: 3360-368.

Srivastava, Swami Prakash, and Surat Prakash Srivastava."Solar Energy and its Future Role."*International Journal of Environmental Science: Development and Monitoring* 4(3): 81-88.

Stevens, Paul. 2008. "National Oil Companies and International Oil Companies in the Middle East: Under the Shadow of Government and the Resource Nationalism Cycle." *Journal of World Energy Law & Business* 1(1) May: 5-30.

Stringer, Kevin. D. 2008. "Energy Security: Applying a Portfolio Approach." *Baltic Security & Defence Review.* 10: 121-142.

Subramanian, T.S. 2003. "Nuclear Safety, The Kalpakkam 'incident'." *Frontline* 20 (17): August 16 – 29, 2003.

The Economic Times. 2017. "Iraq replaces Saudi Arabia as India's lead oil supplier." December 18, 2017.

The Economic Times. 2018. "India needs 600 MMT refinery capacity by 2040." January 13, 2018.https://economictimes.indiatimes.com/industry/energy/oil-gas/india-needs-600-mmt-refinery-capacity-by-2040-dharmendra-pradhan/articleshow/62487735.cms.

The Economic Times. 2018. "India set to achieve 20GW solar energy capacities this fiscal itself." March 8, 2018. https://economictimes.indiatimes.com/ industry/energy/power/india-set-to-achieve-20gw-solar-energy-capacities-this-fiscal-itself/articleshow/63218130.cms.

The Hindu. 2017. "Powered by a pause: delay in Indo-U.S. nuclear deal." March 28, 2017.

The Hindu. 2018. "Why has coal mining been opened up." February 25, 2018.

The Telegraph. 2016. "OVL also bought 11% Stake in Venkor Field."September 29, 2016.

The Telegraph. 2017. "OVL suffers Sudan setback." May 3, 2017.

The Telegraph. 2018. "Nuclear capacity to triple by 2031". August 10, 2018. https://www.telegraphindia.com/india/nuclear-capacity-to-triple-by-2031/cid/1216719.

The Times of India. 2017. "Coal import from Canada may rise as steelmaking makes headway." July 19, 2017.

The Times of India. 2018. "India discusses 'Oil Buyers Club' with China; seeks US crude to counter OPEC." June 13, 2018. https://timesofindia.indiatimes.com/business/india-business/india-discusses-oil-buyers-club-with-china-seeks-us-crude-to-counter-opec/articleshow/64575528.cms.

Tiwary R.K, and B.B Dhar.1994. "Effect of coal mining and coal based industrial activities on water quality of the river Damodar with specific reference to heavy metals." *International Journal of Surface Mining, Reclamation and Environment* 8(3): 111-115.

Tripathi, Bhasker. 2018. "Now, India is the third largest electricity producer ahead of Russia, Japan." *Business Standard*. March 26, 2018.

Trombetta, Maria Julia. 2008. "Environmental Security and Climate Change: Analysing the Discourse." *Cambridge Review of International Affairs* 21(4):585-602.

Vanderheiden, Steve. 2011. "The Politics of Energy: An Introduction." *Environmental Politics* 20(5): 607–16. Routledge.

Verma, Nidhi. 2018."India's Oil imports in 2017 surged into a record 4.4 million barrels per day." *The Economic Times,* January 17, 2018.

Verrastro, Frank, and Sarah Ladislaw. 2007. "Providing Energy Security in an Interdependent World."*The Washington Quarterly* 30(4) November: 95-104.

Vivoda, Vlado. 2009. "Resource Nationalism, Bargaining and International Oil Companies: Challenges and Change in the New Millennium." *New Political Economy* 14(4) December: 517–534.

Walde, T. 2008. "Renegotiating Acquired Rights in the Oil and Gas Industries: Industry and Political Cycles Meet the Rule of Law." *Journal of World Energy Law & Business* 1(1) May: 55-97.

Wheeler, Deborah. 2011. "Freedom from Want, and Freedom from Fear: A Human Security Approach to a New Middle East?." *Journal of Human Security* 7(1): 37-52.

Yergin, Daniel. 2006. "Ensuring Energy Security." *Foreign Affairs* 85(2) March/April: 69-82.

Ziegler, Charles. E, and Rajan Menon. 2014. "Neomercantilism and Great- Power Energy Competition in Central Asia and the Caspian."*Strategic Studies Quarterly* 8(2): 17-41.

Documents

Abbott, Derek. 2011. "Is Nuclear Power Globally Scalable?." In the *Proceedings of the IEEE (Institute of Electrical and Electronics Engineers)* University of Adelaide, October, 1611-1617.99(10):1611-1617. Adelaide, Australia: IEEE.

APERC (Asia Pacific Energy Research Centre). 2007. *A Quest for Energy Security in the 21st Century: Resources and Constraints*. Japan: APERC. https:// aperc.ieej.or.jp/ file/2010/9/26/APERC 2007 A Quest for Energy Security.pdf.

ASP (United States American Security Project). 2017. *Fact Sheet: Climate Change and Energy Securityin Alaska*. Washington, DC: ASP.

ASSOCHAM (Associated Chambers of Commerce and Industry of India). 2016. *Hydropower @ Crossroads.*https://www.pwc.in/assets/pdfs/publications/ 2016/ hydropower-at-crossroads-pwc-assocham-report.pdf.

B P (British Petroleum). 2017. *B P Stistical Review of World Energy 2017*, https:// www.bp.com/content/dam/bp-country/de ch/PDF/bp-statistical-review-of-world-energy-2017-full-report.pdf .

Bandyopadhyay, Bibek. 2013. *Prospects and challenges of Solar Power in India.* Under Industry Institution Interaction Programme of TEQIP Phase II, Jadavpur University. October 28. http://teqip.jdvu.ac.in/for_website/Program%2028.10.2013/Presentation_Dr.%20Bibek%20Bandyopadhyay.pdf.

BARC (Bhabha Atomic Research Centre). 2006. *50 Years of Apsara Reactor*. http://www.barc.gov.in/publications/tb/apsara.pdf.

BEE (Bureau of Energy Efficiency).(2017). *Energy Conservation Building Code.* Ministry of Power, Government of India. http://www.aeee.in/wp-content/uploads/2017/05/ECBC-presentation-by-BEE.pdf.

BEE (Bureau of Energy Efficiency).2018. *Energy Conservation Building Code Rules 2019.* Ministry of Power, Government of India. https://beeindia.gov.in/news-events/energy-conservation-building-code-rules-2018.

Bose, Srinjoy. 2007. *Energy Politics: India-Bangladesh-Myanmar Relations. Institute* of *Peace* and *Conflict Studies* (IPCS) Special Report 45 (July). http://www.burmalibrary.org/docs09/IPCS-Special-Report-India-Myanmar.pdf.

BP (British Petroleum). 2017. *B P Statistical Review of World Energy 2017*. https://www.bp.com/content/dam/bp-country/de ch/PDF/bp-statistical-review-of-world-energy-2017-full-report.pdf.

BP (British Petroleum). 2018. *B P Energy Outlook.* B.P Energy Economics. https://www.bp.com/content/dam/bp/business-sites/en/global/corporate/pdfs/energy-economics/energy-outlook/bp-energy-outlook-2018.pdf.

BP (British Petroleum). 2018. B P *Statistical Review of World Energy 2018.* https://www.bp.com/en/global/corporate/energy-economics/statistical-review-of-world-energy.html.

BP (British Petroleum). 2018. *BP Energy Outlook Country and Regional Insights – India*. https://www.bp.com/content/dam/bp/en/corporate/pdf/energy-economics/energy-outlook/bp-energy-outlook-2018-country-insight-india.pdf.

BP (British Petroleum). 2018. *Energy Demand by sector*. Accessed January 12, 2019. https://www.bp.com/en/global/corporate/energy-economics/energy-outlook.html.

CEA (Central ElectricityAuthority). 2016. *Draft National Electricity Plan.* Ministry of Power. http://www.cea.nic.in/reports/committee/nep/nep dec.pdf.

CEE (Community Energy in England). 2017. *Community Energy State of The Sector: A study of community energy in England, Wales and Northern Ireland.* https://communityenergyengland.org/files/document/51/1499247266 Community Energy-StateoftheSectorReport.pdf.

Central Statistics Office. 2017. *Energy Statistics.* New Delhi: Ministry of Statistics and Programme Implementation, Government of India. http://www.mospi.nic.in/sites/default/files/publication reports/Energy Statistics 2017r.pdf.pdf.

Central Statistics Office. 2018. *Energy Statistics.* New Delhi: Ministry of Statistics and Programme Implementation, Government of India. http://mospi.nic.in/sites/default/files/publication reports/Energy Statistics 2018.pdf.

Chenoy, Dilip. 2009. "Overview of Indian Hydrogen Programme & Key Safety Issues on Hydrogen Fuel." In *Workshop on Compressed Natural Gas and Hydrogen Fuels Lessons Learned for the Safe Deployment of Vehicles.* December 10-

11. Washington D C: US Department of Transportation and US Department of Energy.

CIL (Coal India Limited). 2018. *Coal Vision 2030*. https://www.coalindia.in/DesktopModules/DocumentList/documents/Coal Vision 2030 document for Coal Sector Stakeholders Consultation 27012018.pdf.

Cilliers, Jakkie. 2004. *Human Security in Africa: A Conceptual Framework for Review*. Nairobi, Kenya: African Human Security Initiative.

Cilliers, Jakkie. 2015. *Future (im)perfect? Mapping conflict, violence and extremism in Africa.* Pretoria, South Africa: Institute for Security Studies.

EAI (Energy Alternatives India). 2017. *India Biomass Energy.* Chennai: Energy Alternatives India.

Ebinger, Charles. 2016. *India's Energy and Climate Policy: Can India Meet the Challenge of Industrialization and Climate Change?*. Brookings. https://www.brookings.edu/research/indias-energy-and-climate-policy-can-india-meet-the-challenge-of-industrialization-and-climate-change.

EIA (United States Energy Information Administration). 2015. *Russia's Key Energy Statitics.* Washington, D.C: EIA.

EIA (United States Energy Information Administration). 2016. *Country Analysis Brief: India.* Washington D.C: EIA.

EIA (United States Energy Information Administration). 2017. *Beyond China and India, Energy Consumption in non- OECD Asia Continues to Grow.* US: EIA. https://www.eia.gov/todayinenergy/detail.php?id=32972.

EIA (US Energy Information Administration). 2016. *Annual Energy Outlook 2016 with Projections to 2040.* Washington D.C: EIA. https://www.eia.gov/outlooks/aeo/pdf/0383(2016).pdf.

EIA (US Energy Information Administration). 2016. *International Energy Outlook 2016 with Projections to 2040.* Washington DC: Office of Energy Analysis, U.S. Department of Energy. https://www.eia.gov/outlooks/ieo/pdf/0484(2016).pdf

EIA (US Energy Information Administration). 2016. *World Shale Resource Assessment.* Washington D.C: EIA. https://www.eia.gov/analysis/studies/worldshalegas/.

ENVIS (Environmental Information System Network).2016.*Statewise Installed Capacity of Biomass Power in India 2012-2016 (Grid Connected).* Centre on Renewable Energy and Environment. Ministry of Environment, Forest and Climate Change (MoEFCC), Government of India,http://terienvis.nic.in/index3.aspx?sslid=3252&subsublinkid=850&langid=1&mid=1.

EUEI PDF (European Union Energy Initiative Partnership Dialogue Facility). 2014. *Mini Grid Policy Toolkit:Policy and Business Framework for Successful Mini Grid Roll outs.*http://www.ren21.net/Portals/0/documents/Resources/MGT/MinigridPolicyToolkit Sep2014 EN.pdf.

Fattouh, Bassam and Coby van der Linde. 2011. *The International Energy Forum: Twenty Years of Producer-Consumer Dialogue in a Changing World.* Riyadh: International Energy Forum.

Gault, John C. 2006. "*Energy Security, Globalization and Global Security*." In the Program on the Geopolitical Implications of Globalization and Transnational Security GCSP Policy Brief Serics.no.8. September 28. Geneva: Geneva Centre for Security Policy.

ICC (Indian Chamber of Commerce). 2016. *Bridging the gap Increasing Coal Production and Sector Augmentation.*https://www.pwc.in/assets/pdfs/publications/2016/icc-pwc-coal-report-june.pdf

ICVL (International Coal Ventures (P) Ltd). n.d. "*Company Background*" https://icvl.in/aboutus.php?tag=company-background.

IEA (International Energy Agency). 2015. "*India Energy Outlook: World Energy Outlook Special Report.*" Accessed July 1, 2018.https://www.iea.org/publications/freepublications/publication/IndiaEnergyOutlook WEO2015.pdf.

IEA (International Energy Agency). 2017. *Energy Access Outlook 2017.https://www.iea.org/access2017/.*

IEA (International Energy Agency). 2017. *World Energy Outlook 2017.*https://www.iea.org/weo2017/.

Indian Bureau of Mines. (2015). *Indian Minerals Yearbook 2015.* Indian Bureau of Mines, Government of India, https://ibm.gov.in/index. php?c = pages & m= index & id=852.

IRENA (International Renewable Energy Agency). 2015. *Off-Grid Renewable Energy Solutions, Global and Regional Status and Trends.*https://www.irena.org/-/media/Files/IRENA/Agency/Publication/2018/Jul/IRENA Off-grid RE Solutions 2018.pdf.

IRENA (International Renewable Energy Agency). 2018. *Renewable Capacity Statistics 2018.*Abu Dhabi: IRENA. https://www.irena.org/publications/2018/Mar/Renewable-Capacity-Statistics-2018.

IRENA (International Renewable Energy Agency). 2018. *Renewable Energy Policies in a Time of Transition*. Abu Dhabi: IRENA.

ITE Group. 2017. *Russian Energy in 2016: Russia: The Figure*. ITE Oil and Gas.http://www.oilgas-events.com/market-insights/MIOGE-Preview/Russia-Oil-Gas-Statistics

Jagniti, Sharinee. 2012. *India's Africa Policy: Towards a More Coherent Engagement.* Nanyang Avenue, Singapore: S Rajaratnam School of International Studies.

Kesharwani, Manoj Kumar. 2006. "Overview of Small Hydro Power Development in Himalyan Region." In International Himalayan Small Hydropower Summit. October 12-13: 44-57.

Leverett,Flynt. 2007. *The Geopolitics of OilandAmerica's International Standing.* United States: Committee on Energy and Natural Resources,US Senate.January 10.

Mallya, Sameer and Shreyas D Deshmukh. 2015. *Viability of India's Gas Pipeline Options: A Geo-political Perspective: (Pakistan as a spoiler in TAPI and IPI venture)*. New Delhi: The Centre for Land Warfare Studies.

MFA (Ministry of Foreign Affairs Iceland 2018).*Icelandic Foreign Affairs 2018.*https://www.government.is/library/01-Ministries/Ministry-for-Foreign-Affairs/PDF-skjol/MFA%20-%20Icelandic%20Foreign%20Affairs%202018.pdf.

MHA (Ministry of Home Affairs). 2011. *Census of India 2011: Rural Urban Distribution of Population, Provisional Population Totals*. New Delhi: MHA, Government of India. http://censusindia.gov.in/2011-prov-results/paper2/data files/india/Rural Urban 2011.pdf.

Ministry of Coal. 2017. *Coal Directory of India 2016-17*. Government of India.http://www.coalcontroller.gov.in/pages/display/16-coal-directory.

Ministry of Coal. 2018. *Provisional Coal Statistics 2017-18*. Government of India. http://www.coalcontroller.gov.in/writereaddata/files/download/provisional coalstat/ProvisionalCoalStat2017-18.pdf.

Ministry of Coal. 2019. *Annual Report 2017-18*. https://coal.nic.in/content/annual-reports.

Ministry of Mines. 2018. Indian Minerals Yearbook 2017, Coal and Lignite. Nagpur: Government of India.

Ministry of Petroleum and Natural Gas. 2017. *Indian Petroleum & Natural Gas Statistics 2015-16*. New Delhi: Economic and Statistics Division, Government of India. http://petroleum.nic.in/more/indian-png-statistics.

Ministry of Railways. 2017. *Facts & Figures 2016-17*. Government of India http://www.indianrailways.gov.in/railwayboard/uploads/directorate/stat econ/IRSP 2016-17/ Facts Figure/Fact Figures%20English%202016-17.pdf.

Ministry of Statistics and Programme Implementation. 2011. *Statistical Year Book 2011*. Central Statistical Office, Government of India. http://www.mospi.gov.in.

Mishra, Niharranjan. 2015. *Coal Mining, Displacement and Rural Livelihoods: A Study in Mahanadi Coalfield Odisha*. Rourkela, Odisha: Department of Humanities and Social Sciences National Institute of Technology.

MNRE (Ministry of New and Renewable Energy). 2017. *Annual Report 2016-17*. Government of India.https://mnre.gov.in/annual-report.

MNRE (Ministry of New and Renewable Energy). 2017. *Year End Review 2017*. New Delhi: Press Information Bureau, MNRE, Government of India.

MNRE (Ministry of New and Renewable Energy). *2018*. Year End Review 2018. New Delhi: Press Information Bureau, MNRE, Government of India.

Moss, Jeremy, Michael McMann, Jessica Rae, Andrea Zipprich, Darryl R.J. Macer, Aori R. Nyambati, Diana Ngo, MingMing Cheng, N Manohar and Gregor Wolbring. 2011. *Energy Equity and Environmental Security*. Bangkok: The United Nations Educational, Scientific and Cultural Organization (UNESCO).

Müller-Kraenner, Sascha. 2008. *China's and India's Emerging Energy Foreign Policy*. Bonn: German Development Institute.

Nakamura, Yuji. 2002. *The Historical Flow of Black Gold: Two Approaches to Energy Security*. Institute for International Policy Studies Policy Paper. 282 E (January). Tokyo: IIPS.

Nakano, Jane, David Pumphrey, Robert Price and Molly A. Walton. 2012. *Prospects for Shale Gas Development in Asia: Examining potentials and Challenges in China and India*. Washington D.C: Center for Strategic and International Studies.

NITI Aayog and BCG (NITI Aayog and the Boston Consulting Group). 2018. *Transforming India's Mobility: A perspective*. http://niti.gov.in/writereaddata/files/document_publication/BCG.pdf.

NITI Aayog. 2017. *Draft National Energy Policy*. Government of India. June 27. https://niti.gov.in/writereaddata/files/new_initiatives/NEP-ID_27.06.2017.pdf.

NRDC (National Resource Defense Council). 2017. *The Road from Paris: India's Progress toward its Climate Pledge*.https://www.nrdc.org/sites/default/files/paris-climate-conference-India-IB.pdf.

ORKUSTOFNUN. 2017. *Energy Statistics in Iceland 2017*. https://orkustofnun.is/gogn/os-onnur-rit/Orkutolur-2017-enska-A4.pdf.

Pattanaik, Smruti S.n.d. *Nepal-Bhutan Bilateral Talks and Repatriation of Bhutanese Refugees*. New Delhi: The Institute for Defence Studies and Analyses, (IDSA). https://www.idsa-india.org/an-jan9-11.html

Perera, Pradeep.2018.*Challenges of Integrating 175 GW of Renewable Energy in India and Policy Options.*Philippines: Asian Development Bank.

Pethiyagoda, Kadira. 2017. *India-GCC Relations:Delhi's Strategic Opportunity.* Brookings Doha Center Analysis Paper. Washington D. C: The Brooking Institution.

Philibert, Cedric. 2017. *Renewable Energy for Industry From green energy to green materials and fuels.*International Energy Agency.

https://www.iea.org/publications/insights/insightpublications/Renewable Energy for Industry.pdf.

Planning Commission. 2006. *Integrated Energy Policy.* Report of the Expert Committee, New Delhi: Government of India.

Planning Commission. 2014. *India-US Energy Dialogue.* Press Information Bureau, Government of India. http://pib.nic.in/newsite/PrintRelease.aspx?relid=104569.

PPAC (Petroleum Planning & Analysis Cell). 2018. *Ready Reckoner Snapshot of India's Oil & Gas Data.*Ministry of Petroleum & Natural Gas.

https://www.ppac.gov.in/WriteReadData/Reports/20190 122055 43813 40355 Snaps hotofIndia%E2%80%99sOil&Gasdata,December2018.pdf.

PPAC (Petroleum Planning and Analysis Cell). 2013. "All India Study on Sectoral Demand of Petrol & Diesel." Nielsen, PPAC. Government of India.

http://ppac.org.in/WriteReadData/Reports/2014111 103294 50069740 All India Study on Sectoral Demand of Diesel. pdf.

PPAC (Petroleum Planning and Analysis Cell). 2016. *Assessment report: Primary survey on household cooking fuel usage and willingness to convert to LPG*. Ministry of Petroleum and Natural Gas.Government of India.

http://www.ppac.org.in/WriteReadData/Reports/2017 103 10449 342512219 Primary Survey Report PPAC.pdf.

PPAC (Petroleum Planning and Analysis Cell). 2018. *Monthly Report on Indigenous Crude Oil Production, Import and Processing & Production, Import and Export of Petroleum Products.*Ministry of Petroleum and Natural Gas, Government of India

https://www.ppac.gov.in/WriteReadData/Reports/20190 228060 109872 5033WebVersion MonthlyReportJan2019.pdf.

Rahman, Salma and Zaki Hussain. 2017. *Renewable Energy Governance in India: Challenges and Prospects for Achieving the 2022 Energy Goals*. Munich, Germany: Munich Personal RePEc Archive.

Rajagopalan, Rajeswari Pillai. 2008. *Indo-US Nuclear Deal: Implications for India and the Global N-Regime*, New Delhi: Institute of Peace and Conflict Studies.

Ramana M.V. 2009.*The Indian Nuclear Industry: Status and Prospects, Nuclear Energy Futures*. The Centre for International Governance Innovation Nuclear energy Futures Papers, The Nuclear Energy Futures Project: 1-34,

https://www.cigionline.org/sites/default/files/nuclear energy wp9.pdf.

Reja, Binyam. 2016.*China's Green Freight Initiative.*Conference Report, Busan: South Korea..The World Bank Group.http://cleanairasia.org/wp-content/uploads/2016/09/03 Binyam-Reja World-Bank1.pdf.

Remme, Uwe, Nathalie Trudeau, Dagmar Graczyk and Peter Taylor, 2011.*Technology Development Prospects for the Indian Power Sector.* IEA Energy Papers 2011/4: OECD Publishing.

REN 21(Renewable Energy Policy Network for the 21st Century). 2018. *Renewables 2018 Global Status Report.* http://www.ren21.net/wp-content/uploads/2018/06/17-8652 GSR2018 Full Report web final.pdf.

REN 21(Renewable Energy Policy Network for the 21st Century). 2018. *Distributed Renewables for Energy Access.* http://www.ren21.net/gsr-2018/chapters/chapter 04/chapter 04/.

RIS (Research and Information System for Developing Countries).2013. *A Dialogue on India-Canada Economic Cooperation.*In the Proceedings of India Canada Cooperation Dialogue. February 12-13. New Delhi: RIS.

Saghir, Jamal. 2004. *Energy and poverty: myths, links, and policy issues*. Energy and Mining Sector Board.World Bank.http://siteresources.worldbank.org/INTENERGY/Resources/EnergyWorkingNotes 4.pdf.

Sahel and West Africa Club/OECD. 2006. "Workshop on Human Security in West Africa: Challenges, Synergies and Action for Regional Agenda." Lome,Togo, March 26–28. Governance, Conflicts Dynamics, Peace and Security Unit, Sahel and West Africa Club/OECD. https://www.oecd.org/swac/events/38522284.pdf.

Sethi, Girish. 2017. "Industrial Energy Efficiency." In *Workshop on SDG7: Affordable and Clean Energy,* New Delhi, February 23: TERI and NITI Aayog.

Shakthi Sustainable Energy Foundation. 2017. *Thermal comfort for all. Sustainable and Smart Space cooling.*https://shaktifoundation.in/wp-content/uploads/2017/09/Brochure-Thermal-Comfort-For-All.pdf.

Singh, Hemant K. and Aman R Khanna. 2012. *India's Energy Options: the Road Ahead: an Analysis of the Prospects of Shale Gas in India's Energy Future*. New Delhi: Indian Council for Research on International Economic Relations.

TERI (*The Energy and Resources Institute)*. 2017. *Transitions in Indian Electricity Sector 2017–2030*. New Delhi: TERI. http://www.teriin.org/files/transition-report/files/downloads/Transitions-in-Indian-Electricity-Sector Report.pdf.

Thambi Simi, Anindya Bhatacharya, and Oliver Fricko. 2018. *India's Energy and Emissions Outlook: Results from India Energy Mode ,Energy, Climate Change and Overseas Engagement Division.* NITI Aayog, Government of India.
http://www.niti.gov.in/writereaddata/files/document publication/India % E2 % 80%99s-Energy-and-Emissions-Outlook.pdf.

Thampi, Simi. 2017. *Access to Clean Cooking for Rural Women: Food for Thought*. NITI Aayog, Government of India. http://niti.gov.in/content/access-clean-cooking-rural-women-food-thought.

UNCTAD (United Nations Conference on Trade and Development). 2015. *Sustainable Freight Transport systems: Opportunities for Developing Countries.*https://unctad.org/meetings/en/SessionalDocuments/cimem7d11en.pdf.

UNDP (United Nations Development Program). (1994). *Human Development report: New Dimensions of Human Security.* Oxford: Oxford University Press.

UNEP (United Nations Environmental Programme). 2015. *District Energy in Cities, Unlocking the Potential of Energy Efficiency and Renewable Energy*. https://wedocs.unep.org/bitstream/handle/20.500.11822/9317/-District energy in cities unlocking the potential of energy efficiency and renewable ene.pdf?sequence=2&.

United States Environmental Protection Agency. 2016. "Learn about Smart Way." In the *17th World Clean Air Congress and 9 th Better Air Quality (BAQ) Conference.* Busan, South Korea. https://www.epa.gov/smartway/learn-about-smartway.

Vesterinen, Pirkko, Eija Alakangas, Kati Veijonen, and VTT Martin Junginger. 2010. *Prospects of bioenergy in new industrial sectors – D2.3.* Utrecht University.

Victor, David. G. 2006. *National Security Consequences of U.S. Oil Dependency.* New York: Council on Foreign Relations.

Zoback, Mark, Saya Kitasei and Brad Copithorne. 2010. *Addressing the Environmental Risks from Shale Gas Development.* World Watch Institute, Natural Gas and Sustainable Energy Initiative.

Websites

AERB (Atomic Energy Regulatory Board). 2010. "Convention on Nuclear Safety." AERB, Government of India. Accessed February 10, 2018.https://aerb.gov.in/index.php/english/convention-on-nuclear-safety.

BMBF (Federal Ministry of Education and Research). 2017. "German Energy Transition." Accessed May 18, 2018.https://www.bmbf.de/en/german-energy-transition-2319. html.

BMWi (Federal Ministry for Economic Affairs and Energy). 2017. "The Renewable Energy." Accessed April 13, 2018.https://www.bmwi.de/Redaktion/EN/Dossier/renewable-energy.html.

DAE (Department of Atomic Energy). n.d. "Important Agreements" DAE, Government of India.Accessed November 2, 2018.http://www.dae.nic.in/?q=node/75.

DAE (Department of Atomic Energy). n.d. "Myths and Facts." DAE, Government of India. Accessed February 16, 2019.http://www.dae.nic.in/?q=node/926.

EEAS (European External Action Service). 2016. "India-European Union Partnerships for Sustainability, Clean Energy & Climate Action". Accessed November 31, 2018. https://eeas.europa.eu/sites/eeas/files/india-eu partnerships for sustainability clean energy and climate action.pdf

FAO (Food and Agricultural Organization).n.d. "India at a Glance." FAO, United Nations.http://www.fao.org/india/fao-in-india/india-at-a-glance/en/.

FOWPI (First Offshore Wind Farm Project in India). 2017. "Oveview."Gurugram: FOWPI.Accessed November 30, 2018.https://www.fowpi.in/

GRIHA (Green Rating for Integrated Habitat Assessment) n.d "Infosys Green Building: GRIHA." Accessed March 15, 2018.http://www.grihaindia.org/images/case studies/pdf/Infosys-hyderabad.pdf.

Human Rights Watch. 2003. "Sudan, Oil, and Human Rights." https://www.hrw.org/reports/2003/sudan1103/sudanprint.pdf.

IBEF (India Brand Equity Foundation). 2018. "Oil & Gas Industry in India." IBEF. Accessed November 12, 2018.https://www.ibef.org/industry/oil-gas-india. aspx.

IBEF (India Brand Equity Foundation). 2018. "Road Infrastructure in India." IBEF.Accessed January 2, 2017. https://www.ibef.org/industry/roads-india.aspx.

IEA (International Energy Agency). 2006. "Energy for Cooking in Developing Countries." IEA.Accessed June 5, 2018.https://www.iea.org/publications/free publications/publication/cooking.pdf.

IESD (Indo European Sustainable Development). 2017. Diplomatic Mission for the Indian Photovoltaic Market Development." New Delhi: IESD. http://www.iesd.eu/news/i-e-s-d-partecipated-in-the-diplomatic-mission-for-the-indian-photovoltaic-market-development/.

India Energy Portal.n.d. "Agriculture, Energy Sectors." Government of India, Accessed December 13, 2018.

http://www.indiaenergyportal.org/subthemes link. php? text = agriculture & themeid = 15.

Infosys. n.d. "Commercial radiant cooled building: A first in India."Accessed April 24, 2018.https://www.infosys.com/newsroom/features/Pages/commercial-radiant-cooling-building.aspx.

Jadugoda Uranium Mine – 1. 2009. Jharkhand Forum, April 22. https://www. youtube.com/watch?v=-2z8EsV748I.

Ministry of Coal. 2018. "Production and Supplies." Accessed October 20 2018. https://coal.nic.in/content/production-and-supplies.

Ministry of Coal. 2018. *Production, Supply and Import of Coal.* New Delhi: Press Information Bureau, Government of India. http://pib.nic.in/newsite/Print Release.aspx?relid=186616.

Ministry of Petroleum &Natural Gas. 2014. "70% of Diesel, 99.6 % of Petrol consumed by Transport Sector: M/s Nielsen submits All India Study Report to PPAC on sale of Diesel and Petrol." Press Information Bureau, Government of India. January 28. http://pib.nic.in/newsite/PrintRelease.aspx?relid=102799.

Ministry of Petroleum and Natural Gas.n.d. "Pradhan Mantri Ujjwala Yojana." National Portal, Government of India. https://www.india.gov.in/spotlight/pradhan-mantri-ujjwala-yojana#tab=tab-1.

Ministry of Power. 2008. "Power Generation, Overview." Government of India. Accessed August 19, 2018.https://powermin.nic.in/en/content/overview.

Ministry of Power. 2016. Energy Cooperation to be the Defining Feature of India-Australia Relationshiphttp://pib.nic.in/newsite/PrintRelease.aspx?relid=136293.

Ministry of Power. 2017. "Power Sector at a Glance: All India." Governmant of India, https://powermin.nic.in/en/content/power-sector-glance-all-india.

Ministry of Power. 2017. 1st 'India Indonesia Energy Forum' held in Jakarta. http://pib.nic.in/newsite/PrintRelease.aspx?relid=161220.

Ministry of Power. n.d. "Power Sector at a Glance All India". Accessed June15, 2018. https://powermin.nic.in/en/content/power-sector-glance-all-india 2018

Ministry of Road Transport & Highways. 2017. "Methanol Economy for India: Energy Security, Make in India and Zero Carbon Foot Print." 28-December, Government of India: Press Information Bureau.http://pib.nic.in/newsite/Print Release. aspx?relid=174919.

MOEF (Ministry of Environment, Forest and Climate Change). 2015. "India First Biennial Update Report to the United Nations Framework Convention on Climate Change."http://www.moef.gov.in/sites/default/files/indbur10.pdf.

MOT (Ministry of Motor Transport Singapore).n.d. "Infographics."Accessed April 9, 2018. https://www.mot.gov.sg/transport-matters/motoring/infographics.

National Portal of India.n.d. "Power & Energy."Government of India.Accessed June 2, 2018.https://www.india.gov.in/topics/power-energy.

Natural Resource Canada. (2014). *What are the Oil Sands.* Government of Canada. https://www.nrcan.gc.ca/energy/oil-sands/18089.

NPCIL (Nuclear Power Corporation of India Limited). 2017. *Plants under Operation.* http://www.npcil.nic.in/content/3021 AllPlants.aspx.

OPEC (Organization of the Petroleum Exporting Countries). 2017.OPEC Share of World Crude Oil Reserves 2017, OPEC.https://www.opec.org/opec web/en/data graphs/330.htm.

OPEC (Organization of the Petroleum Exporting Countries). n.d. *Member Countries,* OPEC. https://www.opec.org/opec web/en/about us/25.htm.

Petronet. 2017. "Corporate Profile." https://www.petronetlng.com/PDF/AR2016-17.pdf

Rajya Sabha. 2016. "Per Capita Consumption of Power." Rajya Sabha Unstarred Question No.2392. Ministry of Power, Government of India.

http://www.indiaenvironmentportal.org.in/files/file/Per % 20 capita % 20consumption%20of%20power.pdf.

Rajya Sabha. 2017. "Disposal of Radioactive Waste Materials." Rajya Sabha Unstarred Question No.2086. Department of Atomic Energy, Government of India.http://dae.nic.in/writereaddata/parl/monsoon2017/rsus2086.pdf.

Rajya Sabha. 2017. "Production and Import of Uranium." Rajya Sabha Starred Question No.368. Department of Atomic Energy, Government of India.

Sastry, Guruprakash. "Integrated Design Approach Question all assumptions 2011."Accessed April 23, 2018.http://www.grihaindia.org/images/casestudies/pdf/Infosys-hyderabad.pdf.

Sastry, Guruprakash. n. d. "First Radiant Cooled Commercial Building in India – Critical Analysis of Energy, Comfort and Cost. Green Initiatives Infosys Limited." Bangalore, India. Accessed April 23, 2018.http://portal.aeecenter.org/files/newsletters/ESMS/Sastry.pdf.

Saubhagya. 2018. "House Electrification Status." Pradhan Mantri Sahaj Bijli Har Ghar Yojana, Saubhagya Dashboard, Ministry of Power, Government of India.https://powermin.nic.in/en/content/saubhagya.

Sharma, Oum Prakash and Poonam Trikha. 2013. Geothermal Energy and its Potential in India. *Renewable Energy, Akshaya Urja:* Ministry of New and Renewable Energy. https://mnre.gov.in/file-manager/akshay-urja/july-august-2013/EN/14-18.pdf.

Smith, Rob. 2018. "Three countries are leading the renewable energy revolution." *World Economic Forum*.https://www.weforum.org/agenda/2018/02/countries-behind-global-renewable-energy-growth/.

The Danish Wind Turbine Owners' Association, n.d. "Cooperatives - a local and democratic ownership to wind turbines."Accessed April 5, 2018.http://dkvind.dk/html/eng/cooperatives.html.

World Bank. 2005. "Energy Security Issues." Accessed April 23, 2018.

http://documents.worldbank.org/curated/en/464811468175435408/Energy-security-issues.

World Bank. 2017. "Solar Powers India's Clean Energy Revolution."https://www.worldbank.org/en/news/immersive-story/2017/06/29/solar-powers-india-s-clean-energy-revolution.

World Bank. 2018. "Understanding Poverty, Overview."

https://www.worldbank.org/en/topic/energy/overview.

World Nuclear Association (n.d). "Nuclear Power in Germany." Accessed June 16, 2018. http://www.world-nuclear.org/information-library/country-profiles/countries-g-n/germany.aspx.

Index

C

L

M